The
CIVIC BARGAIN

The
CIVIC
BARGAIN

HOW
DEMOCRACY
SURVIVES

BROOK MANVILLE
and JOSIAH OBER

PRINCETON UNIVERSITY PRESS

PRINCETON & OXFORD

Published by Princeton University Press
41 William Street, Princeton, New Jersey 08540
99 Banbury Road, Oxford OX2 6JX

press.princeton.edu

Library of Congress Cataloging-in-Publication Data

Names: Manville, Brook, 1950– author. | Ober, Josiah, author.
Title: The civic bargain : how democracy survives / Brook Manville and Josiah Ober.
Description: Princeton : Princeton University Press, [2023] | Includes bibliographical
    references and index.
Identifiers: LCCN 2022050950 (print) | LCCN 2022050951 (ebook) |
    ISBN 9780691218601 (hardcover) | ISBN 9780691230443 (ebook)
Subjects: LCSH: Democracy—Case studies. | Civics—Study and teaching—
    Case studies. | Citizenship—Social aspects—Case studies. | Political participation—
    Case studies. | BISAC: POLITICAL SCIENCE / Political Ideologies / Democracy |
    HISTORY / World
Classification: LCC JC423 .M2127 2023 (print) | LCC JC423 (ebook) |
    DDC 321.8072/3—dc23/eng/20230214
LC record available at https://lccn.loc.gov/2022050950
LC ebook record available at https://lccn.loc.gov/2022050951

British Library Cataloging-in-Publication Data is available

Editorial: Rob Tempio and Chloe Coy
Production Editorial: Kathleen Cioffi
Text and Jacket Design: Karl Spurzem
Production: Erin Suydam
Publicity: James Schneider and Carmen Jimenez
Copyeditor: Cindy Milstein

This book has been composed in Arno and Bulmer MT

Printed on acid-free paper. ∞

Printed in the United States of America

10 9 8 7 6 5 4 3 2 1

Looking ahead, to my family—with bright hopes for the future;
looking back, to Donald Kagan—with fond memories of the past.

BROOK MANVILLE

To my teachers: friends and family, mentors and colleagues, and
students who never realized how much I was learning from them.

JOSIAH OBER

CONTENTS

PREFACE

This book is a coproduction of our thirty-year personal and civic friendship. Over that time, we have periodically converted our various discussions about democracy—both ancient and modern—into collaborative publications, including a previous book about rethinking the modern corporation as a "company of citizens."[1]

The notion of undertaking this second book together emerged after a 2018 National Geographic Society panel discussion about democracy's future. That day, our conversation with our fellow panelists and members of the public audience—government employees, students, various concerned citizens, and even a US Supreme Court justice—demonstrated to us the wide range of understanding and opinion that any similar group of citizens will bring to a discussion about the state of their nation's democracy. In the context of what seemed to be an eroding political climate, it also showed great hunger among citizens to talk about how democracy survives or fails. The course of events since that panel, plus the growing challenges faced by all modern democracies, have only increased that craving.

We wrote this book in the hope of providing some answers to pressing questions about democracy's fate. We offer a guardedly optimistic vision for how democracy might be kept. That vision was drawn from a combined theoretical and historical analysis to better understand what democracy is, and how it emerged and developed in several highly influential historical cases. In each case that meant fulfilling several essential conditions, agreed on by people who chose to govern themselves without any "boss"—except one another. Securing democracy's future can be achieved if today's citizens recommit to a civic bargain—the practice of good faith compromise, aimed at sustaining the common goods of security and welfare along with the institutions that support them. The bargain is made by the members of a defined citizen body who regard one another as friends rather than enemies. It is sustained by civic education.

Our thesis has been shaped by ideas and suggestions offered by friends, colleagues, students, and pretty much anyone who wanted to share their two cents about democracy's past and future (and there were many!). This page hereby indemnifies them all, with our promise of no-fault insurance.

Those named below are a small subset of what grew into a wide network of friendly helpers. With gratitude for all, we would also like to especially recognize, and very much thank, those who read and commented on part or all of the manuscript in progress: Danielle Allen, Jenna Bednar, Clive Dickinson, Margarita Egan, Sara Forsdyke, Roselyn Fuller, Jennifer Futernick, William Gormley, Bruce Hitchner, David Johnson, Jethro K. Lieberman, Jonathan Lipman, Adrienne Mayor, Ian Morris, Norman Sandridge, Avshalom Schwartz, David Stasavage, Doug Smith, Barry Strauss, Barry Weingast, and Rosemary Zagarri. We owe special thanks to our superb research assistants, Julian Hong, Philip Petrov, and Garrett Walker; our talented agent, Jill Marsal; our visionary editor, Rob Tempio; and above all Margarita and Adrienne, who offered advice as well as encouragement, and put up with our many long Zoom calls in the course of writing this book.

Brook Manville and Josiah Ober
September 2022

The
CIVIC BARGAIN

INTRODUCTION

DEMOCRACY'S REAL DEAL

In September 1787, Dr. Benjamin Franklin emerged from the Pennsylvania statehouse—today's Independence Hall. The summerlong Constitutional Convention, at which the Constitution of the United States of America was drafted, had just ended. After Franklin exited the building, he was confronted by Mrs. Elizabeth Powel, a prominent member of Philadelphia's intellectual and social elite. Eager for Franklin's take on the closed-door deliberations, she asked, "Well Doctor what have we got? A republic or a monarchy?" That is, would it be self-government by citizens or the rule of a boss? Franklin famously replied, "A republic—if you can keep it." It was both a promise and a warning.[1]

At first glance, this often-repeated story portrays the eighty-one-year-old scientist, diplomat, and constitutional framer as a stern grandparent, surrendering keys to an inexperienced and perhaps irresponsible child: "OK, the new red, white, and blue family car is now yours, but don't crash it!" Franklin and his fellow "founding fathers" were leaving the convention, about to hand over a masterpiece of governmental design to American citizens, first for ratification and then making it work. They just hoped their fellow citizens would be up to those challenges.

But look again: Was it a masterpiece? The common answer has frequently been an unabashed "yes": the US Constitution has been revered as both the source and most perfect embodiment of America's democratic republic. But of the seventy delegates appointed by the thirteen states, only thirty-nine ultimately signed the document. Some of the most prominent of the founders had deep doubts about the viability of their collective enterprise. More recently, the landmark document has been a target of skeptical critique and source of disappointment. Many Americans now complain that the Constitution was fatally flawed from the beginning—in its vague and awkward language, elitist avoidance of majority rule, and authorship by slave-owning hypocrites. For these critics, it is no masterpiece that Franklin helped design; indeed, it is a mess.

Reframing Pessimism

Negativity about the Constitution is part of a current trend of democratic pessimism. A generation ago, the collapse of the Soviet Union led to a wave of enthusiasm for democracy, and launched the spread of free and liberal governments around the world. Yet today, democratic systems everywhere are under pressure, polarized, and struggling with both internal and external authoritarian challenges. The worry is that democracy is dying. Commentary across national and global media suggests that its demise may be inevitable.

History offers a corrective. Yes, some democracies are faltering today, and many others collapsed in the past. But four exceptionally well-documented and highly influential democratic experiments—classical Athens, republican Rome, British parliamentarianism, and US constitutionalism—endured, or continue to endure, for multiple centuries. What can be learned from these cases about how democracies can, at least sometimes, survive? Could historical insights be applied to help save today's struggling democracies?

Those questions launched this book. We began by turning current pessimism on its head. Instead of inquiring into the causes of democracy's death, we looked to history's long survivors for clues to democracy's emergence, evolution, and strategies for persistence. Ancient Athenian democracy lasted close to two hundred years; republican Rome twice that; and British parliamentary governance developed slowly, but it started early and ever since the seventeenth century has evolved toward a democratic system. The United States' constitutional government has held on through sharp partisan dissension and a bloody civil war for over two centuries. We asked ourselves how these systems of citizen self-government survived (or still survive) for so long: Is there some general pattern, some adaptive strategy, that enabled and sustained (even if unevenly) democracy across multiple generations? Can insight from comparative political history be harnessed to help renew modern democracy?

Democracy's Essence, Rise, and Survival

To tackle those issues, we posed two more basic questions. First, what *is* democracy? What essentially has it meant to those who created and sustained democratic societies? Second, how does it come into being?

Taking history as a guide to political theorizing, we concluded that democracy in its most basic sense means "no boss." Democracy pertains when extensive, socially diverse bodies of citizens govern themselves, accepting no ruler except for one another. That is no mean feat, especially once societies grow beyond the tiny face-to-face communities that were the norm before the development of agriculture. Decision-making in any large organization is always difficult, but it is particularly complex when no individual or small group is in charge. A "bossless" community will always struggle to make decisions that are sufficiently pleasing to enough people to be supported with action. Because choices must be made, and because they cannot please everyone, the outcome will never be perfect. By its very nature, democratic governance is indeed messy— but not necessarily chaotic. Decisions can be made and followed if citizens devise the right procedures. But even the best procedures are useless unless citizens bring the right mindset and behaviors to the task: working together as political equals who prioritize finding common ground in spite of differing preferences and interests. That is to say, democracy can succeed if and when it is understood as a fundamental bargain among free and equal citizens—an agreement to work together to defend the things we the citizens hold in common.

Instead of viewing democracy as a static collection of laws and institutions, we reimagine it as an organic, living system—messy indeed, but also purposeful. It operates to include and bond many diverse people who choose the freedom to make their own decisions and live by what they, together, decide. Democracy as bossless self-governance survives when citizens keep constructively and peacefully interacting and learning from one another, and when they reach for the benefits of freedom and shoulder the burdens of defending them. When they don't, democracy fails, and before long once free citizens find themselves answering to a boss.

On the second question—how democracy arises—we drew again on the rich historical record of our four cases. We sought to honor the best scholarly interpretations of political development in each case while going beyond a focus on democratic leaders and revolutions. Standard histories often underappreciate the process of negotiation that follows when the fighting stops—or that avoids fighting altogether. The centrality of bargaining to democracy, to its emergence and persistence, is the major theme of our book.

The Civic Bargain and Its Essential Conditions

Based on our analysis of historical cases, we contend that democracy is made possible and preserved over time by dealmaking and compromises. Democracy usually must be fought for (bosses like being bosses), but also requires bargaining. To consolidate and sustain self-government, citizens must agree to a *civic bargain*. Historically, civic bargains of different kinds have been struck and revised by democracies; we describe four of them in our case studies. Whether it is a written document like the US Constitution, coherent body of laws and legal precedents, or unwritten set of norms, the civic bargain specifies who is a citizen, how decisions are made, and what citizens owe one another. It determines how the "gives and gets"—the benefits and costs of ruling together for the common good—are distributed.

The civic bargain depends on and must in turn actively promote what we call the *essential conditions* of democracy—the conditions that are necessary for citizen self-governance. The seven conditions listed below are discussed in detail in chapter 1. They are elucidated in the historical case studies of chapters 2–5 and revisited in our summary of findings in chapter 6.

1. **No Boss**—except one another: citizens govern themselves, directly or through accountable representatives
2. **Security and Welfare**: ensure common safety, freedom from harm, and basic means of living as a common good for all
3. **Citizenship Defined**: formally specify who is a citizen, and what that means, including the extent of citizens' equality, freedoms, and responsibilities
4. **Citizen-Led Institutions**: maintain institutions of decision-making and conflict resolution under the charge of members of the democracy
5. **Good Faith Compromise**: prefer common good compromise in political decisions over unilateral demands for perfection
6. **Civic Friendship**: act as "civic friends" with one another, not as enemies, smoothing the way to renegotiate bargains with one another and meet future challenges
7. **Civic Education**: provide civic learning and experiences for citizens, instilling the values and practices they need to keep bossless self-governance

Before those seven conditions are achieved, democracy remains at best an aspiration. The conditions come about, when they do, through a sequence of prior political bargains. When they are robustly sustained, democracy flourishes. When they start to break down, democracy struggles. When they are abandoned, democracy fails.

So what enabled long-enduring democracies to create the essential conditions, strike a durable civic bargain, and survive over time? Our answer echoes the evolutionary processes of a living system. The patterns of behavior that allow a system of self-government to take root also enable it to continue to grow and thrive. Democracy must adapt when threatened while still preserving its essential core. Threats may arise from internal dissension, foreign attempts at conquest, or both. Indeed, as we will see, existential threats have historically provided an incentive for citizens with competing interests to bargain with one another.

Democracies survive if and only if their citizens maintain a robust and adaptive civic bargain, making the necessary and necessarily imperfect deals to preserve security, welfare, and self-governance. Faced with new threats and opportunities, citizens must periodically reexamine and renegotiate the bargain, the terms on which they agreed to live together as a democratic community. For that, as we will emphasize throughout, the final condition—education of citizens, by citizens—is essential.

Back to Philadelphia

A less familiar story about Franklin at the 1787 Constitutional Convention is revealing of how a civic bargain is struck. As we detail in chapter 5, many state delegates had come to the convention with a shared assumption about what needed to be done, given the failure of the earlier and ineffective Articles of Confederation, which had failed to adequately ensure for the new nation's security and welfare: a no-boss system of self-government must be capable of competing with autocratic rivals by promoting effective cooperation across a diverse constituency. Other delegates came to share that core assumption as the proceedings unfolded.

But deep disagreements remained about how to do it. Happily, many of the men had previously served in the local colonial and state assemblies, and several had also fought in the revolution. Many were deeply read in history and political philosophy. They brought their beliefs and priorities from those experiences to the bargaining table, and actively attended to and learned from one another's arguments.

Most delegates had a sense of the goals and mechanics of self-governance that either needed to be affirmed or further developed: having just fought for liberation from the British king, they would tolerate no overarching boss. As a new free nation, they had to ensure their ability to defend themselves from external threats. In the aftermath of the recent farm debt rebellion of Daniel Shays and his Massachusetts armed mob, it was vital to secure the internal peace against domestic dissension. The chaos enabled by the earlier Articles of Confederation—

multiple currencies, local taxes, and inconsistent trade regulations—was impeding collective welfare by hampering economic development. There must be a shared understanding of who would be a citizen in the new nation, and what would be their rights and responsibilities. There had to be a framework for how public decisions would be made and conflicts resolved in order to coordinate local, state, and central administration—without a king. And there needed to be mechanisms of enforcing collective decisions.

But with the backdrop of the proverbial smiling devil, there was little shared agreement about how to accomplish such things. And there remained the burning issue of slavery, thought by many southern delegates to be essential to their state economies, and despised by others as contrary to the natural rights of all people, as proclaimed in the Declaration of Independence of 1776. The delegates tackled all of those questions as best as they could through three long months of heated argument, punctuated by negotiation, compromise, and renegotiation.

On the afternoon of September 17, a final draft of a new constitution lay before them. Most delegates saw it as an improvement over the old Articles of Confederation, but the level of support to approve it, and seek ratification and implementation, was unclear. Franklin came to the front of the room to signal his assent to the draft, hoping to encourage others to also vote "yea." To add to his plea, he offered his personal reflections about what it had taken, from all of them working together, to reach this moment. In his aged frailty, he was seated beside his fellow Pennsylvania delegate, John Wilson, who read the speech aloud on Franklin's behalf.

The Perfect Is the Enemy of the Common Good

The speech conveyed a tone humbler than Franklin would display the next day, when he blurted out his answer about "keeping the republic." This day, still behind closed doors, he signaled more painful practicality, an eighty-one-year-old man chastened by the experience of a long and eventful career.

The speech began by asserting his agreement "to this Constitution with all its faults, if they are such," but conceding as well that "there are several parts which I do not at present approve." He then commented on the ego and irrationality of human nature, which he acknowledged no less for himself than others now listening: "Most men . . . think themselves in possession of all truth, and that wherever others differ from them it is for error." Franklin next suggested the disputes arising from such assumptions often in fact worsen when many are gathered together for "joint wisdom" because they also bring to their tasks "their prejudices, their passions, their errors of opinion, their local interests, and their selfish views." With all of that, Franklin expressed astonishment at how close to perfection the delegates had come with this draft of the Constitution—close, but not 100 percent, because perfection, he further implied, was not attainable in human endeavor. With still some lingering doubt, the speech nonetheless concluded with Franklin's approval, as he acknowledged that important practical matters now hung in the balance: "I consent because I am not sure, that this [Constitution] is not the best. The opinions I have had of its errors, I sacrifice to the public good."[2]

As the delegates mulled Franklin's words, they knew all too well the specific controversies his carefully chosen philosophical language alluded to without naming. They had hammered out an agreement through disputes about the branches of government, central versus local financial authority, voting rights, and the fraught issue of slavery. Franklin was congratulating them for finding the compromise that was the best available while acknowledging its imperfections.

The delegates had agreed on a system *that ensured no overall boss*: the specific authority of the new president was critically constrained to minimize that risk, and the "balance of powers" would similarly limit any domineering attempts by the court or legislatures. They had *provided for the citizens' collective security and basic welfare* by strengthening the financial and military authority of a national federal government over the local states—not too much, but enough, a majority believed, to remedy the weakness of the Articles of Confederation. They had *defined who would be a citizen and what that meant*, with rules and requirements about voting, immigration, and certain responsibilities and freedoms (albeit with, among other limits, a painful compromise about slaves). And they had designed *institutions of governance led wholly by citizens*, with a careful detail about the requirements and selection of officeholders and representatives for the presidency, legislature, and courts. They were able to *negotiate in good faith* because they treated each other as *civic friends* rather than enemies, and because they had been *educated* by formal learning, experience, and one another in the essentials of civic life.

Of course, there were still loopholes and loose ends, but the draft was overall good enough to move forward to the still-uncertain process of ratification. And Franklin reminded them of that. His speech emphasized what it took to strike a civic bargain among ambitious and opinionated human beings—*to prefer a common good compromise in political decisions over unilateral demands for perfection.*

Franklin and his fellow delegates recognized that the agreement was not a timeless masterpiece; they knew that it would be revised. It was an imperfect but living civic bargain for a living democracy; the search for a "more perfect union" (in the words of the Constitution's famous prologue) would continue. The founding document set out a framework of self-governance that had the capacity to evolve, and it would have to do so if it were to survive. The challenges, tragedies, and successes of America in doing that are the subject of chapter 5.

In the aftermath of the convention, the thirty-nine delegates who signed the new Constitution were indeed eager to sell it to the citizens of the new nation; the Constitution was only a proposal until it was ratified by the states. Ratification was achieved through a public process of education—through reasoned arguments presented by citizens to citizens in newspapers and pamphlets about the nature of the governance proposed, and the rationale for the choices that were made in its design. Other forms and forums of the education of citizens have since been essential in sustaining American democracy. Civic education, both formal and informal, was also basic to striking and keeping the civic bargains of our other three historical cases. It was and is crucial to sustaining democracy.

With history as our guide, this book explains the fundamentals of democracy as collective self-governance. Our goal is to help you understand the key assumptions and imperatives that enable self-governance by citizens, and how democracy survives. It is a book not only about imperfection, compromise, and dealmaking, and how imminent and existential threats are an incentive to negotiation, but also about civic virtue and friendship. Bargaining must be pursued in a climate of goodwill if it is to meet inevitable steep challenges. We hope that having read this book, you will think differently about democracy's future—and about your own role as a citizen or would-be citizen in helping it to survive or letting it die.

1

FUNDAMENTALS

Essential Conditions for Democracy

To understand how democracy survives, we must get back to fundamentals. We must have a clear idea of what we mean by democracy. And we must understand what it takes to have and keep a democratic republic. This book claims that a successful democracy is sustained by a grand civic bargain. The civic bargain is a negotiated agreement among citizens about the terms of their collective self-governance, enabled by practices of civic friendship and supported by civic education. It is achieved through a history of predemocratic political bargains. And it is sustained over time by ongoing, incremental bargaining. It was by getting back to the fundamentals of the civic bargain and tracing the history of political bargaining that we developed our theory of what democracy is and how it survives. Sketching that theory is the work we undertake in this chapter. In the next four chapters, we apply our framework to four great cases of democratic development.

A word on method: our approach is circular in that our theory of democracy arose from our study of history, and it is tested by the light it sheds on specific historical cases. We hope that readers will find the circularity to be virtuous rather than vicious, because the learning that comes from the process is iterative and progressively clarifying. We can and must learn from the past. What we learn must come from a detailed examination of the specifics of what happened over time in particular parts of the world. By comparing local histories, general patterns may emerge. Identifying a pattern then allows us to return to each local history with new insights. If those insights are valid, we will better understand the historical development of diverse times and places; we can make better sense of obscure or confusing aspects of history; and we can use history for building a realistic theory of democracy.

Our Theory in Brief

In the introduction, we listed seven essential conditions for the civic bargain, which in turn enables and sustains democracy. When these conditions are fulfilled, democracy is robust. When they are lacking, democracy is impossible. When they are degraded, democracy is in danger.

1. No boss—except one another
2. Security and welfare
3. Citizenship defined
4. Citizen-led institutions
5. Good faith compromise
6. Civic friendship
7. Civic education

Most books concerned with the problems faced by democracy today focus on number 4: the formal legislative, executive, and judicial institutions of government. But we believe that formal institutions are only part of the story.

Using the metaphor of architecture, democracy, in its most basic sense, provides a foundation for various kinds of institutional superstructure. The superstructure of every real-world democracy, ancient and modern, includes a complex array of constitutional arrangements specifying how rules are made (legislative action), put into practice (executive action), and interpreted and enforced (judicial action). The institutional superstructure is important. We will discuss formal rules in some detail below. But democracy requires more than formal institutions. Focusing exclusively on the details of institutional superstructure can be misleading and distracting. Very different governmental edifices have been erected on a democratic foundation—that is, on a civic bargain. As we will see in chapters 2–5 below, even when we restrict ourselves to just four particularly well-known and influential democracies, we find different decision-making methods, systems of legal judgment, and kinds and levels of administrative bureaucracy.

If we concentrate on the institutional superstructure in isolation from a close examination of the foundations, we risk losing sight of democracy's most basic features. And without a firm grasp of those fundamentals, we will never understand how things can go wrong at the base, and why. Or alternatively, how, because the foundation was solid, the superstructure weathered storms, and why it could be modified and added to without catastrophe. Ignorance of the fundamentals leaves citizens ill prepared to rebuild their own political home before it collapses. So this book pays a lot of attention to the foundation: to what a civic bargain is, how it comes about, and how it is maintained over time.

Conditions 1–3 are foundational in that they clarify what democracy is in its most basic sense, what it must deliver in terms of people's expectations about their individual and collective well-being, and what it means to be a citizen. Once we have those basic understandings in hand, we can better recognize what formal democratic institutions are intended to achieve, and how formal rules can either facilitate or impede that achievement. But creating and sustaining democratic institutions depends on another set of foundational understandings. Conditions 5–6 concern the practices that democratic citizens employ in successful bargaining and the attitudes they develop toward their fellow citizens. Condition 7 establishes why the education of citizens by other citizens is essential for saving democracy.

Our theory of democracy starts with an understanding of what *democracy* is: in its most basic sense, as noted above, democracy means "no boss." The alternative to rule by a boss is collective self-government by people who refuse to be ruled by anyone but themselves. Democracy as no-boss self-government arises when subjects become citizens who strike a bargain among themselves: they set the rules and devise the norms of their shared political project. This is the civic bargain. It may subsequently be revised, but meanwhile the bargain settles the question of who gets and who must give what so as to enable and then sustain self-governance. Democracy survives if and only if citizens can and do rule themselves under the terms of their civic bargain, accepting no boss but themselves. So to grasp how democracy is saved, we must understand the conditions that pertain when citizens govern themselves. The seven primary conditions, detailed below, are the main subject of this chapter.

By specifying the conditions that make it *possible* to sustain self-government, we also reveal the problems that must be solved if democracy is to survive and flourish over time. Among the most important problems are what we call *the challenges of scale*: a democratic state must get and stay big enough to achieve an adequate level of security and material welfare. But the growth of wealth, growth in the number of citizens, and increased diversity puts strain on the capacity of any body of citizens to rule themselves. Once we have grasped why and how scale presents both opportunities and problems for democracy, we can better understand how citizens might go about solving those problems.

Abstracting general principles from the details of historical cases shows us that what allows democracy to survive is what first gave it birth: citizens bargaining with one another about the fundamental terms of self-governance, accepting trade-offs about gives and gets, and coming to understand how it works in practice. In sum, democracy survives when the challenges of scale are met, when citizens achieve and then maintain a civic bargain, agreeing to renegotiate the terms of the bargain as needed while still preserving the conditions of self-governance. The rest of this chapter unpacks this brief statement of our theory, first by exploring each of the seven fundamental conditions, then highlighting some of the civic bargain's less obvious features, and finally answering why alternative approaches to understanding democracy seem to us less satisfactory.

Condition 1: No Boss—Except One Another

Democracy is one solution to the problem of social order: How can people with diverse viewpoints and goals, whose interests are not identical, join forces to work together, effectively, to build and inhabit a peaceful and prosperous society? Social order emerges as a problem that must be solved as soon as a human community exceeds the tiny scale of a few dozen individuals; indeed the problem may arise even in the smallest human groups. Any solution must answer several questions: Who makes decisions on the formal rules or informal norms determining who gets what (powers, resources, or honors) and who gives what (duties, responsibilities, or taxes)? How are those rules and norms enforced (violators punished or excellence rewarded)? Why do people obey the rules (if they do)? The democratic solution is "collective self-government by citizens." The answers to the questions about who decides, who gives and gets, who enforces rules, and why people obey all flow from that basic premise.

In the simplest and bluntest terms, democracy is a no-boss condition. That means there is no absolute king, no ruling elite, and no political party permanently in power. The alternative to rule by a boss is self-government by an active, participatory citizenship. A democracy will make use of leaders and educated elites, but these people will not be the rulers. A democracy will employ a majority decision rule, but the composition of that majority is not fixed.

The democratic solution to the problem of social order is difficult, especially as communities grow larger. The easy and historically common (although never universal) solution is some form of autocracy: the decision-making ruler is the boss. Often the ruler is a dominant individual: a king, tyrant, or dictator. In other cases, it may be a small coalition of powerful individuals: an aristocracy, oligarchy, or junta. Or it may be a wider network of people who use violence to quash lawful civic decision-making. In yet other circumstances, the boss may be an extensive minority or even majority of enfranchised citizens organized as a permanent ruling party. A ruling party may advertise itself as a "democracy." But when one organized body of citizens systematically excludes the rest of the citizens from effective participation in making, carrying out, and interpreting the rules, those who are excluded are citizens in name alone. They are subjects in fact. One-party government is thus also the rule of a (collective) boss.

Under the rule of any boss, the rules are enforced by persuasion, or as necessary, force. People obey because they are afraid to do otherwise or believe the boss is in some way legitimate. In the latter case, the boss is held to have a *right* to rule and others have a *duty* to obey. So the rule of a boss may be based on consent—the active or passive acceptance by many subjects to the condition of being ruled over. The rule of a boss may be nasty or relatively benevolent. Despite whatever name it gives itself, though, a boss-rule regime is not a democracy.

Individual citizens choose to reject any ruler other than their fellow citizens for a variety of reasons. We will detail those in the chapters to come. Briefly, those reasons may be characterized as negative and positive. On the negative side is a dislike, distrust, and distaste for authoritarian rule. On the positive side is the recognition that self-government is a good thing, in and of itself. That positive evaluation is combined with the belief that democracy can be an effective instrument in gaining other valued ends and common interests. In material terms, common interests include security and welfare. In ethical terms, common values include freedom, equality, and as we will see (condition 6), civic friendship and dignity.

We believe that there are strong negative *and* positive reasons for preferring democracy to the rule of a boss, and that at least as an aspiration, a consideration of these reasons should foster a willingness to enter a civic bargain. On the negative side, it suffices to cite Lord Acton's famous dictum: absolute power corrupts absolutely. Democratic citizens are convinced that a boss with absolute power will be absolutely corrupt. Positively, democrats believe that democracy is desirable as an end in itself because the "gets" are great, ethically as well as materially. Free, equal, dignified citizens live lives that are, all things being equal, better than the alternative. At least some of those gets are unavailable, as a package, outside democracy.

Democracy is, of course, a hotly contested term. Autocrats who claim the name democracy for boss rule are simply using a socially favorable term to mask the true nature of their government. But many serious students of democracy have offered definitions that are either more or less demanding than ours. One set of less demanding definitions holds that democracy pertains whenever existing forms of social control are rejected or contested in a social movement, or when forms of power are more or less widely dispersed in a community, whether or not it takes the form of a state. A second less demanding definition maintains that democracy pertains when the ruler (say, a monarch or elite coalition) is advised by a council of persons not appointed by the rulers themselves. On those accounts, democracy is a widespread, common, and persistent phenomenon, readily observed in all periods of human history and across the globe. Although our concern in this book is the democratic state, we agree that democracy is manifest below the level of the state. Indeed in an earlier book, we argued in detail for the practical and ethical value of democracy in firms and voluntary organizations. And we also concur that there are meaningful differences between absolutist forms of centralized rule and, for example, consultative rulers who avail themselves of an advisory council. An illustration of the latter is the Anglo-Saxon kings in early medieval England (chapter 5).

Consultative rule, by bosses who accept some limits on their authority, arises from political bargaining, and it may lead, eventually, to democracy. Much can be learned by carefully studying the differences been consultative and absolute forms of centralized, boss-dominated government. Democracy is compatible with modern, strictly limited forms of constitutional monarchy. Yet we resist using the term *democracy* for the rule of powerful hereditary monarchs, who periodically consult with those they did not personally appoint but are also not bound by the council's advice. When the ruler's decision is informed, yet not actually constrained, by the input of others, when the ruler is the ultimate source of law and legal interpretation, then the ruler is still a boss. Describing that sort of ruling as democracy runs up against a long tradition, stretching from the ancient Greeks to the Declaration of Independence, of sharply distinguishing monarchy and oligarchy from democracy.

The two less demanding approaches to defining democracy noted above have been applied to prehistoric and ancient societies as well as, at least potentially, modernity. A third, less demanding approach to democracy is that adopted by political scientists concerned uniquely with modern states. So-called minimalist approaches to democracy treat it as a rule-constrained electoral contest for power between established political parties. Power transitions are orderly because losers of elections do not resort to violence in an attempt to remain in power. While we agree that for modern democracies these are imperatives, the minimalist approach allows for (and in some cases, insists on) a passive citizenry. This opens the way to boss rule between elections.

Our definition of democracy as no boss—as a system of collective self-governance by citizens—means that democracy has historically been less common than the first two less demanding definitions imply, but historically more common than is indicated by the third. By our definition, there are many examples of nonabsolutist government that fall short of self-government by citizens. But on the other hand, our definition does not require electoral contests between political parties.

Other serious students of democracy offer definitions that are in various ways more demanding than ours. First, in the modern era, democracy is often equated with "liberal democracy," requiring, among other things, a commitment to an extensive set of universal human rights. Indeed, the project of advancing universal rights is sometimes given priority over self-government in the understanding of what democracy demands. Next, democracy is said to require organized political parties. Parties are assumed to be an essential feature of self-government because they facilitate the focalization of citizen interests into coherent voting patterns by providing for organized leadership. Finally, some prominent political thinkers have asserted that democracy is incompatible with republicanism. They argue that rules are made in a republic by representatives who are chosen (directly or indirectly) by the citizens, whereas in democracies rules are made by direct (referendum-type) voting by the citizens themselves, and that democracy is liable to be unstable because its citizens lack the courage, self-control, and knowledge required to participate effectively in governance. Later in this chapter, we address why we think these alternative definitions are too demanding.

Condition 2: Security and Welfare

Sustaining adequate levels of physical security and material welfare for those who inhabit a bounded territory is at least one reason that governments exist. Some theorists, like the great seventeenth-century English political writer Thomas Hobbes, would say it is *the only* reason. The definition of what level of safety or material well-being is adequate varies considerably over time and space. Today, in a globalizing world of hostile powers and cross-border economies, it is impossible for a state to ensure that everyone is always safe and prosperous. But every successful, independent state must build the capacity to deliver conditions of everyday life that most residents see as safe and prosperous enough. This means, at a minimum, that residents do not live in constant fear of attacks on themselves or their property. Successful states must sustain lawful and peaceful conditions internally, and must also be able to defend themselves from external threats. Residents must have ample opportunity at least to feed, clothe, and house themselves. In a regime without a boss, the essential public goods of security and general welfare must be maintained by the citizens themselves. While there are always trade-offs between security and economic welfare (guns versus butter), both safety and prosperity must be treated by democratic citizens as matters of common interest. When people live in constant fear for their safety, when they are starving and exposed to the elements, they are likely to look to a boss to fix it.

Historically, states contend with bandits and criminals, and are faced with sometimes-hostile rival states; such existential threats provide a strong incentive to create effective responses. Autocratic states can grow their capacity for confronting those threats as well as enlarging their territory and wealth by exploiting their more efficient command-and-control organizations. Autocrats who devise effective hierarchical systems of authority can build large police forces and armies capable of dominating less capable neighbors. If neighboring states are to retain their independence, they too must gain capacity. Given interstate rivalry, all involved find themselves in a race in which each entrant must run faster and faster just to stay even with the others. So democracies, just like autocracies, must "scale up"—must grow their capacity to a level that suffices to provide citizens with at least as much security and economic welfare as the autocratic alternative. They must meet this challenge of scale without recourse to the command-and-control inherent to autocracy.

Democracy can, however, deliver real advantages in capacity building, and existential threats can motivate social cohesion. Free citizens have historically proven to be highly motivated and effective warriors, accepting mandatory military service as a duty owed to their country and fellow citizens. Democracies promote economic development by advancing the free exchange of knowledge and lowering the fear of arbitrary expropriation of property by a predatory boss. Well-motivated democratic citizens willingly pay taxes to provide for both safety and material welfare for all. As we will see, democracies have historically featured impressive levels of economic growth and military might. Yet growth must somehow be managed. Unconstrained economic growth can result in severe inequalities in wealth among citizens, putting pressure on civic relations. Rapid growth in military capacity can lead to the transformation of a leader into a warlord ambitious to become the boss.

Supplying conditions of safety and collective self-government by citizens in a competitive world has been achieved either by increasing the productivity of the incumbent citizens (through technical and economic innovations) or more effectively exploiting noncitizens (for example, through slavery), or both. But it may also entail expanding the number of productive citizens. Historically, in democratic communities, the citizens themselves are especially efficient producers. Citizens have a stake in the current form of governance of their community; they willingly bear the high costs of sustaining their own security and welfare. And that in turn introduces a practical reason for expanding the citizen body. The imperative to "grow or fail" has often (although as we will see, not always) pushed the incremental expansion of the citizen body.

Condition 3: Citizenship Defined

Democracy as collective, no-boss self-government takes citizens to be much more than "legally resident passport holders" or "those obedient to and protected by the civil law within a certain territory." Citizens in a democracy are rulers of themselves and each other. They are active and ultimately authoritative participants in making important decisions on behalf of their political community as voters or activists, and also in interpreting, implementing, and enforcing those rules as jurors or democratically appointed officials. The participation of the citizens in making and enforcing decisions may be direct (voting on policy) or indirect (voting for representatives or selecting them by lottery). Citizens are active participants too, along with others in their community, in sustaining and revising social norms. The norms most relevant to democracy, detailed in conditions 5–7, are the expectations that citizens have of one another.

In a democratic state, citizenship is *extensive* in that it is larger than face-to-face. That means the civic community is not a place where "everybody knows your name"—nor do others always "have their eyes on you." And that in turn means that the rules and norms must be made and sustained without everyone knowing just what everyone else is doing, or how they are behaving on a day-to-day basis. For democracy to survive, citizens must internalize rules and norms. They must voluntarily choose to moderate their behavior when it threatens the social order. The citizenship is also socially *diverse* in that different people have different social identities, different life experiences, and to some degree different interests. That means that decisions cannot be made based on the assumption that "we all agree on pretty much everything most of the time." Negotiating among diverse interests (condition 5) is necessary in a democracy because it is *not* the case that all interests are common ones, although importantly, it is the case that there must be *some* interests that are held in common. As we have seen (condition 2), security and welfare must be treated as shared interests by all citizens.

While some citizens will be more privileged than others in various ways due to differences in (at least) wealth, natural talents, and educational achievement, citizens hold one another as political equals in terms of (at least) potential political influence. While the aspiration of equality of influence is never fully achieved in practice, it is exemplified by the individual votes of citizens being held to have equal weight.

Likewise, democratic citizens, from antiquity to today, demand the fundamental conditions of political liberty. Not having a boss means that we are free to express our opinions in public and pursue our interests in private. Freedom does not mean doing just whatever one pleases, irrespective of the consequences for others. Free and equal citizens must also ordinarily be law-abiding and aware of their responsibilities as citizens: they agree to live according to the rules that are established by democratic procedures and norms of civic comity. In philosopher Aristotle's deceptively simple phrase, citizens are those who "share in both ruling and being ruled over"—both in making rules (formal and informal) and being subject to them. But democratic citizens may sometimes disobey the established rules with an aim of saving democracy. They do not break the rules for selfish reasons or because they can get away with it. Rather, they disobey because the system of rules has come to seem unfair. Citizens loyal to the ideal of democracy may engage in disobedience as a way of calling attention to the need for the rules to be revised. Yet loyal disobedience seldom justifies violence; brute force opens the way for boss rule.

In a democracy, the rules are ultimately made, interpreted, and enforced by a relatively large, socially diverse, self-defined body of citizens.[1] People rule in their own common interest within a bounded domain. A democratic state is established within recognized (although often-revisable) borders. Democratic citizenship is, compared with any form of boss rule, inclusive. Yet there are always limits to inclusion. The political domain, the space in which "we the people" rule, always includes some people who are not citizens—at least not in the sense of having an active share in ruling. At a minimum, young children will be excluded from active participation in government. The domain of a democracy has historically also included adults who are ruled over—who are subjects rather than citizens. In aspiration, democracy is inclusive: all persons resident within the political domain who have both the proven capacity and sincere desire to be citizens are given the opportunity to participate fully in the benefits and duties of citizenship. But that aspiration has never been fully realized in any historical democratic state.

As we will see, democracy has, historically, coexisted with exclusions that are rejected by contemporary democratic states, such as slavery, extensive colonial empires, and the exclusion of women and long-term foreign residents from the status of participating citizen. Democracy, collective self-government by citizens, ought not be conflated with just, fair, or even good government. While democratic citizens aspire to make their regime more just and themselves more virtuous, the democratic republic is not an ideal system of just and impartial social order. Democracy is the exercise of political power by an extensive yet bounded body of citizens, among themselves and over others.

Collective self-governance *by citizens* also means that it must be clear who is a citizen and who is not, and what the special privileges and duties of citizens are. Membership in the civic body is formal, and in an important sense, it is exclusionary. Citizens are, collectively and in comparison to other residents of their community, a differentiated and politically privileged body. The citizen is a person with a special, desirable status. That status grants the citizens certain political rights not held by noncitizens. It likewise imposes special duties on them in the form of civic responsibilities. Some people, but not others, hold these specific rights and responsibilities. Membership in that body is, at the moment of democratic foundation, historically contingent: it is determined by the social norms of the time, not by abstract justice. Subsequently, there must be some way for those who are currently "the citizens" to decide on whether to include in the citizen body others who desire citizenship but do not presently have that status. If the process leading to inclusion is not done in a way that is widely perceived as fair by both incumbents and those seeking civic membership, then noncitizens will be a constant source of potential threat. Preserving democracy means achieving some level of fairness at the level of democratic inclusion. Yet finding that level is often politically difficult.

Democracies betray their own fundamental principles as well as threaten their own survival when one group of citizens seeks to deprive other citizens of the rights of full and participatory citizenship. Historically, democratic citizenship has usually been a one-way ratchet: those who gain citizenship expect to keep it. When that is not the case, citizens thrust into the role of subjects are likely to fight and democracy is put at risk. Consequently, the citizenship tends to grow in both absolute size and diversity as new categories of persons are admitted to the ranks of the citizens. Both size and diversity put pressure on the instruments of self-government. The question of how to scale up the citizenship while sustaining civic norms and values is one of the primary challenges that a democracy must address if it is to survive. That challenge is met, in part, through institutional innovation.

Condition 4: Citizen-Led Institutions

Institutions answer questions about the form of decision-making bodies (for example, the legislature, executive, and judiciary) and their respective powers. They also do so about the processes by which decisions are actually made and implemented—the internal procedures governing those bodies, and how they relate to one another—and the formal and informal mechanisms that facilitate or impede implementation. Both historical and contemporary democratic institutional systems vary considerably. Decision-making may be by the assembled citizens themselves, or representatives appointed by lottery or election. Mechanisms for enabling a subset of the citizenry to represent the others addresses one major problem of scale, although it introduces another: at some point the ratio of those represented to representative becomes so high that the individual citizen is no longer a political agent. But the constant among democratic institutions is that power is not concentrated in a boss. This sets limits on the scope of authority wielded by the executive and unelected administrators. It requires a degree of transparency in public processes. It necessitates accountability, such as periodic elections and conduct reviews for public officials. Limits on the concentration of official power have historically been achieved through distributing authority among state officials by the separation of powers among branches of government as well as the authority of the citizen body to recall officials and make rules (regularly or occasionally) by public referendum.

Well-functioning democratic institutions sustain political equality and freedom, provide for adequate public goods of common interest (say, security from invasion), and allow for fair-minded bargaining over interests that are not shared. Moreover, democratic systems of government have, at least potentially, a relative advantage over autocratic ones: they can leverage the diversity of the citizen body by making a wide range of knowledge and information available for problem-solving. Democratic success has historically been facilitated by the often-overlooked ability of democratic institutions to bring more diverse knowledge and problem-solving skills to bear.

The design and reform of the formal institutions of government is where most writing on "how democracy fails or thrives" tends to concentrate. Yet there are limits on what can be accomplished by formal institutions alone. The balance of power and rule of law can be corrupted when a boss captures the relevant branches. The legislature or judiciary may be monopolized by an organized political party. The executive may become entrenched, nontransparent, and resistant to being called to account. Partisanship and party spirit may lead to gridlock, such that new rules cannot be made. The aspiration of a democratic government to be a kind of "machine that runs by itself" has never been achieved or even approached in practice.

Self-governance means, as we have seen, that the citizens rule themselves. They answer to no one except each other for the decisions that concern their shared community. They may choose to rule themselves indirectly, by naming representatives—legislators to whom the authority to make decisions is delegated and judges to weigh decisions against democratically established laws. When representatives are effectively held to account during their term of office or after it, self-governance is preserved. Likewise, self-government is not threatened by the legitimate exercise of authority by those to whom authority is delegated, such as to police or tax collectors. If, on the other hand, the rights of free and equal citizens to free speech and public assembly are infringed, then the infringing authority is taking the role of the boss. In that case, those exercising authority are acting illegitimately and must be resisted. A democracy must establish the boundary within which authority delegated by the people to our representatives is legitimately exercised and obedience to authority is a civic duty. And likewise, democracy must define the bright line beyond which the exercise of authority is a violation and resistance to violators becomes a civic duty. Maintaining those boundaries is a difficult and vital part of establishing and enforcing democratic rules and norms.

Citizen self-government must, by definition, be *self-enforcing*; instead of depending on a third-party boss to enforce the terms of the bargain, it is the citizens themselves, acting in their individual and collective interest as citizens, who ultimately make the rules and provide for their enforcement. As we have seen, they may, and in modernity usually do, make, interpret, and enforce rules through representatives and administrators—that is, through a government. But the government of a democracy is not a third-party enforcer with an abstract will and interests of its own. Its powers are delegated by the citizenry, and government officials are accountable to the citizens. In every case in which democracy has survived, representatives govern in the name of the people, in the interests of the people, and at the pleasure of the people. In Abraham Lincoln's resonant phrase, in a democracy government is "of, by, and for the people." By contrast, when the representatives or administrators govern in their own selfish interest, when the government is no longer of, by, and for the people, democracy perishes. The officials running the government have become the boss, and the citizens are their subjects.

Collective self-governance signifies the ability of citizens to achieve ongoing, effective, collective action. In an important sense, citizens remain individuals as they fulfill their duty to preserve democracy through self-governance. Unlike ants or bees, the individual members of the community do not merge into an organic group entity. They do not have a hive mind. But that said, the collective must be able to function as a choice maker in certain ways just as does a rational individual. The group, directly or through representatives, must be able to formulate orderly preferences such that *this or that* option is preferred to the available alternatives. And like a rational individual, the collective must have coherent beliefs—that is, the beliefs that lead the group to decide what options are available must not be contradictory in the sense of believing X and not-X simultaneously. It is not the case that all will prefer just the same outcome, nor will all believe just the same things about the availability of options. Yet the choice (however made) must plausibly represent a choice of the citizenry: disagreement must allow closure, with all agreeing to follow legitimately enacted group decisions regardless of their preferences.

Acting together is not easy. The forms, processes, and mechanisms of democratic institutions must ensure that there is no permanent majority or empowered minority that acts to consistently secure the interests of some at the expense of the rest. For democracy to work, all must accept getting less than they desire. All must subordinate certain of their personal or subgroup interests to the good of the whole. A choice that is made collectively will typically lay heavier burdens on some than others. My (or my subgroup's) interests will sometimes be sacrificed for yours. I will rationally accept that if I believe that your interests will in turn someday be sacrificed for mine and that we are both willing to be persuaded by good arguments about common goods.

The willingness to accept that kind of sacrifice and trust in others is an important part of the responsibilities that self-governance imposes on each citizen. It is a duty to self-regulate the impulse to act selfishly on desires that conflict with common interests. An important part of democratic freedom is the freedom to pursue one's personal goals through the established institutions with the expectation that others will likewise be pursuing theirs. But citizens must moderate the natural urge to act to satisfy their private desires in full, when acting that way precludes the collective achievement of an essential public good. In ethical terms, for democracy to work, citizens must cultivate a *virtue* of civic moderation. The practice of that virtue is good faith compromise when negotiating with others seeking different goals.

Condition 5: Good Faith Compromise

Democracy, as bossless self-government capable of maintaining social order and promoting public goods, depends fundamentally on bargaining. It also relies on negotiating in good faith with one's fellow citizens over divergent interests and accepting the result of the negotiation while recognizing that in the future there will be further negotiations over other issues. The survival of democracy depends on the capacity of citizens to make and revise the agreements by which they regulate their shared community, decide who gets and who gives what, and sustain their joint capacity to create and preserve common goods. The agreements negotiated among participatory citizens as *civic bargains* are a subset of the larger category of *political bargains*. In nondemocratic or predemocratic communities, political bargains are made between rulers and subjects, or between leaders to build a ruling coalition. Political bargains are in turn a subset of the yet-larger category of *bargains*: negotiated agreements between interested parties in which each party expects to get more from making the bargain than they could expect if they did not make it.

Zero-Sum versus Positive-Sum Agreements

If we are to understand the gives and gets of political bargains, and ultimately of the democratic civic bargain, we must first understand how bargains work. Bargaining, in its most basic sense, is an alternative to the use of violence to determine who gets what and who gives what. Behind every bargain lies a potential resort to force. The crudest form of bargain is that of the armed robber who, instead of just shooting you in the back and taking your wallet, offers you the choice of "your money or your life." This gangsters' bargain is *zero-sum*: what they take, you lose. The losses and gains in that kind of bargain sum to nothing. But it could be worse. Suppose you decide not to take the gangsters' bargain; you instead choose to fight, grabbing for the gun. In that case, you may be killed, and the gangsters may be imprisoned for life. That is a *negative-sum* result: both parties are worse off than they were before the bargaining began. If all bargains were based on overt threats or devolved into violence, if bargaining offered at best the chance of a zero-sum outcome, there would be no chance of social or political development, and indeed no possibility of civilization as we know it.

Piracy and gangsterism, which tend to flourish when there is no government capable of suppressing them, represent an organized form of the armed robber's bargain: groups of pirates and gangsters may be organized either autocratically or in a rough form of self-government. In either case, however, the purpose of their organization is to seize the goods and require services from the weak: the bargain they make with their victims is zero-sum. As historian Thucydides realized twenty-four hundred years ago, in a world of zero-sum bargains defined by piracy and gangsterism, there is no large-scale social development or economic growth. Happily, the armed robber's bargain is not the only kind of bargain.

We are all familiar with economic bargains; we make them every time we buy or sell something. Economic bargains among peaceful traders in goods and services offer a productive alternative to piracy and gangsterism. Peaceful traders do not fear the resort to violence if they know that there are some background rules or norms that give them that assurance. Under those conditions, the traders can freely bargain over an exchange of goods. If they come to agreement on a price, it means that each expects to be better off after the deal is made than they would have been if no agreement had been reached. That is, the traders expect a *positive-sum* result from the successful conclusion of their negotiations. Their agreement is expected to be productive; it is "win-win." It is those kinds of productive bargains that make civilization possible.

It is important to note that the wins may be unequal; one party may walk away having gained more than the other. But each expects to get something of value, and that value was not available to them outside the bargain. If the bargain is successfully concluded, what each gives is more than made up for by what each gets. Moreover, if things go well the first time around, the traders may initiate a longer-term relationship. As they continue to productively exchange with one another, they come to trust one another more. As a result, each can afford to invest more in the goods and services that will be exchanged. The costs of peaceful transactions drop as trust grows and the risk of being cheated declines. The potential profits on both sides consequently increase.

If they develop deep enough trust, the two parties may take the next step and form a partnership. In that case, each of the partners is expected to willingly make some personal sacrifices and give more than they get in the short run in order to preserve the valuable partnership. When we extrapolate those kinds of positive-sum, productive relationships to a world of markets and firms, we can better understand the dynamics of economic growth and social development.

Political Bargains

Political bargains are like economic ones in that the parties to the bargain believe they are better off inside the bargain than outside it. Historically, political bargains have been struck between (for example) monarchs and nobles, kings and towns, and oligarchic rulers and those they rule over. Political bargains are also struck between citizens and those who aspire to become citizens. A political bargain is an agreement about specific gives and gets—that is, who *gets* what in terms of rights and privileges, material benefits, and protection from violence from a system of government. And equally important but often ignored, it concerns who *gives* what in order to build and sustain the system: who pays what costs in terms of duties and responsibilities.

Political bargains settle (for the time being at least) the questions of who gets and who gives what in terms of ruling and being ruled. And by so doing, political bargains establish and maintain social order. They reduce the level of overt violence. They create conditions that can reduce piracy and gangsterism. Political bargains bring about legitimacy and rule of law. They tend to promote common goods (for example, security) that benefit the wider community. And those conditions in turn facilitate making positive-sum economic bargains. Throughout history, every successful state that is not simply a top-down autocracy, maintained by ideological mystification or brute force, has been built and sustained through beneficial political bargains. These include early bargains between powerful rulers and a limited number of their subjects.

In the following chapters, we will consider in detail the historical conditions in positive-sum political bargains that were made among rulers and subjects. Then, when people rejected being ruled by a boss, positive-sum civic bargains were struck among citizens. We need to keep in mind that as in our simple model of the armed robber's bargain, for people within a given political community, the alternative to making a political bargain is the use of force. If one side is narrowly self-interested, willing to fight, and expects to win, and if the other side has no chance of surviving a fight, then the outcome is political domination. In the most extreme case, it is the zero-sum equivalent of handing over your wallet to the gangster.

If, on the other hand, those who are being threatened with violence believe that they have a chance of winning, if they expect to lose less by fighting than by agreeing to the harsh terms of a bad bargain, there will be open conflict. The result of the fight is likely to be, once again, at best zero-sum: one side wins and takes what it wants from the other side. Or it will be negative sum: both sides will be harmed in the fight and will be worse off than when they began. In the extreme case, failing to strike a political bargain among parties within a single political community leads to full-on civil war. Civil wars, as any student of history knows, are typically destructive for both sides.

The goal of political bargaining is a positive-sum outcome that avoids the costs of fighting. To be mutually beneficial, political bargains, like bargains between traders, must be regarded as "fair enough" by those who enter into them. When both sides have some bargaining power—that is, each can credibly threaten to walk away from the bargaining table—any resulting bargain will have to be seen as fair enough. That means that unlike the armed robber's bargain, neither side will get all it wants. Each will have to give something to get something. This means that fair enough seldom, if ever, establishes conditions that are regarded as ideal by either side. And for some people, that is a deal breaker.

Political bargains involve trade-offs. Given the pluralistic preferences of those at the bargaining table, they do not achieve ideal justice. Good faith negotiating becomes difficult, or even impossible, when people refuse to accept anything less than what they believe is perfectly good or right. The attempt at bargaining will fail if the parties come to the bargaining table inflexibly committed to rejecting any agreement that does not fully instantiate their own conception of what a perfectly just (or happy, pious, or moral) outcome would be. Inflexible demands might stem from bargainers' expectation of certain property rights, demands for the righting of particular wrongs, or insistence on the needs of divine justice. From the point of view of those who demand perfection here and now—as opposed to those who see their ideal outcome as a regulative ideal or a goal to strive for—a political bargain that falls short of the ideal is a contemptible compromise.

Value absolutists may come to regard democracy as a sham. They may advocate for the autocratic rule of a boss—whether an individual, junta, or political party—because they expect bosses will use the power of government to impose their preferred outcome on all others. When that attitude becomes prevalent, democracy as collective self-government is crowded out by competing absolutisms. The political question devolves to, "What boss wins?" We will return to that all-too-readily imaginable scenario below.

Negotiated solutions can be hard to accept, even by those who recognize the necessity of compromise, because "fair enough" does not mean that everyone does equally well out of a bargain. The negotiations that lead to a political bargain are invariably carried out among parties whose bargaining strength is in some ways unequal. One party is likely to start the negotiation in a stronger position. They may have better information or greater patience, or be better at bluffing. In any case, the advantaged party in political bargaining, like the trader in a market who is more willing than another to walk away from the table, is likely to get more and give less than the other party.

But when the conditions are right, the fair enough bargain will be recognized by all parties as advancing their position. In that case, the process of coming to the bargaining table and expecting to come out with a mutually beneficial outcome can be repeated indefinitely. Through that repeated process, the parties engaged in political bargaining may come to regard one another differently: not just as rivals with competing interests, but as partners in a shared enterprise. They will need to accept that democracy is self-government, not ideal justice. Yet they may, together, achieve conditions that each party can recognize as more just than would otherwise be available.

The Democratic Civic Bargain

Democracy arises when a substantial and socially diverse body of persons, having chosen to be citizens rather than subjects, strikes a civic bargain and pays the costs of sustaining it. These citizens agree to accept the trade-offs and do what is necessary to govern themselves. The bargain may be formalized, as in a written constitution. But every civic bargain depends on unwritten norms and social practices in order to sustain the seven conditions necessary for citizens to govern themselves. The bargain is always imperfect with respect to justice and always open to revision. Revisions may be made by a complex process of constitutional amendment (for fundamental issues), or ordinary legislation along with the interpretation of rules by judicial process, or in the day-to-day practice of citizens living together. As we will see in the next four chapters, the civic bargain is historically preceded by a series of political bargains that culminate in the choice not to be ruled by a boss.

It is essential to realize, though, that the costs of the democratic gives are also great: the civic bargain demands that citizens themselves do a lot of the work that would otherwise be done by the boss. Citizens must willingly offer to one another some of their precious time and energy. They may be asked to contribute a substantial part of their private wealth. The preservation of democracy may even, in times of crisis, require the ultimate sacrifice of their lives.

The history of democracy is one of political bargains, culminating in a civic bargain that may itself be revised over time. The specifics of the civic bargain struck in different times and places vary considerably. But every civic bargain rests on the seven fundamental conditions. And every civic bargain resembles other productive bargains: it is a positive-sum, win-win agreement and part of an ongoing relationship defined by compromise. That relationship builds trust over time. Finally, every civic bargain creates shared ethical goods as well as individual payoffs and shared material goods. While at least some of the material goods and individual payoffs can be provided to subjects by autocratic bosses, the democratic moral goods of political freedom, civic equality, and dignity cannot.

The People at the Bargaining Table

While the history of democracy is a history of bargains, it is also one of people, of *who* is at the bargaining table, and importantly, who is not invited to the table. In a democracy, it is citizens who are at the bargaining table; noncitizens are excluded. As such, the history of democratic citizenship is a history of relations based on power, on inclusion and exclusion. Ultimately, to be a citizen is to have a right to a place at the bargaining table. It is to be one of those who decides what will be put on the table, what is up for negotiation—and what is not. It is to be one of those whose input into decisions is regarded as especially valuable. It is to be granted the civic dignity that commands respect and recognition from the other citizens. Those at the table expect their rights to be protected by the rules established by the bargain. And they expect to pay the costs of sustaining those rules.

Just as positive-sum bargains must be regarded by those who make them as fair enough, the question of who is at the bargaining table, as a citizen, must be answered in terms that are regarded as fair enough. While excluded from the civic bargaining table, noncitizens in a democracy are nonetheless involved in political bargains with the citizens. Those who were not at the table and yet are subject to the rules made by those at the table remain in the condition of subjects. Yet even if not participating as sharers in ruling, they are participants in a political bargain. They are ruled over, but not powerless. When the political bargains that regulate relations between citizens and noncitizens are not seen as fair enough, the noncitizens may choose to fight. Recognizing that, the citizens must offer noncitizens enough gets to keep them in a productive, positive-sum political bargain. The gets may be limited to certain protections under the law and access to economic opportunities. But considering their exclusion and the disadvantages that entails, noncitizens may demand a seat at the table, which means gaining the status of citizen.

In response, the incumbent citizens have a choice. They may jealously seek to maintain their exclusive hold on the rights and privileges—and special duties and responsibilities—of citizenship. On the other hand, and under the right conditions, they may come to recognize the claims of those who have been excluded as legitimate—and see that expanding citizenship brings them benefits. Current citizens may act according to what they have come to see as rightful demands in expanding the franchise. Even if they are not moved by moral considerations, they may find that they have a compelling practical reason to invite some noncitizens to share in their citizenship. When the citizen body is expanded, the capacity of the community is increased: more human capital is available, in the form of more information, knowledge, and experience. The space in which answers are found to the problems that face the community is expanded. As a result, more innovative and effective solutions can be discovered and implemented. But expanding the citizen body means more and more diverse members at the bargaining table. And that means that there may be more and different issues on the table.

Expanding the number of issues under negotiation can, under the right conditions, make bargaining easier. It may allow matters that are highly salient for group A, but not particularly important to group B, to be traded off against matters of great salience to group B, but unimportant to group A. Alternatively, groups A and B may seek mutually exclusive outcomes. If those outcomes matter a lot to each group, it will be harder to hammer out positive-sum bargains. Democracies have historically expanded their citizenship both because the exclusions have come to seem unfair and bringing more people into citizenship allows the democratic community to better achieve its ends. At the same time, a larger, more diverse citizenry can make it more difficult to find a bargaining solution that is regarded as fair enough. The scale challenge can be ameliorated not only by institutional innovations (for example, representation and federalism) but also by fostering friendship among citizens.

Condition 6: Civic Friendship

The civic bargain can be struck and sustained because those who enter into it recognize that they have some interests in common, share certain norms and civic values, and have certain civic attitudes toward one another. They are, at least, not enemies who seek to destroy their opponents, not ruthless competitors who see all human interactions in zero-sum terms, or con artists who regard others as potential marks. Rather, they are *civic friends*. Civic friendship, as Aristotle (who coined the concept) realized, has a transactional aspect, but also has an aspect of mutual care: civic friends seek not only their own good but the good of the others too.[2] Political bargains are, as we have seen, positive-sum bargains. They are based on a recognition that all are better off within the bargain. But as we have seen as well, the payoffs to any given agreement are likely to be unequal, so the ongoing negotiations that characterize civic bargains must likewise be built on a foundation of mutual trust. Not unquestioning trust, but rather trust among persons who, first, have good reason to believe that those with whom they enter into an agreement are committed to keeping their promises because they regard the bargain as fair enough and believe that what is produced by their agreement is of intrinsic value.

Next, citizens trust that the ongoing process of negotiation will not formalize the domination of one faction or party (even if it is a majority) over all others. Citizens must trust that other citizens, with different values and goals, will not seek to set up themselves or their leader as a boss. The bargains they make with one another build trust not only by positive-sum outcomes but also by defining and refining a civic identity: a sense of certain shared interests and norms as well as a shared fate— that is, "being in this together for the long run." Civic identities do not go all the way down. Citizens retain strong personal and group identities grounded in, for example, religion, ethnicity, gender, occupation, and locality. Civic identity remains relatively thin in that it is noncomprehensive: it does not fully define "who I am." But it must be thick enough to allow the presumption that my fellow citizen is my friend—in the sense that we are engaged in the same civic project, and that project includes sustaining democracy.

Civic friendship is therefore not simply another kind of personal friendship. It is not even a matter of liking others; it is both more and less than that. According to Aristotle, civic friends regard one another as useful (like traders in a market). Yet they do not see each other merely as instruments to narrowly selfish ends. The key point is that civic friends regard one another as sharers in a common enterprise. They have some concern for one another's good, even if they disagree on many things and seek some different goals. Civic friends come to see the advantages they gain through civic bargaining not only as their personal gains but also as common goods. The good of the civic community becomes, for them, a good for themselves.

Citizens in a working democracy recognize themselves and their civic friend as deserving of *dignity*. By this we mean the kind of respect and recognition that each of us accords those we regard as our moral equals. The respect and recognition that constitutes civic dignity means that unless I have violated a fundamental norm, I expect my fellow citizens not to seek to publicly humiliate me and not to cancel me when I offer an opinion that is other than their own. My civic friends may not like what I have to say, but they grant me the space in which to say it. And for my part, I grant them a similar space. Even if I am less highly educated, less adept at public expression, I expect my fellow citizen to treat me as an adult rather than as a child in need of paternalistic care. That means, among other things, that when it comes to voting, my fellow citizens also accept that my vote counts. They accept that my vote has a weight equal to their own, even if they regard my opinions as misguided and my choice as foolish.

Importantly, the civic dignity that civic friends offer one another does not preclude vigorous debate and strongly expressed disagreement. Indeed, dignity is the precondition of democratic public discourse. It is when citizens recognize one another as civic friends, worthy of respect and recognition, that they can honestly, frankly, and even heatedly confront one another's positions. And they can do so without running the risk of endangering the civic bargain. On the other hand, when civic friendship erodes, when citizens come to regard their fellow citizens as unworthy of respect, as enemies to be beaten, they have taken the first and potentially fatal step toward treating them as subjects to be dominated. When enmity rather than friendship characterizes the public domain, and public debate devolves into verbal or even physical fighting, the rule of a boss looms. Violence has no place among civic friends.

Condition 7: Civic Education

The final condition of the civic bargain is civic education: the mutual teaching and learning that citizens provide to one another, generation on generation. Civic education seeks, one way or another, to elucidate and make real the civic bargain. Schools, colleges, and universities have an important role to play in the process of civic education, but in a well-functioning democracy their role is only one part of a larger ecology in which citizens engage in the ongoing process of better understanding and internalizing the democratic project along with their own role in it.

Civic education includes a knowledge of the content of, in the case of the United States, the Constitution, federalism, and the democratic political process. That kind of knowledge is featured in, for example, the test that the US government requires for the naturalization of new citizens and the curriculum of high school civics classes (where they still exist). But the nuts and bolts of government mechanics are clearly not enough. Civic education also includes, for Americans, a knowledge of our national political and social history. Historical knowledge includes both the country's greatest positive achievements and its profoundest mistakes, from which citizens must learn and work to make "a more perfect union." It includes both American aspirations—expressed, for instance, in the Declaration of Independence—and the nation's failure to live up to those aspirations as well as its most eloquent patriotic partisans and its sternest patriotic critics. But that is still not enough. An adequate democratic civic education must also explain why democracy is difficult to get and keep, and how it is preserved. In short, we suppose that civic education ought to address the subject matter of this book—and we offer the book as a contribution to that effort.

And yet that is still not enough: civic education must go beyond the classroom and schools, beyond what we can learn from reading books, to the process of active participative learning and skills building. It includes civic engagement and volunteerism. For most citizens, most of their educative engagement will be at the local and organizational level. Tocqueville's mid-nineteenth-century insight that democracy in America was sustained by local associations and activities is just as valid now as it was then. Finally, civic education happens in popular rituals and celebrations linked to our history—whether that is fireworks on the July 4 Independence Day, or gathering on Juneteenth to remember the painful history of slavery and deep scars that remain from racial oppression. It may be public recognition for the national and local heroes who devote their energy and sacrifice their lives so that "a government of the people, by the people, for the people, shall not perish from the earth."

Civic education must teach citizens and would-be citizens something about "who 'we the people' are" and "where we've come from." That education should not be entirely celebratory. Education must not be propagandistic. But in its honesty and civic aspiration, it must also bind us together more closely. It need not be built or managed by a federal government. Local jurisdictions (states, counties, towns, and neighborhoods) have a central role to play in educating citizens, as do a wide range of nongovernmental organizations. Education, broadly so understood, is the key to promoting civic friendship and the willingness to bargain under imperfect conditions. It is crucial to accepting with good grace results that are always imperfect for every party to the bargain, yet always open to revision. Civic education is essential to building and rebuilding the shared political culture without which formal institutions are doomed to fail. Education is ultimately how the civic bargain is preserved and democracy is saved—or lost. As the ongoing responsibility of all citizens, it acknowledges the basic fact that democracy is never finished.

But What About . . . ?

Our review of the seven conditions sustaining the democratic civic bargain includes some familiar features: notably the requirement that a government provide adequate levels of security and welfare for the resident population, and the importance of a reasonably stable set of well-designed formal institutions along with the processes and mechanisms that facilitate or impede their proper functioning. But our survey also surfaced some issues that are less prominently featured in the existing literature. These include the definition of democracy as the simple condition of no boss, and the hard truth that democratic citizenship is not only inclusive (when compared to boss rule) but also and necessarily exclusive, predicated on clearly established political boundaries. It includes the centrality of political bargaining and reality that the civic bargain does not achieve anyone's idea of justice. And it involves the essential roles of civic friendship and civic education. Each of these less commonly discussed principles and practices will be documented in the next four chapters as we turn from theory to history.

Three points are likely to be particularly controversial. First, there is the sharp distinction we make between essential civic rights (including free speech and association as well as equal votes) and universal human rights that may or may not be recognized. Next, that political parties are nonessential features of a democratic state and threaten to devolve into boss rule. Finally, our claim that republicanism is a form of democracy, and vice versa.

Democracy and Human Rights

Civic rights are the rights of citizens, necessary for them to participate on an equal footing with their fellow citizens and resist would-be bosses. A familiar example is the first ten amendments to the American Constitution, canonized as the Bill of Rights. While that list incorporates rights that were taken by the framers as natural or God-given, the purpose of the list was to ensure the fundamental goal of citizen self-government as enshrined in the Constitution's preamble, "We the people . . ." Every right, civic or human, held by an individual or group imposes a corresponding duty on others to respect that right. Civic rights impose duties on citizens with respect to their political community and one another as citizens; those duties are, as we have seen, quite demanding. But the demands that come with civic rights are circumscribed by a political domain—the space in which the rules and norms of the political community are enforced.

Human rights are, at least in principle, different in scope and scale: they are more extensive than the civic rights of citizens to participate in government or be free from unnecessary government interference in their private affairs. Human rights are also, by definition, universal: they are the rights of all humans, not just of enfranchised citizens. And so the duties that come with human rights fall, in principle, on everyone, everywhere. Human rights do not stop at the border of the political domain.

Moreover, the duties imposed by human rights are moral duties. Insofar as moral duties are taken as making strict demands of each of us, they are not legitimately the subject of *political* bargaining. Once again, in principle, the moral duties that arise from human rights are nonnegotiable. All of this means that human rights can come into conflict with self-government. The extension of nonnegotiable rights naturally restricts the space in which citizens can negotiate over their diverse interests. It reduces the scope for making and amending the bargains that enable democracy to survive. For the rights absolutist, that may not matter. Philosopher Immanuel Kant famously believed that moral law was strict and proclaimed, "Let justice reign even if all the rascals in the world should perish from it."[3] For the democrat, that is likely to be regarded as too high a price to pay; most of us are rascals by Kant's lights.

The potential conflicts between bargain-based self-government by citizens and moral demands intensify with the multiplication of rights taken as inherent and inalienable. Such rights are definitive of the modern, liberal form of social order. They include, for example, rights to property as well as a wide range of human rights. Secure possession of rights, whether of property or persons, is regarded by rights holders as a matter of justice. The violation of a right is injustice, and as such, demands rectification. When rights come into conflict, compromise can become impossible, such as when the right to control private property comes into conflict with the right of a person not to be in various ways exploited.

The American Bill of Rights protects the rights of individuals against the tendency of the government, even the democratic government, to act as anyone's boss (chapter 5). These rights, along with those guaranteed in subsequent constitutional amendments—for instance, equal protection under the law guaranteed in the Fourteenth Amendment—are compatible with democracy. The list of human rights recognized in, for example, the United Nations' Universal Declaration of Human Rights, is much longer and more demanding.[4] A reasonably broad set of human rights and democracy as self-government can be compatible—as proved by the policies of various liberal democracies currently in existence. But democracy as collective self-government requires that the list of rights that democratic citizens have a duty to defend be limited to those rights that citizens can and will defend. Democracy is, in any case, not coextensive with or dependent on the recognition of a specific list of property rights or human rights that extend beyond the domain of rights of citizens to participate in self-government. As we will see, while in some cases the histories of rights and self-government go hand in hand, the history of self-government by citizens long antedates the conception of rights as morally required, inherent in humanity, and therefore universal and nonnegotiable.

Democracy and Political Parties

Modern political scientists often equate democracy with competition among organized political parties. Indeed, many standard definitions and measures of democracy assume that without competition among parties, democracy is impossible. That argument has been elaborated in a substantial body of recent work. But it was made most forcefully by political scientist E. E. Schattschneider in *Party Government*, a book written in 1942. Because his book remains so enduringly influential, Schattschneider's work serves as a model of the idea that democracy must necessarily be based on political parties.

Schattschneider began with the obvious fact that modern democracies feature political parties. He defined the political party as an organization whose purpose is seeking political power, with the goal of controlling the government. Schattschneider noted that the US Constitution does not recognize parties, and moreover that the framers of the Constitution were hostile to the very idea. So Schattschneider admitted, American political parties exist in the interstices of the law and are not effectively controlled by constitutional law. In addition, he recognized that the ultimate purpose of the party, monopolistic control of government, is antithetical to the power-limiting and power-balancing mechanisms of constitutional order.

We think Schattschneider was right in all of that. In light of the last sixty years of political history, though, perhaps he did not go far enough: modern autocracy is also (almost) always associated with political parties; the few exceptions (for instance, Saudi Arabia, where power is based instead on kinship) do not change the overall picture. Schattschneider supposed that the difference between political parties in a democracy and an autocracy was that democratic parties compete for power. The competition is reasonably fair and peaceful. It is conducted according to a set of cultural practices and norms that Schattschneider called *comity*. By this he meant that democratic political parties and their leaders agreed on voting procedures. They conceded elections when they did not win the necessary number of votes. They did not resort to extraordinary legal maneuvers or incite violence to overturn the results.

At least until recently, political parties in modern democracies usually competed for power in ways that fit Schattschneider's idea of comity. But there was nothing in Schattschneider's theory to explain why an organization that aims at control would *necessarily* be dedicated to the ideal of peaceful competition or willingly give up power. For those seeking power, *permanent* control of government is better than temporary control. So why would a power-seeking political party ever wish for its control to end? Norms that are not enforceable in law can change over time. If the norm of comity is degraded, if it is ineffective in regulating the behavior of the leaders of power-seeking parties, if law fails to restrain the power-seeking activities of parties, we should not be surprised when a party tries to get and keep control of government "by whatever means necessary."

Political economist Joseph Schumpeter, another midcentury theorist of democracy and political parties, went one step further in his own immensely influential book, *Capitalism, Socialism, and Democracy* (3rd ed., 1950). Schumpeter's model for party politics was warfare, not comity. He asserted that "the first and foremost aim of each political party is to prevail over the others in order to get into power or to stay in it." Schumpeter went beyond Schattschneider in arguing that the party (that is, a successful, unified party) is identified with its leader: the popular vote puts a "whip into the hand of the leader," who thereby dominates the party and the government; this is the "normal relation . . . the essence of the democratic method." Schumpeter concludes that the "political boss" is the very essence of politics.[5]

Together, these twentieth-century theories suggest that political parties may have as their goal the control of government by a boss. If democracy is, by our definition, no boss, then political parties and democracy can have opposing goals. When democracy pertains, the power-seeking party is frustrated in its ambitions. If a party achieves the goal of permanently controlling the government, democracy is thereby ended. Ultimately, the difference between democratic and autocratic parties may not lie in their goals but rather in their character, in their willingness to employ deception and violence to gain their ends. The conflict and competition that Schattschneider identified as the essence of democracy could be suppressed by a party willing to do whatever it takes to gain and keep power.

Modern democracies have consistently featured competition among political parties. For a long time, the norm of comity was strong enough to ensure that competition was for the most part peaceful. Losers acknowledged their defeat in the assurance that they might win next time. But in the twenty-first century, it is a mistake to see political parties as *effectively* controlled by norms of comity. Nor are parties a necessary feature of a theory of democracy. As we will see, classical Athens and republican Rome fit our definition of democracy as no-boss self-government, yet they lacked organized political parties. Local and regional governments in America in the seventeenth and eighteenth centuries had strongly democratic features long before the first American political parties had emerged. The question of whether a modern democracy *could* in principle operate effectively in the absence of parties remains open. For now, the key question about parties and democracy is how citizens who are determined to resist the rule of a boss can preserve democracy by preserving norms of comity and preventing the leader of a political party from becoming their boss.

Democracy and Republic

It is sometimes said, on the authority of constitutional founder James Madison, that "America is a republic, not a democracy." Madison's statements to that effect, in the brilliant, coauthored collection of essays published in 1788 as *The Federalist*, were strategic: he sought to draw a sharp contrast between his federal plan for the United States and what he characterized as the turbulent, troubled, and short-lived forms of popular government characteristic of Greek and Roman antiquity. To draw his contrast, Madison focused on decision-making institutions, lawfulness, factionalism, and scale.[6]

Madison's eighteenth-century model of democracy was drawn from his reading of ancient Greek writers on the history of democratic government in Athens. Noting that in Athens, decisions were made by the votes of citizens in an assembly open to all citizens, Madison argued that political decision-making in ancient democracies was always direct: citizens decided policy in mass gatherings, where they voted on proposals brought forward by self-interested demagogues, who played on popular passions and ignored the common good. As such, democracy was necessarily turbulent: the unruly mob that gathered in assembly was led hither and yon by whims and momentary enthusiasms; it had no way to make use of expertise or cool deliberation.

The decisions of these citizen assemblies were, Madison claimed, unconstrained by law: there was no separation of powers within government, so whatever the mob decided at a given moment just was the law; if it decided something different tomorrow, then *that* was the law. Furthermore, ancient democracies were necessarily small—since every citizen had the right to attend the decision-making assemblies, the scale of democracy could not be expanded. Small size meant that the space for factions was likewise constrained. Madison supposed that in any kind of popular government, factions would always arise. In small democracies there was room for only a few factions—and that meant that faction fighting tended to be violent and deadly.

By contrast, Madison suggested, a law-respecting republic employed indirect forms of political representation, whereby citizens do not themselves make rules or vote on matters of policy. Rather the citizens choose representatives to make decisions in their stead. Ideally, representatives are especially virtuous persons who will consider both the particular interests of those they represent and the common good. Taking properly into account the common concerns of the community as a whole, these wise representatives would bargain in good faith, advancing the interests of local or regional groups only insofar as those interests were compatible with the good of the whole.

Taking over a distinction from ancient writers, Madison also contrasted "lawless" democracy with law-respecting republics: in a republic, fundamental law (for example, the recently drafted and not-yet-ratified Constitution that the *Federalist* was written to defend and promote) would constrain the fleeting whims and self-interested strategic moves of any majority of the moment. Meanwhile, a principle of separation of powers would ensure that judicial and executive officials, their powers guaranteed within an established institutional order, would limit the chance that the majority would act tyrannically as a boss.

Finally and importantly, Madison emphasized that a republic could be scaled up. The practice of representation allowed a great many citizens to participate in self-government through periodic elections. Those elections would appoint a small enough number of representatives to allow for deliberation and good faith bargaining among them. As the republic grew, there was also more space for factions. That too conduced to preserve public order because with more factions, there was more room for "faction to counter faction." There was less chance that any one faction would come to control the government and rule tyrannically in the interest of only a part of the citizenry over the rest. Madison concluded his contrast of democracy with republic by asserting that "had every Athenian citizen been a Socrates, every Athenian assembly would still have been a mob."[7]

Madison's "republic not democracy" position has been influential, not only among conservatives, because of his stature as a political thinker and constitutional framer, but also among self-described radical democrats, who follow the lead of another highly influential Enlightenment writer, Jean-Jacques Rousseau. Writing a short generation before Madison, Rousseau's most influential work on politics was *The Social Contract* (1762). In that book, he described and advocated for a form of direct democracy. Like Madison, Rousseau looked to ancient Greece, but in Rousseau's case, it was Sparta rather than Athens that provided his model—and in Rousseau's mind the ancient model was not a nightmare but instead an ideal.

Rousseau urged that the purpose of democracy was to bring about the "general will" as binding rules on a body of citizens, understood as natural and political equals. He defined the general will as the genuine interest of the entire community, exemplified in the vote of an assembly at which all citizens would gather. Once gathered, citizens would not deliberate with one another over the issue in question; there would be no speeches and no debate—they just voted on the matter brought before them. Deliberation was not, for Rousseau, a matter of publicly offering reasons for or against a proposal. That left open too much room for corruption in the form of undue influence of some over others. Instead, in Rousseau's view, deliberation was an internal matter: each citizen was to reflect privately on what was best for all and choose, by voting, accordingly.

The majority vote in this "all-citizen" assembly just was the general will; citizens who had voted the other way were shown to be in error—recognizing that, they ought to adopt the will of the majority as their own private will. If they did not, they must be punished. That is what Rousseau supposed happened in Sparta, and he thought it both reflected and promoted the kind of civic virtue that was essential for sustaining a democratic community. Rousseau anticipated Madison's argument about scale. He was sure that no democracy could have a population of more than several thousand—the size of his native town of Geneva, where he imagined his ideal democracy might be established. But he saw that as a good thing: small was beautiful. Rousseau was adamantly opposed to representation of any kind—and so his advocacy for democracy tended to support the notion that insofar as republican government is characterized by representation, it is something other than democracy.

With all due respect, neither Madison nor Rousseau knew enough about the real history of citizen self-government in ancient Greece to make the historical case for the distinction between democracy and republic. Both were selective in the ancient texts to which they referred in describing what they imagined as model (terrible or wonderful) early democracies. Historians of antiquity now have a wider range of evidence to use in the reconstruction of ancient political theory and practice. Madison and Rousseau were right to say that Greek-style democracies were limited in scale—although not nearly so limited as is sometimes claimed. They were wrong to assert that representation was unknown in Greek antiquity. By the time of philosophers Plato and Aristotle, moreover, policy decisions of the Athenian citizen assembly were self-consciously constrained by a set of fundamental laws, which could only be changed through an intentionally cumbersome legal process.

The sharp distinction between democracy and republic does not hold at the level of either history or theory. Premodern societies that called themselves "democracies" and those that called themselves "republics" were equally committed to the principle of no boss, and developing institutions and norms that would keep the bosses at bay. The ancient Greek term that is the root of democracy, *demokratia*, means "the power (in the sense of the capacity) of the citizenry to accomplish things." The ancient Latin term that is the root of republic, *res publica*, means "the public thing"—a good that is valued and shared, in common, by the citizens: in brief, "the common good."

A democratic republic preserves that common good by depending on the capacity of the citizens to act together in its defense, and the citizens employ their own capacity to preserve the common good. That common good includes, at a minimum, security, welfare, and keeping would-be bosses at bay. Those goods are secured, in the absence of a boss, by citizen self-government. Therefore in this book, we use the terms *democracy* and *republic* as near synonyms, while respecting the residual difference in connotation as well as the fact that different communities of citizens, or would-be citizens, use one term or the other for historically contingent reasons.

Looking Ahead: Four Influential Cases of Democratic Development

Establishing and sustaining democracy, as bossless self-government by an extensive and diverse body of citizens, is not easy. It requires a set of demanding conditions that allow for developing and continuously revising civic bargains. The difficulty is compounded by scale challenges: the democratic community must grow in capacity, meaning that there are likely to be more citizens, with more diverse social and cultural identities, participating in self-government. When either the pace of innovative new mechanisms for facilitating decision-making or the strength of a shared civic identity fails to keep up with the growing size and diversity of the citizenry, the risk of bargaining failures increases. Meanwhile, in modernity, the quickening rate of technological change drives up expectations and wealth inequality, thereby increasing pressure for more frequent and more profound changes. An expanding menu of rights regarded as universal and inherent in humanity limits the community's capacity to strike positive-sum bargains. It becomes harder to find a stable bargaining solution that increases the overall set of gets for all parties without intolerably multiplying the gives demanded of any individual or group. Meanwhile, the existential threats that have historically provided an incentive to subordinate personal and factional goals to the common good have become less imminent (climate change) or less amendable to citizen action (nuclear war).

For those who care about keeping democracy, well-documented historical cases of democratic emergence and long-term persistence are precious sources of evidence for understanding what worked and what failed. Those cases allow us to study the process of developing and revising the bargains that made it possible for citizens to govern themselves, without a boss, for extended periods. They let us see how it is possible for citizens to govern themselves over time without sacrificing security or welfare. In short, history can help us explain how democracy survives, and what citizens do to keep it alive.

This chapter has laid out our theory of democracy. In social science, theories are difficult to prove. No social theory ever explains all the relevant phenomena. But if our theory illuminates the history of democratic success and failure, if it brings to light otherwise obscure aspects of what happened and why, then we can claim that the theory is supported by evidence. And in that case, at the very least, it is worth testing further. The next four chapters start the work of testing our theory of democracy against the evidence of history. We hope some readers will want to go further—digging deeper into our four cases (we offer suggestions for additional reading) and examining other cases that we were not able to take on here.

In chapters 2–5, we focus on what we regard as the four greatest democratic experiments in Western history: classical Athens, republican Rome, the British parliamentary system, and America's constitutional federalism. We recognize that some would reject the proposition that any of these is properly described as a democracy. We know that others would insist that to gain any insight from history, we would need to add many other cases, from other eras and other parts of the world. We defend our choice of cases, first, in terms of feasibility: more than four cases would make a bigger book than we are able to write. But more important, we defend our choice based on suitability: these four well-documented, long-duration cases are, we claim, especially valuable for understanding democracy *as collective self-government by citizens*. We call them "experiments" because the democratic systems of self-governance built in each of these states were characterized by bold innovations and marked by both successes and failures. And their extinction, actual or possible, is also part of the story; experiments sometimes end in failure. The two ancient democracies, Athens and Rome, have long since passed away. The future viability of the two modern examples is hardly guaranteed.

Even those who object to our choices may admit that the four cases we have selected are among the most influential instances of self-government in world history. The fact that they are all drawn from what is conventionally described (and now sometimes derided) as the history of Western civilization is not accidental. It is determined by our own limited knowledge and resources, but it is not a product of simple chauvinism. We emphatically do not assume that the insights gained from these cases are uniquely applicable to current or future democratic experiments in the Western world. There is no reason to doubt that under the right conditions, the relevant sort of civic bargain could be struck in diverse parts of the globe. But given our definition of democracy as self-government (a definition that others are, of course, free to contest), we know of no other comparable and influential historical examples.

Each of our four cases is distinctive. Yet our four cases are in some ways interwoven in that after the emergence of democracy in ancient Greece, those involved in subsequent experiments could draw on the memory of previous ones. The Athenians first invented the term *democracy*; they had no obvious models to draw on. But the Romans were well aware of political developments in the Greek world. In the early modern period, the British drew on both Greek and Roman history. And the American founders took all of that on board as well as borrowing much from the British parliamentary system. The historical pathways to government by citizens in our four cases are nonetheless quite different. They suggest a range of possibilities open to citizens seeking to govern themselves. Moreover, as we follow the twists and turns, the backtracking and frequent lack of guideposts along those pathways, we realize that democracy was never a simple accomplishment or foregone conclusion.

In the chapters that follow, we discuss the rise and development of citizen government in each of the four cases in light of the seven conditions of the civic bargain. As historians, we are sharply aware that each case must be viewed in its own chronological and cultural context. Yet we seek to gain generalizable insights by looking at underlying features that we conclude are common to all four cases. To draw out those commonalities, we pose a few basic questions. We have sought to pitch those questions at the right level of generality, honoring differences across the cases, but also probing for common themes with transhistorical validity that could illuminate how democracy survives. In that spirit, we bring this set of "how and why" questions to each case:

> What developments led up to the emergence of democracy?
> At what point in each state's history was democracy, as collective self-government by citizens, achieved? How and why did that happen just when it did—and not before? And what happened then? How did self-government change after it was first established?
>
> What explains the survival and (in some cases) failure of citizen government? What allowed it to thrive when it did? When it struggled or faltered, did it then successfully evolve and adapt to whatever circumstances threatened it? And if so, how? If not, what went wrong?
>
> How and why did the scale of the democracy (the size and diversity of the citizen body), and content of the bargains among citizens, understood as both benefits and costs incurred by them, change over time? What external and internal forces drove those changes? How do the changes in citizenship and bargains among citizens bear on the issue of democratic success and failure?

2

ATHENS

The Bargain That Invented the Power of the Citizenry

In Greek, the word *democracy* literally means "the power of the citizenry." It was first coined in the city-state of Athens, about 2,500 years ago, in the aftermath of a popular revolution that set the stage for a civic bargain. The people of Athens rejected rule by a boss, established a remarkably wide franchise, and publicly embraced values of liberty and equality. The history of democratic Athens, before and after the revolution, is marked by ongoing political and civic bargaining. Those agreements resulted in the creation of innovative political institutions. The experience of citizens in "working the machine" of democratic self-governance fostered a public culture that replaced suspicion and enmity among those from different walks of life with trust. It built civic friendship even in the face of deep differences. As a result, Athens flourished economically for 180 years, leaving a legacy of high culture that remains unique and enduringly influential in Western history. But in the end, the Athenians failed to meet a scale challenge: fearing that greater diversity would degrade morale, they refused to enlarge their civic community by freeing slaves, acknowledging women as participatory citizens, and enfranchising new citizens whose ancestors were other than Athenian. And so the native, free men of Athens found themselves outnumbered on the battlefield as well as outmaneuvered by clever and ambitious autocrats.

Toward Citizenship

The historical journey that culminated in the revolution and institutional reforms that established self-government in Athens begins in the twelfth century BCE with the sudden collapse of the palace-centered civilization of the Greek Bronze Age. Before that catastrophic fall, Greece had been chopped up into several small kingdoms, centered on a palace and ruled by monarchs who legitimated their rule, notably the authority to tax their subjects and conscript soldiers, by claiming to have a special relationship with the divine order. It was just the kind of political, social, religious, and economic organization that would be familiar to anyone living in the neighboring cultures of Egypt, Syria, and Mesopotamia—or for that matter in much of the rest of the world across most of human history: the king ruled with the support of warrior-aristocrats and bureaucrats; ordinary people were subjects whose labor and rents sustained the hierarchical system.

Greece's Bronze Age civilization was devastated by a "perfect storm" of natural catastrophes: climate change, disease, earthquakes, and volcanoes. The crisis led to mass migrations and considerable violence. When the dust had finally settled, the population of Greece was smaller and poorer than it had been under the Bronze Age kings. Survivors gathered in tiny, impoverished, illiterate communities, seeking to defend and feed themselves as best they could. Imports of luxury goods and raw materials from abroad were curtailed. Cheap iron replaced bronze as the metal of choice, leading to modern archaeologists' term for this era: the Early Iron Age. The art of writing was entirely lost. Scribes in the service of the king, tasked with keeping track of goods coming into and leaving the palace, had kept records on clay tablets, utilizing a complex writing system that was known to only a few. As the palaces went, so too went scribal literacy. Most of these small Greek communities were relatively egalitarian: there simply was not enough surplus for anyone to become wealthy. Moreover, there was no single, powerful boss: the small scale of a typical Early Iron Age Greek village meant that local affairs could be handled communally; elders with a reputation for wisdom collaborated with those with a reputation as skilled fighters to decide whatever issues faced the community. This era of relative poverty lasted for several hundred years.

By the eighth century BCE, however, many Greek communities were doing better economically; Greece had crawled its way back to something like the material level that had pertained before the collapse. Surprisingly, the institution of centralized, divinely sanctioned monarchy had not returned. The more successful of the growing towns brought nearby villages under their sway; they were well on their way to becoming city-states—in Greek, *poleis* (singular, *polis*). The rulers of these emerging poleis were not kings but instead coalitions of local notables who had managed to acquire more wealth and prestige than their fellows. They were aristocrats in aspiration and soon enough in practice. Aristocrats distinguished themselves by their dress, hairstyles, and cultural tastes—for fine tableware, fancy armor, and knowledge of poetry. Literacy returned when the Greeks borrowed a writing system from their neighbors in Phoenicia (modern Lebanon). Greeks added vowels to the consonant-based Phoenician alphabet, which meant that writing could readily represent oral speech and literacy was much more easily acquired. The new technology was quickly taken up by poets and traders.

As the population grew, ambitious aristocrats alleviated demographic pressure on local resources by leading colonizing expeditions to the western Mediterranean and then to the Black Sea in the northeast. By the early sixth century BCE, much of Sicily, southern Italy, and the coastal areas of the Aegean and Black Seas were occupied by Greeks living in poleis. The takeover of these areas was facilitated by innovations in weaponry and military organization. A coordinated phalanx of heavy-armed infantry—called hoplites—proved to be highly effective.

In some poleis, most notably Sparta, the relatively numerous hoplites organized themselves into a body of citizen-warriors who embraced an ethos of social equality and made rules forbidding ostentatious displays of private wealth. That social ethos served as a counterweight to the power of the aristocratic leaders of the community. It allowed for coordinated activities across a substantially larger population. Spartan citizen-soldiers used their monopoly on efficient violence to enslave other, more numerous but less organized local residents. They extracted agricultural rents from their subjects by developing institutions that allowed for domination by systematic terrorism. That in turn enabled Spartan hoplites to train full-time and thus become an especially effective military force. Sparta's strictly limited and circumscribed approach to citizenship was a form of collective self-government, and was much admired by Enlightenment era European intellectuals, but it was a long way from anything the Greeks regarded as democracy.

Social Crisis and First Political Bargain in Athens

By the early sixth century BCE, Athens was facing a challenge of scale that threatened the coherence of the emerging state: compared to most other city-states, Athens had a large territory, extending across several agriculturally productive valleys, and including uplands and a long coast. Separated from one another by geography, Athenians tended to prize local identity over their national identity. They had little motivation to cooperate on risky ventures with strangers who lived in far-flung parts of the Athenian homeland. As a result, Athens's western border and its claim to the nearby island of Salamis were threatened by a much smaller yet better organized rival state, Megara. The scale challenge was exacerbated by a growing social crisis. Some Athenian aristocrats had done well from the opportunities offered by the expanding Greek world; other Athenians had fared badly, falling deeply into debt and then into debt slavery. The poor were increasingly desperate, numerous, and ready to fight for their freedom. The wealthy seemed equally ready to fight to keep what they had. Athens was teetering on the brink of a civil war, and Megara was poised to take advantage of the chaos.

But rather than collapse into a bloody, destructive civil conflict and fight each other as enemies, the Athenians found a way forward through a political bargain. It was not yet a democratic civic bargain—that was still two long generations in the future. Nonetheless, the political bargain put Athens on a road that made democracy possible by establishing basic rights for Athenians—the vital first step toward shared member-

ship in a community of free and equal citizens. The bargain was brokered by an unexpected leader: a middle-class poet named Solon. He
had risen to prominence and earned the respect of both sides for his
stirring patriotic odes and dedication to the cause of defending Athenian assets against Megarian intrusion. Solon was accepted as an arbitra-
tor by rich and poor Athenians alike; both sides agreed to allow him to
propose new rules for their community. Each side would, however, accept those new rules only if they offered a payoff that appeared to be the
best that each could hope for. The alternative to a bargain was fighting:
if either side rejected Solon's offer, in effect walking away from the bargaining table, they would be choosing to wage a civil war.

Faced with these daunting conditions, Solon came up with a plan
that fully pleased neither side but was indeed the best that each side
could hope for. He abolished debt slavery and mandated a onetime can-
cellation of existing debts. Athenians who had been sold into slavery by
their creditors were freed and repatriated. Those measures obviously
advantaged the poor and in effect created a baseline of citizenship. Now,
being an Athenian meant having a right not to be enslaved by a fellow
Athenian. Slavery remained legal, but from then on, all slaves owned by
Athenians would be foreigners. On the other hand, Solon refused to
expropriate the property of the rich or redistribute Athenian agricultural lands to the poor—the radical economic goal that the poor eagerly
advocated and the rich feared.

After some grumbling, the Athenians, rich and poor alike, admitted
that Solon had offered them as much as they could reasonably expect,
and they gave him the authority to make new rules. In favor of the rich,
he organized access to public offices on the basis of annual income: the
highest offices went to those with the highest incomes. But in favor of
ordinary citizens, he made all state officials accountable and subject to
legal prosecution. The jury in the trial of a corrupt magistrate would be
a public assembly of all Athenian citizens, and the poor would be in the
majority. Moreover, Solon allowed any Athenian to serve as prosecutor
for crimes committed against any other citizen; in essence, he made
every Athenian personally responsible for the public safety and dignity
of every other citizen. In so doing, he offered his fellow citizens a

positive-sum, win-win bargain and laid a foundation for civic friendship. And so although the ordinary Athenian citizens still had no real say in policy making, they had gained important civil rights and could begin to think of themselves as members of a shared community. The bargain was sealed by a sacred oath: all Athenians swore to their gods to abide by the laws of Solon for a period of time.

Solon himself was well aware of the importance of what he had accomplished, and he boasted of his success in poems that were long remembered. According to his Roman era biographer, Plutarch, Solon was also well aware of the constraints he confronted given that either side would have chosen to fight if they felt they were better off outside the bargain than within it. According to Plutarch, Solon replied to a critic who claimed that his reforms would fail by noting that "men keep their bargains with each other when for neither party is there profit in breaking them, and he was adapting his laws to the citizens in such a manner as to make it clear to all that the practice of justice was preferable to the transgression of the laws."[1] The "justice" that Solon refers to here is sticking by an agreement rather than a moral standard. Plutarch also reports that "when [Solon] was afterward asked if he had enacted the best laws for the Athenians, he replied, 'The best they would receive.'"[2] As we will see (chapter 5), this line acknowledging the impossibility of perfect justice in a political bargain was quoted at least twice in the constitutional era of early American history.

Tyrannical Interlude and Democratic Revolution

Solon's new rules were intended to preempt the takeover by a boss in the form of a monarch-like despot. In many other Greek poleis, political power had been seized by a local *tyrant* (Greek, *tyrannos*)—a word the Greeks borrowed from their Middle Eastern neighbors to refer to a leader who took power and ruled by force. But Solon's new laws could not prevent tyranny. An ambitious Athenian aristocrat with a large local following along with social and economic connections across the Greek world tried three times to seize control of the polis. In his third attempt, in 546 BCE, Peisistratus employed a mercenary army to take Athens by force of arms.

Peisistratus was wise enough, however, to maintain the framework of the Solonian bargain; he respected the laws that had been made by Solon and sought to co-opt members of leading families by offering them a role in the government. He also tried to co-opt ordinary people, emphasizing their shared Athenian identity by building massive public projects as well as organizing parades and a new, annual "All-Athens" festival. While sponsored by a boss, the festival was an early example of civic education. All of that was aimed, first, at celebrating Athenian culture by encouraging identification with the polis, and next, encouraging loyalty to the tyrant's family, which claimed a special relationship with both Athena, the city's patron deity, and Zeus, the king of the gods.

For his own purposes, then, Peisistratus addressed the scale challenge and promoted civic friendship by giving each Athenian a stronger sense of belonging to a single community with a unique and shared communal identity—and a benevolent boss. Peisistratus successfully passed his tyrannical authority on to his sons. But in 514 BCE, when one of them was assassinated, the surviving son, Hippias, turned tyrannical in fact as well as in name. Other Athenian aristocratic families fled into exile and began to work actively for Hippias's downfall. Their machinations eventually bore fruit: Sparta was convinced to send a military force against Hippias, who finally fled Athens—ending up in the court of the king of Persia, the great empire to the east.

The tyrant was out, but the Spartans did not have the spare manpower to rule Athens while still controlling their immense local slave population. They hoped that a friendly Athenian aristocrat would run Athens in Sparta's interest; they found their man in Isagoras, a prominent aristocrat. Isagoras had substantial local support among other Athenian aristocrats. But he was opposed by Cleisthenes, the leader of the Athenians who had gone into exile in opposition to the tyrant. When Isagoras gained control of the most important public office, Cleisthenes was left without a move in the old intraelite game of "whose faction will be boss?" The background conditions had changed, though. The Athenians had gained the status of rights holders under Solon, formed a stronger shared Athenian identity under the benevolent tyrant Peisistratus, and then experienced under Hippias what it meant to have a boss who did not respect the norms and rules. The way was open for a dramatic next step.

Breaking sharply with the norms of aristocratic politics, Cleisthenes built a big popular coalition by promising major changes that would give the people more say in the government. This propelled Cleisthenes into prominence. Isagoras, however, had a countermove: he begged for help from the Spartans. The Spartan leader agreed to back Isagoras and ordered the expulsion from Athenian territory of Isagoras's political opponents. With a Spartan army marching toward Athens in support of Isagoras, Cleisthenes prudently fled into exile along with his family and aristocratic supporters. When the Spartan-led force arrived, Isagoras sought to replace the Athenian government council with his own minions. But the people of Athens had been inspired by Cleisthenes's promises, and they'd had enough of bosses. They also had the advantage of both numbers and motivation. Caught off guard by a sudden mass uprising, Isagoras and his Spartan mercenaries retreated to the sacred Acropolis, a natural fortress in the center of the town. Three days later, after a successful siege of the Acropolis, it was over. Isagoras surrendered; he and the Spartans left Athens under a truce. The victorious Athenian people then recalled Cleisthenes from exile.

Back in Athens, Cleisthenes was called to deliver on the promises that he had made before he fled: a new kind of regime in which ordinary people would be active and participatory citizens, not mere subjects of the powerful few. His plan would need to be put into place quickly. It would need to harness the energy of the revolutionary uprising, shared civic identity built through Solon's political bargain, and emerging civic friendship promoted by Peisistratus's All-Athens festival. Sparta was hungry for military revenge, and only a massive, effective mobilization of armed Athenians would keep the Spartans and their military allies from bringing back Isagoras as Athens's boss. If that happened, Athens would be transformed into a puppet state, and Athenian citizens reduced to subjects.

The Athenian Civic Bargain

Cleisthenes's plan was a civic bargain, a new, citizen-centered approach to government, and a new definition of citizenship: nothing short of universal free male franchise. That is, *all* adult free men who were resident in Athens at the time of the revolution—some thirty thousand or more—would now be participating members of the civic community— rich and poor, educated and ignorant, and recent newcomers and those who could claim that their ancestors were born of the earth itself. While the idea of participatory citizenship was in the air in other Greek city-states in the late sixth century BCE, universal free male franchise was still unheard of. According to Cleisthenes's plan, there would be no boss, neither a monarch nor a gang of ruling aristocrats. Athenian men would be fellow citizens, and as citizens they would enjoy freedom, political equality, and civic dignity. In exchange, they offered their service as soldiers, but also as legislators and judges. They debated and voted on policy in a legislative citizen assembly, and each agreed to be bound by the decisions made by a majority of his fellow citizens—even when the decision was to his own disadvantage. In people's courts, Athenians punished those who violated the bargain, either by free riding on others' service or attacking the dignity of the weak. The costs of citizenship were not trivial: each citizen was expected to devote a significant part of his energies to sustaining the democratic community and risk his life in war when called on to do so.

The meaningful participation of citizens in the work of government was made possible by new civic institutions. Prominent among these was a citizen council of five hundred men. The councillors were chosen by a lottery and served for a single year. It was a startling innovation to place so much responsibility in ordinary men, chosen at random from among the male population over age thirty. The councillors would undertake some of the most important functions of government. Moreover, the working of the new council depended on an even more remarkable innovation. Aristotle notes that Cleisthenes's goal was to "mix together" the citizens, subordinating traditional local, village-based identities to a new, shared civic identity. Based on his village or neighborhood of residence, each Athenian was now assigned to one of ten newly organized "tribes," each named for a hero of Athenian mythology. Each tribe drew its membership from villages in three distinct geographic regions within Athens's homeland—the urbanized center, agricultural inland, and coasts. The new citizen council was made up of ten teams of fifty men—with each team drawn from one of the tribes. That meant that each tribe team had roughly equal numbers of men whose home neighborhoods were far from one another and whose livelihoods (industry, fishing and trade, and agriculture) were different. Yet the members of those diverse tribe delegations had to work together as high-performing teams; the council was responsible for most of the day-to-day business of the city-state.

Most important, the councillors were tasked with preparing the agenda for regular meetings of the reorganized citizen assembly. That assembly was open to every citizen, honoring the fundamental principle of free association. The citizen assembly was responsible for all public policy. In council and assembly, debates were conducted according to the principle of free speech, although those who wasted the time of their fellow citizens by speaking out on issues on which they were not well-informed could expect to be called out. After debate, decisions were made by counting equal votes.

That was not all. Cleisthenes's plan was based on a radical expansion of the very idea of who could be a citizen and what citizenship meant in practice. The new tribes were also the basis for military recruitment: the land army was now composed of ten tribal regiments. Like the council teams, each tribal regiment had the feature of drawing together men from three different parts of the Athenian homeland. Athenian soldiers depended on their tribe mates for their survival in brutal hand-to-hand combat. Furthermore, major state-sponsored religious rituals were now reorganized according to the new tribes: men from the city, inland, and coasts joined together in honoring the gods of the community in song and dance with dramatic theatrical performances as well as sharing the sacred meat from public animal sacrifices.

Cleisthenes's master plan, as mentioned above, was to mix together the Athenians—and through mixing, break down established prejudices based on locality and livelihood. He aimed to build a strong core of civic friendship by promoting trust and virtuous interdependence among the much-expanded body of citizens. Experience on the council as well as in war and public rituals would serve as a practice-based form of civic education. In addition, Cleisthenes sought to ensure that the agreement on "who is a citizen" held: any citizen from a long-established aristocratic family who claimed that some recent arrival did not deserve the honorable status of Athenian citizen would have to face the ire of his fellow tribe mates, who had learned to depend on one another in war and peace. Although the word *democracy* was yet to be coined, the Athenian revolution and Cleisthenes's reforms had created a system of collective self-government by citizens. But questions remained: Would it work? Could it provide security and welfare? Would the new bargain hold in the face of a military crisis?

From Strength to Strength:
The Growth of Democratic Athens

The answer was a resounding yes. In 506 BCE, just two years after the Athenian revolution and the siege of the Acropolis, the Spartans prepared to invade Athens from the west. Sparta led a coalition of southern Greek city-states and worked in coordination with Athens's rival city-states to the north and east. But just as the Spartan coalition forces were about to march across Athens's western border, the soldiers sent by one of Sparta's most important coalition partners, the city-state of Corinth, suddenly pulled out. The Spartan war leader quickly aborted the mission. What had apparently happened is that the Athenian force the invaders faced was not the small body of aristocrats in fancy armor plus some mercenaries that had passed for an Athenian army before the revolution. Rather it was a new, national Athenian army, vastly larger and hypermotivated. Newly enfranchised Athenians were ready to fight to the death for the ideals of personal freedom and national autonomy gained and held through active citizenship. That was a kind of army the Corinthians were not prepared to take on. Moreover, without their allies, neither were the Spartans. Once the threat of invasion from the west dissipated, the Athenian forces pivoted to the north and east, quickly defeating armies of the rival city-states that had planned to divide the spoils of war with the Spartan coalition. It was a glorious Athenian victory, long remembered and celebrated.

Democratic citizenship had passed its first test: the challenge of scaling up—mobilizing the numbers of highly motivated men necessary to meet the invaders—had been met through innovations in social identity and government institutions. Those innovations transformed the large size of Athens's territory and the social diversity of Athens's population from costly burdens into vital assets.

The next great test faced by the young Athenian democracy was even steeper. It began when the king of the mighty Persian Empire turned his attention westward. In 490 BCE, a large invasion fleet appeared on the northeastern coast of the Athenian territory, making landfall near the village of Marathon. The ex-tyrant Hippias was with them; the Persian plan was to make him the governor of a new Persian province. The Athenian army, led by their democratically chosen commanders, quickly mobilized, marching the twenty-six miles across the hill lands north and east of the city. The epic battle that followed was a lopsided Athenian victory. Once again Athenian citizen-soldiers proved their worth, this time against a much larger force. The victory at Marathon bought Athens some time, but foresighted Athenian leaders saw that the Persians would be back before long.

Fortuitously, a few years after Marathon a rich vein of silver ore was discovered in the southern part of Athens's territory. The mineral rights belonged to the state, so there was a large public windfall. The citizens gathered in assembly to decide how the windfall should be used. Two proposals were offered. In the first, a substantial payoff, roughly a month's wages, would be made to each Athenian family. The second proposal held that the silver would be used to build a big fleet of two hundred trireme warships. Each trireme had a total crew of about two hundred, most of whom pulled the oars and propelled the ship rapidly through the waves. As befitted civic friends who had learned to trust one another, the Athenians chose the second option, preferring the long-term public good of a great navy for national security over the short-term private good of hefty individual payoffs. The new ships were built and then staffed, mostly by poorer Athenian citizens—men without the resources to purchase the heavy arms and armor necessary to fight as hoplites. With the completion of the new fleet, virtually the entire Athenian citizenry could be mobilized for military service—the rowers who staffed the fleet would complement the hoplite spear fighters of the land army—each playing an essential role in the defense of their country.

In 480 BCE, the Persian king Xerxes led an invasion force west across the Hellespont strait separating northwestern Anatolia from northern Greece. The Persians advanced south into Greece. A famous, desperate attempt by the Spartans failed to stop the invaders at the pass of Thermopylae. The Persian land army was much too large for any conceivable Greek force. The Athenian citizens gathered in assembly to decide what to do.

Three options were put on the table by the citizen council. First, put as many Athenians as possible on boats and flee to the western Mediterranean, hoping to establish a new colonial polis far from the Persian threat. Next, fortify the Acropolis and hope to weather a Persian siege. Finally, evacuate the civilian population to friendly towns in southern Greece and use the new navy to confront the Persian warships in the straits around the island of Salamis. A big enough victory at sea would incapacitate the Persian fleet. Then, since the fleet was essential for resupplying the huge Persian army, the Persians would be forced to evacuate most of their forces. But abandoning the city would mean that the religious temples and private homes would be sacked and plundered by the enemy. Furthermore, defeat at sea would mean the end of Athens as a state. Again the question was posed, Could the civic bargain hold? Was Athenian civic friendship strong enough to allow the polis to gamble its future on the motivation and skill of its poorer citizens, the oarsmen of the fleet? After serious public debate, the decision was made and affirmed by the assembled citizenry. Athens would fight at sea. The subsequent victory in the naval battle of Salamis proved decisive: King Xerxes retreated back to Persia with the bulk of his forces. The much-reduced Persian forces that remained in Greece were later defeated in a land battle in which Spartans and Athenians, along with citizens from other Greek city-states, fought side by side against their common foe.

The Greek victory over King Xerxes was astounding, but the Athenians were sure that the Persian king would try again if he could, and they were determined to stop him. They proposed a joint Athens-Sparta defense plan, aimed at preempting Persian naval operations anywhere in the Mediterranean Sea. The Spartans demurred, though; they could not see their way to keeping control of their big local slave population while simultaneously leading in a long-term overseas effort at containing Persia. So democratic Athens took on the job. Athenian leaders devised a sophisticated plan for the joint defense of the Greek homeland: the Greek poleis of coastal northern Greece, the Aegean Islands, and the western Anatolian coast were organized into a defensive league under Athenian leadership. The residents of most of those city-states had little experience in shipbuilding or large-scale naval operations. So a bargain was struck: Athens would provide the bulk of the ships and rowers; the allied states would pay war taxes into a common treasury. The plan worked brilliantly. Within a generation, and after Athenian warships had repeatedly defeated his attempts to rebuild a war fleet, the Persian king gave up his western ambitions. The Aegean Sea became, in effect, an Athenian lake.

With Persia out of the picture, some of Athens's allies now hoped to quit paying their war taxes. But the Athenians saw little advantage to themselves in dissolving the league: the taxes paid by the allies employed tens of thousands of Athenians in the shipyards and the fleet itself. Why give that up, when Athenian ships ruled the waves of the eastern Mediterranean?

By the mid-fifth century BCE, the defensive league had morphed into an Athenian Empire—the first, but not the last, historical example of a democracy running an empire. Recalcitrant city-states that sought to go their own way were faced with quick, harsh reprisals and Athenian garrisons. At its height, Athens ruled over hundreds of city-states and perhaps 2.5 million persons. States within the empire were subject to Athenian law, and disputes were adjudicated in Athenian courts. Yet the status of citizen was jealously guarded by the Athenians. After the initial inclusive moment following the revolution of 508 BCE, citizenship was largely limited to native-born Athenians. Indeed in 451 BCE, democratic leader Pericles passed a new law in the assembly that limited citizenship to those men whose fathers *and* mothers were born of Athenian parents. Naturalization of foreign-born residents was rare and required a special vote of the citizen assembly.

Nonetheless, with growing prosperity from imperial revenues and increased trade, the population of Athenian citizens grew in the fifth century, to about 50,000. Many non-Athenians chose to move to Athens and were welcome to do so. But with few exceptions, they and their offspring were permanent *metics*—resident aliens who paid a special tax for the privilege of long-term residency. In exchange for paying their taxes, metics enjoyed various civil rights in law, but they were not participatory citizens. They could not hold office, nor could they share in making rules in the assembly or interpreting law in the courts. They helped drive the Athenian economy to new heights. By excluding them from the civic community, however, Athens lost an opportunity to build up its workforce and knowledge base—resources that could have aided in confronting future challenges.

Meanwhile, growing Athenian wealth led to a growing population of non-Athenian slaves, many of them taken captive in distant wars and transported to the Aegean to feed the burgeoning labor needs of Athens and other city-states. Athenian slaves worked in households, urban industry, agricultural fields, and the silver mines. Although there were enslaved Africans in classical Greece, unlike American slavery (chapter 5), Greek slavery was not race based: Greeks taken in war were often enslaved by other Greeks; many others arrived from the Danubian region and western Asia. While slaves could be manumitted by their Greek masters, and many were, freed slaves were seldom offered citizenship; instead, they joined the ranks of Athenian metics. In common with other self-governing states, the political and personal freedom embraced by Athenian citizens was accompanied by a social and legal system that maintained many others in miserable conditions of enforced servitude.

The imperial age of the mid-fifth century BCE was one of extraordinary prosperity for Athens and produced an efflorescence of high culture. Artists, scientists, thinkers, and poets from around the Greek world flocked to Athens, contributing to the creation of an extraordinary array of new literary genres: historiography, tragedy, comedy, scientific and medical writing, and philosophy in many forms. Architects created amazing buildings—the Parthenon on the Acropolis among them. Sculptors and painters developed remarkable new ways to portray the human body. Music and the performing arts reached new heights. Meanwhile, the city was fortified by a massive wall, and long walls connected the city to the port at Piraeus, with its well-defended commercial and military harbors. The institutions of the democratic government continued to evolve through ongoing bargaining in council and assembly. Panels of two to five hundred citizen-jurors sat in judgment on civil and criminal trials; their decisions were made by simple majority vote and secret ballot. Some officials were either elected at large in the assembly (including generals and state engineers); many others were chosen in an open lottery. Magistrates, councillors, and jurors were paid, so that even the poorest Athenian could participate fully in the self-government of the democratic state. Rich and poor citizens alike walked the streets unarmed, without fear for their physical safety or assaults on civic dignity. The polis climbed to new heights of material welfare, security, and civic engagement.

War with Sparta: The Fall and Rise of Athenian Democracy

As imperial Athens grew in wealth and resources, Sparta and the members of Sparta's coalition became increasingly concerned. Under Pericles's leadership, Athens engaged in an aggressive foreign policy, putting economic and military pressure on Greek states not yet in the empire. By the 430s, the Greek world of the eastern Mediterranean was effectively divided into two major power blocks: Sparta's league in southern and inland central Greece versus Athens's empire of coastal and island states. As historian Thucydides saw, given the continued growth of

Athenian power and the fear this generated in Sparta, interstate peace was not sustainable in equilibrium.

The upshot was the twenty-seven-year Peloponnesian War, a conflict that pitted Athenian sea power against the land power of Sparta, tore apart the Greek world, finally broke the Athenian Empire, and came close to ending the Athenian experiment in democracy. Despite a plague that killed Pericles and a quarter of Athens's population, Athens fought Sparta to a standstill in the first phase of the war. An uneasy truce was made in 421 BCE, but later broken when in 415 BCE, against the advice Pericles had given at the beginning of the war, the Athenian democratic assembly voted to launch an imperialistic seaborne invasion of Sicily. The plan was to address the challenge of "how to defeat the Spartan coalition" by scaling up the empire: expanding the theater of war, adding new resources, and thus finally gaining the wherewithal to break the Spartan alliance.

Athens's grand Sicilian expedition failed massively. Instead of joining Athens, as the Athenians had fondly expected they would, the Greek city-states of Sicily coalesced around the primary target of the Athenian expedition, the polis of Syracuse. Syracuse, like Athens, was a democracy, with a large, highly motivated citizen army and big navy. The Athenian siege of Syracuse failed. Then a great sea battle in Syracuse's harbor ended in an Athenian defeat, followed by a desperate overland retreat by the Athenian land army. In the end, tens of thousands of Athenians, oarsmen and spearmen alike, were killed in battle or died in captivity. In the aftermath of the catastrophe, the Spartans occupied the Athenian countryside. The Athenians were now isolated in their walled city-harbor complex and dependent on imported food, supplied by the empire and protected by the remnants of the navy.

Antidemocratic Athenians saw their chance. They engaged in a campaign of domestic terrorism that ended in a coup that put a body of four hundred oligarchs at the head of the government. Athenian democracy was suspended. But the oligarchic government failed to gain legitimacy. When it came out that the oligarchic leaders were plotting to surrender Athens to Sparta, the Athenian armed forces—army and navy alike—

pushed back and the democracy was restored. The civic bargain had proved resilient.

Athens fought on, but now the war itself scaled up as the Persian Empire entered the conflict on Sparta's side. Persian financial aid enabled Sparta to finally build a fleet capable of challenging Athens's control of the Aegean Sea—and thereby the vital supply lines that fed the population of the walled city. Some of the subject states of the empire seized their opportunity and broke free of Athenian control. After an entire board of generals was sentenced to death by the citizen assembly for the crime of abandoning shipwrecked Athenian oarsmen after a naval victory, Athenian military commanders became excessively cautious, eventually leading to a decisive Spartan naval victory. Athens had lost its last fleet. The Spartans began a siege. Cut off from supplies, starving, the Athenians surrendered in 404 BCE.

The victorious Spartans dismantled the Athenian Empire, tore down Athens's fortification walls, decommissioned the fleet, and ordered the end of the democracy. Thirty antidemocratic Athenians, later dubbed "the Thirty Tyrants," were put in charge of the government and most Athenians were disenfranchised. While some of the Thirty Tyrants were associates of philosopher Socrates and relatives of his greatest student, Plato, they proved to be savage kleptocrats rather than wise philosopher-rulers. The Thirty Tyrants embarked on a reign of terror, exiling their opponents, confiscating property at whim, and murdering anyone who got in their way—or whose possessions they coveted.

A Revised Civic Bargain: Fundamental Law

The viciousness of the oligarchic government stimulated the quick consolidation of a democratic opposition. The forces of the Thirty Tyrants were defeated in a series of battles with the resurgent democrats. The Spartans, divided in their own counsels and occupied elsewhere, did little to help their former partners. In less than a year after the surrender to Sparta, Athens was once again a democracy and free polis. The defeated Athenian oligarchs feared a vengeful bloodbath, but the victorious democrats wisely saw that would lead to a grinding civil war of attrition. Continued conflict would preclude any return to Athenian greatness. So instead, following in the tradition of Solon and Cleisthenes, they returned to the bargaining table. Athenian democrats and their erstwhile Athenian opponents negotiated a revised civic bargain that enabled Athens to recover from a long generation of war and civil conflict, regaining security and welfare in a postimperial era.

The new bargain began with an amnesty: Athenians agreed not to use the legal machinery of the restored democracy to take vengeance on those who had collaborated with the Thirty Tyrants. In brief, the victorious democrats agreed not to treat Athenians who had supported the oligarchs as enemies; this vital first step asserted that civic friendship was possible even in the aftermath of civil war. Anyone who violated the amnesty by seeking vengeance faced public prosecution and the death penalty.

Meanwhile, the previously ad hoc system of making and recording Athenian laws was overhauled. The Athenians recognized that the citizen assembly could all too easily be misled by personally ambitious leaders; to prevent that, they made policy makers accountable for their proposals and distinguished between day-to-day policy making and fundamental, constitutional laws. Fundamental law would now be made by a democratically chosen body of "lawmakers," and the legislative policies voted on and passed in regular meetings of the citizen assembly would now have to conform to those basic laws. All laws and policies were to be recorded and kept in a publicly accessible archive. The new bargain, with its emphasis on a shared Athenian commitment to constitutionalism and the rule of law, ensured relatively wealthy Athenians that they would not be preyed on by the numerically superior poor. And it assured poor Athenians that the wealthy, for their part, would accept the democratic political order and undertake their civic duties by, among other things, paying taxes to sustain the fleet, rebuild the city walls, and restore the central institutions and cultural features of the community.

The new bargain worked well. In the face of adversity—continued Spartan hostility, interference in Greek affairs by the Persian king, and the rise of rival city-states in central Greece—the Athenians came together and turned to the job of rebuilding their community as well as returning it to a high level of security and prosperity. With the empire lost forever, this meant that the Athenians had to find new and innovative ways to persuade other Greeks to come to Athens for business and choose Athenian markets for their commercial activities. And that meant, in practice, expanding the rights and protections offered to noncitizens—metics and short-term visitors alike. The Athenians still stubbornly rejected the option of enfranchising many nonnatives, but they passed new legislation that made Athens an especially attractive place to do business.

The harbor facilities were improved, and warehouses made available to overseas traders. Skilled public slaves, trained to be expert in detecting forged currency, were stationed in key locations. Their services were freely available to anyone engaged in monetary transactions, and their presence assured all traders that the coins they were offered in Athens's market were good. Market regulations and market officials ensured that weights and measures were fair and standard. New laws gave everyone who was engaged in overseas trade—metics, short-term visitors, and even slaves—equal legal standing, assuring them of timely and impartial judgments when contract disputes arose. Meanwhile, despite the notorious trial and execution of Socrates in 399 BCE, Athens was once again a center of culture and especially philosophy; the Academy of Plato and Lyceum of Aristotle were just two of the newly established schools of philosophy that attracted intellectuals to Athens from around the Greek world. The city walls and fleet were rebuilt. Knowledgeable and trusted officials were elected to guide the polis's finances. While never achieving its level of fifth-century BCE imperial dominance, democratic Athens was once again wealthy and a formidable military power in the Greek world. The citizen council, citizen assembly, and law courts all continued to operate much as they had, albeit under the new institutional rules. Democratic Athens was back.

The End of Athenian Democracy

Meanwhile, however, the situation at the margins of the Greek world was changing, and in ways that would present a scale challenge that the

Athenians were finally unable to meet. The Greek culture zone, the wider world in which Greek was spoken, at least as a second language, and in which various aspects of Greek city-state culture were adopted, had expanded in the decades after the Peloponnesian War—among other places into Cyprus, inland Sicily, and southwestern Anatolia. A prime area of Greek cultural expansion lay to the north in Macedonia. The Macedonians had long been engaged with cultural interchange with their central and southern Greek neighbors. The Athenian form of spoken Greek had been adopted as a court language by the kings of Macedon in the fifth century BCE; late in his career, the great tragic poet Euripides performed some of his plays in the Macedonian capital. Yet Macedonian kings had traditionally been weak leaders of a backward country. They had been limited in their authority by local Macedonian nobles. The powerful Greek poleis to the south played their part by backing ambitious rival members of the royal family whenever a Macedonian king appeared dangerously competent. All of that changed after 359 BCE when King Philip II came to the Macedonian throne.

Philip II was, by any account, an organizational genius: a master diplomat as well as superb military tactician and strategist. But he was also smart enough to realize that Macedon could only reach its true potential by importing Greek experts in various domains—not just tragic poets, but experts in military technology and state finance. Moreover, Philip self-consciously incorporated and adapted certain of the features of Greek-style citizenship to a Macedonian context. By ruthlessly crushing internal rivals and diplomatically playing Greek poleis against each other, befriending first one and then another rival state, Philip bought time to build a new Macedonian army. He co-opted nobles while promising new prosperity and land allotments to ordinary Macedonians who joined the king's forces. And he kept his promises. With his growing and highly motivated army, Philip was able to expand Macedon's borders to the south, east, and north—bringing fertile agricultural regions and a rich mining district under his control.

With the help of hired Greek experts, Macedon's state finances were put on a sound footing and new technologies developed—notably advanced forms of catapult artillery. By the 340s, Philip was actively engaged in military actions and diplomacy in various parts of the Greek world. Athens, like other Greek city-states, was slow to recognize the danger. Athenian attempts to limit Philip's expansion to the south came too little and too late. A treaty with Athens, signed in 346 BCE, allowed Philip to consolidate his gains. Several years later the king made his move into central Greece. A last-minute alliance of Athens with long-time rival city-state Thebes set up a decisive land battle in 338 BCE, near the small polis of Chaeronea, just north of Athenian territory. In the event, Philip's forces were too many, too well trained, and too well equipped, and he won handily.

Following his victory at Chaeronea, Philip avoided overplaying his hand. He did not invade Athenian territory, nor did he mandate any change in the Athenian democratic constitution. But the Athenians, like other Greek city-states, saw that their best option was to join his new multistate coalition and thereby accept Philip as their hegemon; Athens lost its freedom to set its own foreign policy. When Philip was assassinated two years after Chaeronea, the Athenians hoped that they might be able to regain their freedom, but Philip's son, Alexander III ("the Great"), proved to be an ever better general than his father. After Alexander sacked Thebes for daring to resist him, the Athenians accepted the young king as their new hegemon.

In 334 BCE, Alexander marched off to Asia to conquer the Persian Empire. Four years later, Athens declined to join an anti-Macedonian uprising led by Sparta. But when Alexander died in Babylon in 323 BCE, the Athenians led a coalition of Greek states in an attempt to throw off Macedonian control. Once again, the Macedonians proved superior on the field of battle. After defeats on land and sea, Athens surrendered, and this time the democracy was forfeit: the victorious Macedonians imposed an oligarchy, closing down the citizen assembly and people's courts. Although over the next few centuries the Athenians sought periodically to reestablish their democratic constitution, the periods of restoration were relatively brief. The last era of democratic government for Athens came in the early first century BCE, when Athens joined a revolt against Rome led by Mithradates of Pontus. After the Romans crushed that revolt, they terminated the Athenian democratic experiment.

Lessons Learned

Athens rose to remarkable heights of power and influence through a series of political and civic bargains. These bargains resulted in a new conception of citizenship, near-universal native, free male franchise, and a series of innovative governmental institutions. The bargains were made possible by civic friendship across a large (by city-state standards) and socially diverse citizen body. Most Athenians refused to treat one another as mortal enemies. They were increasingly willing to recognize one another as fellow members in a shared project, with common interests in security, flourishing as a state and persons, and doing so without a boss. Institutional innovations grounded in shared norms of mutual respect made social diversity into a strength; participation in those institutions and a wide range of civic festivals served as an effective education in citizenship. Richer and poorer Athenians, laborers, artisans, traders, and large landholders all gained from high morale, effective mobilization, and the collective capacity to aggregate dispersed sources of knowledge for problem-solving. But the challenges Athens faced in the fourth century BCE demanded a big leap forward in scale: the Athenians would have needed many more highly motivated people and a much broader knowledge network if they were to address the challenge posed by Macedon and Rome.

Despite periodic proposals to enfranchise loyal metics and liberate slaves, despite the ideas for making women participatory citizens floated by dramatists and philosophers, the Athenians refused to expand their citizenship experiment beyond its original inclusion of adult free men resident in Athenian territory. That initial move—a radical innovation in its day—gave Athens access to a pool of talent, skill, and knowledge that was vastly larger and more diverse than a standard "king's council" of like-minded aristocrats. Along with the high level of civic morale and motivation that enabled the Athenians to mobilize a large force of fighters against external threats, Athens had access to a broad and diverse knowledge set that was put to good use in solving pressing problems. It expanded the zone of creative endeavor, and therefore the state's prestige and influence. That in turn drove the remarkable economic and cultural efflorescence of the democratic period, both in the imperial fifth century and postimperial fourth century BCE. But because Athens failed to devise a way of further boldly enlarging its franchise while still sustaining its unique culture of deep civic participation, it failed to meet the new scale challenges posed by imperial Macedon and Rome.

The Macedonians and later the Romans (chapter 3) fielded large, highly motivated, and well-led armies that were able to beat any force that the Athenians (or any other ancient state for that matter) threw at them. The Macedonian kings, Philip II and Alexander III, solved their own scale problem through an innovative variant on the standard monarchical practice of building a pyramidal structure of hierarchical authority. For Philip and Alexander, the relationship between the monarch and his subjects, whether nobles or ordinary soldiers, was not strictly hierarchical. The kings shared the struggles and dangers of their troops on campaign—and both were frequently wounded in battle. They attended assembly-like gatherings and listened (more or less carefully) to objections and recommendations from the ranks. They were also more than willing to hire Greek experts who had been educated and developed their skill sets within the meritocratic context of a free and open society. In many ways, Macedon, at least in the age of Philip and Alexander, was a sort of monarchical-civic hybrid. Yet it was highly scalable too; lacking the expectations that citizens must be the descendants of citizens, the Macedonian kings were free to expand far beyond their core population base.

What might the Athenians have done when faced with that kind of threat? Most obviously, they might have opened a pathway to citizenship to the thousands of foreign residents and manumitted slaves who legally lived in the polis. Shutting down the hope that immigrants and former slaves would ever be full citizens limited the pool of skills, information, and knowledge available to the Athenian state.

That was a special problem after the Peloponnesian War, when Athens had suffered the double demographic hit of plague and massive military casualties.

Next, the shortfall in highly motivated sharers in the civic project might been made up for by women. Athenian women were in many ways centrally important participants in Athenian society—notably in the vital domains of domestic economy and religion. Women were certainly interested in and knowledgeable about public affairs—as shown, even through the distorting lens of comedy, in Aristophanes's fantasy play, *The Assemblywomen*. But women, along with resident foreigners and slaves, were denied the chance to speak or vote in the institutions of government. No women sat on the council or courts, or in the assembly. Relatedly, women were excluded from military service. Plato, in his dialogue *The Republic*, advocated for women to be full members of the elite guardian class, the highly educated scholar-warriors from whom the philosopher rulers of his imagined ideal state were to be chosen. Plato parried objections that women could not be fighters by citing the experience of the Amazons—warrior women who fought alongside men on the Eurasian Steppe lands that lay to the northeast of the Greek world. His proposal remained at the level of ivory tower philosophical speculation. What if it had not, though? Could the history have gone differently if Athenian citizenship policy had been more inclusive?

Had the Athenians, counterfactually, included at least metics and native women into the ranks of the citizens, had they been more liberal with the manumission of slaves and elevating manumitted slaves to the ranks of full citizen, they would have had a larger and more diverse body of skill and talent to mobilize in the face of the Macedonian threat. And that might, at least hypothetically, have made all the difference at crucial junctures in Athenian history. From time to time, the Athenians did contemplate adding metics and freed slaves to the ranks of citizens, but each time they balked before actually striking that new civic bargain. Arguably, along with entrenched attitudes and habits, the reason they turned back from the path that might have saved their democracy was that they saw that radically expanding the citizen body also threatened to thin down the experience of citizenship.

How could many more citizens be added to the full and active civic community and yet remain fully committed to the common good of the community? How could mobilization be radically expanded while morale and motivation were sustained? What new institutions might make all of that possible? Those were the questions the Athenians failed to answer. And thus the next iteration of the historical experiment with democracy would take place on the other side of the Mediterranean— in republican Rome.

3

ROME

The Compromises That Created the First Great Republic

"Can anyone be so indifferent or idle as not to want to know by what means, and under what kind of government, almost the whole inhabited world was conquered and brought under the dominion of the single city of Rome?"[1] That was the question that Greek historian Polybius asked his prospective readers in the mid-second century BCE. Polybius's idea of the inhabited world was largely limited to the Mediterranean basin. His chronological focus was the half century that culminated in 146 BCE with the Roman conquest of his own Greek homeland. But as he knew, the story of Rome's rise began much earlier. What Polybius cannot have known but might have guessed was that Rome's domains would eventually extend far into inland Europe and western Asia. The "kind of government" under which all that was accomplished was citizen self-government: while Romans called their government a republic, it was, in the terms we are using in this book, a *democratic* republic.

The rise of Rome offers a classic case of the expansive potential of a citizen-centered community that successfully managed the external threats and scale challenges that ultimately doomed Athens's citizen government. The Romans did that through distinctively scalable political bargains between ordinary and elite citizens that resulted in new decision-making institutions, and by building trust through social networks. They extended the scope of civic friendship through demonstrating, first, that "becoming Roman" was a real option for many people, and next, that Romans flourished when they treated each other as fellow sharers in an expansive common project. Rome was never a small, fully participatory democracy on the Athens model. Yet its republican "mixed constitution" was understood by Polybius as fundamentally democratic—in the sense of the bossless rule of citizens in their own collective interest.

The crisis of Roman self-government in the late second and first century BCE was precipitated by the shortsighted selfishness of wealthy elites and ambitions of talented power seekers. That selfishness and ambition undermined key institutional innovations—especially in the adaptation of citizenship—that had enabled the Romans to scale up a city-state to the governance of a huge overseas empire. The crisis that ultimately destroyed the Roman Republic and inaugurated the rule of emperor as boss was both exemplified and precipitated by a bargaining failure: the repeated choice of fighting over negotiation. When Romans began treating fellow citizens as enemies to be defeated rather than as friends with whom one might fruitfully negotiate, the democratic republic collapsed and was replaced by a form of monarchy.

By 146 BCE, the end date of Polybius's half century of extraordinary growth, Rome had become so big and powerful that external enemies no longer posed an existential threat. Scaling up from a city-state to an empire solved Rome's external security problem, but created conditions in which the stakes of discord seemed lower and Romans were ever more ready to view their fellow citizens as public enemies instead of civic friends. Without a credible external threat, powerful Roman elites had less reason to return to the bargaining table. Founded in opposition to one-man rule, the Roman Republic conquered "almost the whole inhabited world." But then through the violence of a brutal civil war, its democracy was undone, replaced by the imperial rule of the Caesars.

In the Beginning

Rome started small. According to Roman tradition, the city was founded in the eighth century BCE. At that time, as modern archaeologists have learned, Rome was an unimposing place, a settlement scattered across a few hills above the Tiber River in central Italy. The town was originally governed by a king, or in Latin, *rex*. So at that time, Romans had a boss, but of a distinctive sort. The kingship was nonhereditary, and Rome's early kings were not even Roman by birth. Each king was chosen by a council of Roman aristocrats called Patricians—"the Fathers." The king was then confirmed by the acclamation of the community's fighting men. Some of the early Roman kings were effective and ambitious. They built security and welfare by developing institutions, embarking on public building projects, and expanding the state's territory. By the late sixth century BCE, Rome had grown to be a substantial and locally prominent city-state. With a total population of some twenty-five to fifty thousand and a territory of about eight hundred square kilometers, Rome was already the largest state in central Italy. It was, however, still only a fraction of the size of classical Athens.

One of Rome's early institutions was unique among well-documented ancient city-states: a regular census. Every five years state officials counted the Roman people—and thereby gauged the number of fighting men who were available to defend the community. Romans capable of arming themselves as infantry gained a civic role when they were organized into the Assembly of Centuries. Each century was a body of men, perhaps originally about a hundred, but not limited to any particular number; the institution was well designed for scaling up as Rome's population grew. Historians guess that this assembly of warriors was first created by the kings as a counterweight to the influence of the aristocratic Patrician council. The assembly evolved over time and long outlasted the kingship. In later years, as we will see, it would be responsible for legislation and the election of officials.

The last of Rome's early kings, Tarquin, continued the pattern of public building and expanding Rome's regional influence. But he also sought to break free of the traditional constraints imposed on the king by the Patrician council—conducting a reign of terror against opponents. The despotic nature of his rule earned him his nickname: "the Proud." A final outrage—when his son raped a noble Roman woman—sparked a revolt against the tyrannical king, and Tarquin fled from the city. The Romans forever after despised the very term *rex*. The accusation, "he seeks to be *rex*"—the equivalent of "he thinks he's our boss"—would be a deadly charge in political struggles to come.

Tarquin was out, but not done; he planned to fight his way back into power. The threat of the return of Tarquin the Proud at the head of an army of Rome's neighbors, suspicious and jealous of Rome's growth, threatened the existence of the Roman community. That threat was a stimulus to striking a bargain between the aristocratic fathers and armed men of the Assembly of Centuries. The result was the foundation of the Roman Republic in 509 BCE.

The New Republic

In the place of the king, the Romans established a republican form of collective self-government by citizens. In principle, the "people of Rome" was the ultimate sovereign, which is why we can describe Rome as a kind of democracy. The first principle of the new government was that no individual would ever be granted an indefinite term of unaccountable authority. The Patrician council that had advised the king became the Senate, composed as before of prominent aristocrats. The Senate had the essential role of advising the officials, who would now take over the king's executive and judicial roles. A formal gathering of all citizens—the Assembly of Tribes—was soon added as a complement to the warriors' Assembly of Centuries. The two assemblies were responsible for electing officials, making major decisions, and passing legislation. The most important officials were two annually elected magistrates later called consuls. Each consul was a check on the authority of the other, and their short term of office prevented them from consolidating power. They jointly convened the Assembly of Centuries, and in times of war, commanded Rome's legionary armies.

Consuls and other important officials were elected, and other matters of great public concern, especially war and peace, were decided by the Assembly of Centuries. The reformed, republican version of the assembly organized adult male citizens into voting groups ("centuries") according to military-related property requirements. Decisions were made by an indirect method of voting: *within* each century, individual citizens cast equal votes; a majority of individual votes determined each century's vote. The outcome of elections and decisions on public policy were determined by a simple majority of century votes. By the era of the Middle Republic there were 193 centuries, and so the matter was decided when 97 of the centuries had cast their collective votes for a candidate, or for or against a policy.

The process was indirectly democratic, yet it was hierarchical too. As Rome grew larger, the centuries came to be vastly different sizes. Each of the top centuries, which voted first, was composed of a small number of the richest and most prominent citizens—so each individual's vote counted for a lot. The bottom few centuries, in which the mass of Romans who owned little or no land were enrolled, were relatively enormous, diluting individual votes. The power of the Assembly of Centuries was also limited in that only high officials could propose legislation. Initially, all Roman officials and all senators were Patricians. All other Romans, rich or poor, were "Plebeians."

In its earliest incarnation, the Roman Republic, while free of any one boss, was in practice a hereditary, aristocratic oligarchy; political power was effectively monopolized by the Patricians as a collective boss. The oligarchy was, however, precarious: the Patricians alone could not muster enough people to fend off Rome's rivals, and the Plebeians were not content to act as dutiful "sons" of the "fathers." Military threats were numerous and serious; Tarquin the Proud sought allies among Rome's neighbors. The other Latin-speaking towns of central Italy feared Rome's increasing size and resented its prestige. Further afield were the rich city-states of Etruria to the north and fierce hill tribes to the east and south. From the moment of its foundation, the Republic confronted existential threats. The proximity of threats lent the Plebeians bargaining strength. But in order to bargain, they had to be united in their aims and collectively willing to take risks.

Early Republican Bargains

Soon after the Republic's founding, in 494 BCE, the Plebeians became collectively aggravated by the domineering behavior of certain

Patricians. Eager to be treated as fellow citizens rather than as naughty children, they chose a moment of military crisis to go on strike (in Latin a *secessio plebis*, literally "withdrawing of the Plebeians"). Sitting down in a field outside the city, they refused to fight for Rome until the rules of the Republic were adjusted in their favor. The Plebeians had a strong bargaining position. Without them, the Patricians could not hold out against their neighbors. So they made a deal. This "first Plebeian secession" led to a new political bargain in which the Patricians acknowledged the official standing of ten Plebeian tribunes, officials whose function would be to protect members of this lower class against mistreatment by state officials and Patrician overreach. Tribunes were to be elected annually by all Plebeians, who were an overwhelming majority in the second citizen assembly, the Assembly of Tribes. Tribunes were also empowered to propose legislation to this assembly. Rome's development as a state, ultimately leading to a democratic civic bargain, was driven by political bargains following a series of Plebeian secessions, and by the counterweighting development of different assemblies and governing bodies.

The tribal assembly, like the Assembly of Centuries, voted by groups. But the tribal groups—originally four "city" tribes and seventeen "rural" ones—were initially roughly equal in size. Each tribe was relatively diverse in membership, including both rich and poor (not all Plebeians were poor). Tribes, unlike centuries, therefore offered the opportunity for social networking and building deeper civic friendship across the lines of wealth inequality.

The powers of the tribunes were both symbolic and operational. In a crisis, the tribune interceded by putting his own body between the victim and oppressor. The new institution was effective because the Plebeians swore to use collective violence against—that is, treat as an enemy rather than a friend—any Roman who laid hands on a tribune. As time went on, tribunes used their power of intercession to stop legislation thought to be harmful to Plebeian interests. Any tribune could effectively prevent legislation from going forward or the election of new officials by declaring his veto. Given the need to hold annual elections and pass new legislation, this veto power encouraged the Patricians to take account of Plebeian interests; Roman political bargaining could thus evolve organically.

The bargain between Patricians and Plebeians ensured that Rome had the military might to fight its wars. That bargain was frequently renegotiated over the course of the next two centuries, resulting in a series of compromises that sustained Roman military might while incrementally changing formal rules, social norms, and the composition of Rome's ruling class. In 451 BCE, a half century after the first secession, Rome's first written law code, the Twelve Tables, was published. Rome had borrowed and adapted the Greek alphabet; publication of the law code meant that in principle, all Romans could know the basic rules. The Twelve Tables was not a democratic constitution, but it was binding on all Romans, including Roman officials. It was a breakthrough in that a principle of "public authority under public law" was firmly established. Among the least equitable of the Twelve Tables was a rule forbidding intermarriage between Patricians and Plebeians. But following Plebeian agitation, this rule was soon set aside. After some unsatisfactory experiments with different forms of military leadership and pressured by hard-bargaining Plebeian tribunes, the Patricians agreed, in 366 BCE, that at least one of the two consuls elected each year would be a Plebeian.

Meanwhile, Rome's armies were on the march, driven by a sense of perpetual threat. The restive Latin towns were beaten into submission, and a long, hard war with the Etruscan city-state of Veii ended in Roman victory. While occasionally the Romans simply destroyed a defeated town, treating its inhabitants as enemies, they usually brought the surviving populace into some form of friendly (albeit dependent) relationship. In some cases, the defeated were granted full Roman citizenship. Others were made semicitizens, with "Latin rights" of intermarriage and commerce. Still others were made "allies"—retaining local independence but when called on they were required to provide men to fight on Rome's side. To secure its ever-expanding zone of control, Rome established new citizen and Latin rights colonies at and beyond its frontiers. Defending those far-flung outposts against local threats led to new wars, new conquests, and new citizens, semicitizens, and alliances.

So a security/citizenship pattern was established. External threats led Rome to scale up its citizenship body. Victories by ever-larger armies led to territorial expansion. Expansion exposed new threats, requiring in turn more citizens. The expansive and inclusive Roman approach to citizenship that made this cycle possible was distinct from that of Athens, where citizenship was jealously guarded by the incumbents. The Roman approach to citizenship was in turn made feasible within the republican constitutional framework by the indirect decision-making process: group voting allowed for more and more people to participate, even while diluting the influence of each individual voter. The question remained, How far could Rome scale up its citizenship and thin down individual participation in decision-making, while still sustaining civic friendship and a virtuous commitment to the common good of the shared community?

Constitutional Equilibrium

It took one more Plebeian secession, in 287 BCE, before the Patricians finally gave up their uniquely privileged place in the social order so that Rome's mature republican civic bargain could be established. This secession was ended with the passing of a compromise agreement, the Lex Hortensia, a law that made all resolutions passed by the Plebeian gathering (a special assembly of the Plebeians, or essentially the Assembly of Tribes minus the Patricians) binding on all citizens.

The civic bargain capped a process of negotiation and social evolution that stabilized Roman politics. By the early third century BCE, the most prominent of the Plebeians had become as rich and influential as any of the "fathers." A new Patrician-Plebeian elite, referred to by historians as "the nobility," now dominated the Senate. Through the collective prestige of its membership, the Senate's advice to officials and recommendations to the assemblies was usually accepted. The Senate gained effective control of Roman foreign policy. But because the senators were by now all former state officials, and officials were elected by the broad Roman citizen franchise, it was not a boss. According to the Roman civic bargain, the Assembly of Centuries elected major officials; the tribal assembly elected minor ones. There was an established order in which offices were to be held: ambitious men needed to work their way up a ladder of elective offices (the so-called *cursus honorum*) before aiming at the consulship. Being elected consul meant not only a year of leadership but also gaining enduring influence in public affairs. Senators who had held the consulship led discussions in the Senate and always spoke first. Tribunes were annually elected, but they now saw little need to intercede. After 287, no major constitutional innovations were deemed necessary for the next 150 years. Polybius rightly associated this era of constitutional stability with Rome's rise to a world-class imperial power.

In the sixth book of his *Histories*, Polybius paused his historical narrative to analyze the Roman constitution of his own time, employing the sophisticated theoretical tool kit of Greek political philosophy. He famously described the Roman political order in the second century BCE as a "mixed constitution"—a concept that was eagerly adopted two millennia later by America's constitutional founders (chapter 5). Polybius argued that the consuls were a "monarchical" element, the Senate was "aristocratic," and the Assemblies of Centuries and Tribes were "democratic." Moreover, Polybius saw that the mix led to a balance of powers among the republican institutions: the power of the consuls to act on their own authority was limited by collegiality of office (each consul could veto any act of the other), their dependence on financing (state finance was effectively controlled by the Senate), and the votes of citizens in the assemblies. Likewise, assemblies were limited by their incapacity to initiate legislation, and the Senate was constrained by its lack of executive or legislative authority. The upshot was, as Polybius saw it, a habit of cooperation across the institutional order—cooperation that was facilitated by persistent external threats along with a shared commitment to the security and welfare of the community. Because the system was based on formal laws, shared norms, and the votes of a broad-based citizenry, it was, in his view, rightly described as a democracy.

Res Publica and Civic Friendship

Rome in the Middle Republic (287–133 BCE) remained a highly unequal society, even within the citizen body. Those Romans who succeeded in being elected to offices were invariably wealthy and typically from families with an established tradition of office holding. The membership of Rome's senatorial class was different in various ways, most obviously in wealth and influence, from the masses of ordinary Roman citizens. Furthermore, like Athens, Rome had a large and growing population of slaves and foreign noncitizens. By democratic Athenian standards, Roman freedom was constrained by law and custom. Romans remained more concerned with collective liberties than individual freedoms. And Roman political equality was likewise constrained by the hierarchy of offices and voting groups. But Roman citizens, from very rich to relatively poor, were socially networked through the tribes, united by a sense of common purpose and motivated by their sense of ever-present external threats. And thus they were willing participants in what they regarded a shared project—one that was essential to the security and welfare of each and all Romans. The English term *republic* comes from the Latin term *res publica*—the public thing, the common interest.

Dedication to res publica was a bond that unified the citizens of Rome—exemplified by shared obedience to the formal laws and informal, ancestral norms. Central among those norms was a willingness to sacrifice one's own short-term interests for the good of the community. The relatively poor served in the ranks of the army—but the wealthy also fought and died in Rome's constant wars. When necessary, the rich were taxed to raise funds to build fortification walls and warships as well as to finance long and hard campaigns at increasingly great distances from the city. The Romans themselves came to believe that norms of public service were an essential part of their deepest traditions: the "way of the ancestors." In one scholarly work now in progress, historian Bruce Hitchner describes the Roman civic psychology as "parochial altruism"—a commitment to the good of Rome and one's fellow Romans that arose as a result of a highly adaptive group-level cultural evolution.[2] That adaptive evolution was facilitated by external threats—a steady stream of security crises at increasing scale, each of which put the survival of the state at risk. Although each crisis threatened the existence of the community, Rome grew stronger as its citizens, together, met each one.

Rome met its challenges by developing habits of strong cooperation among a growing body of persons who trusted one another as civic friends and believed that they owed their lives and loyalty to the Republic. As civic friends, Romans remained concerned with their own interests, whether as individuals or members of social groups (rich/poor, urban/rural, etc.). But their pursuit of individual and group interest was carried on against a background assumption of a shared commitment to res publica. That commitment was manifest in individuals' display of civic virtues: military courage, disciplined self-control, and willing sacrifice of short-term private interests for the long-term public good. Those evidencing extraordinary civic virtue expected and received public honors. This implicit cultural bargain was win-win; it strengthened civic bonds and made Rome a formidable opponent.

Civic Education: Hero Stories and Public Honors

Roman civic education was exemplified in the rigors of military service, shared religious rituals, and especially stories told about virtuous Romans of the past, like Cincinnatus, the brilliant general who, when not fighting on the battlefield, was a simple farmer who plowed his own fields. When an enemy army approached Rome, Cincinnatus was called away from his farm by a desperate Senate and named as dictator. This was an emergency office under which the authority of all other officials was suspended. The dictator's power to command was absolute for the duration of the crisis or six months' time, whichever came first. Cincinnatus rose to the occasion: he led Rome's armies against the enemy, defeated them soundly, laid down his office in a matter of days, and immediately returned to his plowing. The crisis averted, the former dictator was again a simple citizen.

A sharply contrasting story was told of arrogant Coriolanus, also a successful general, but a haughty aristocrat who demanded the deference of all of those he took as his inferiors. When the Roman people declined to elect him consul, he berated them in public and was declared a public enemy by the tribunes. Coriolanus then abandoned Rome, joined forces with Rome's enemies, and led an army against his own city. Only the tearful intercession of Coriolanus's mother saved Rome. Coriolanus himself was assassinated by some of his non-Roman allies, who regarded him as a traitor to their anti-Roman cause.

Or consider the case of Manlius Torquatus, who was three times elected consul and three times appointed dictator at moments of crisis. During a campaign against rebellious Latins, Manlius ordered his son to stay at a certain post. But Manlius's son saw and acted on an opportunity to crush the enemy with a bold forward maneuver. After he proudly presented to his father the armor of his defeated opponents, Manlius's son was executed on his father's order: he had disobeyed his commander by abandoning his position and must suffer the consequences, despite family ties and the success of his sortie. These and similar stories of the early republic were told and retold to exemplify the virtues that Romans were expected to adopt as their own, and the vices they were expected to avoid.

Visible rewards of public honors were another essential part of Rome's education of citizens in civic virtues and friendship. A Roman who saved a fellow citizen's life on the battlefield was awarded a "civic crown"—a distinctive headdress that was worn with pride during public ceremonies. In the case of a siege of an enemy town, the first Roman to climb over the town's fortification wall was granted a "mural (wall) crown." This honor was usually awarded posthumously, given the extreme danger of being first to gain the top of a well-guarded fortification. A Roman commander who himself slew an enemy general, whether in battle or by challenging the opponent to a duel, and who stripped the dead man of his armor, was granted the *spolia opima*—"the finest spoils of battle." A Roman general who won a particularly notable victory over a dangerous foe could be voted a triumph—the right to parade with his army through the city and be lauded as Rome's savior. These coveted honors were remembered and celebrated for generations by the families of those who won them. The death masks of honored ancestors were prominently displayed during political campaigns by candidates for high offices. So honors granted publicly to those who had benefited the community also benefited one's own family; public and private interests were deeply intertwined in the Roman system of civic education. In sum, Romans were given good reasons to emulate modest Cincinnatus and stern Manlius, and avoid the fates of arrogant Coriolanus and Manlius's impetuous son.

Public Works and Altruistic Competition

Dedication to the good of the community was further manifest in the public works that were sponsored and paid for by leading Romans. These included increasingly numerous and elaborate temples to Rome's many gods. Roman religion had as its focal point the good of the community rather than the salvation of individual souls. Although religious rituals were sometimes manipulated by the nobles who dominated specialized priesthoods, reverence for the gods who preserved the state and its people bound the Romans together in a single community of fate under a stern but responsive divine order. Shared belief and the public performance of religious rituals sustained Rome through times of extreme crisis.

Other public works that promoted both security and welfare included a monumental defensive wall around the city—built in the early fourth century BCE in the aftermath of an attack on the city by a marauding party of Gauls. Carefully engineered and well-paved roads facilitated trade—and served as highways along which Rome's armies marched out to the frontiers. Aqueducts provided the residents of the growing city with the fresh water they required for drinking and bathing; storm sewers prevented floods and carried away waste. As in the case of heroic military achievement, individual sponsors of these works were remembered as public benefactors for generations. Their descendants, when candidates for public office, sought votes on the strength of the demonstrated devotion of their family to the highest standard of public sacrifice and service.

What so impressed Polybius about Roman successes during the third and second centuries BCE is a tale of many political bargains culminating in a civic bargain. As we have seen, the exclusive Patricians were forced to negotiate away many of their unique privileges in exchange for an ongoing role in a "noble" senatorial class that included wealthy and prominent Plebeians. Meanwhile, individual members of the noble families engaged in fierce competition for offices. In the annual elections, they were compelled to seek the votes and therefore consider the interests of ordinary Romans. Would-be leaders competed for scarce public honors, and winning those honors required that they sacrifice personal wealth and risk their lives to demonstrate their devotion to the ideal of res publica. Balanced between hard bargaining and a commitment to the collective good, between competition and cooperation, between interest and parochial altruism, the Roman Republic flourished and grew.

Scale Challenges

This Middle Republic period was an era of relative constitutional stability in which the civic virtues and shared ideals of res publica were consolidated. But it also was an age of new and daunting scale challenges. As Rome grew in size and influence, it faced bigger and more sophisticated opponents. By the early third century BCE, Rome was the dominant state in central Italy, but the Greek cities of southern Italy remained independent.

That independence came to the fore in a treaty dispute in 282 BCE, pitting the Romans against the Greek city of Tarentum. When events escalated into the threat of war, the Tarentines summoned help from a foreign power: Pyrrhus, the king of Epirus (modern Albania). Pyrrhus was a Macedonian and heir to the brilliant military tradition of Alexander the Great. In 280 BC, he went on the attack against the Romans, arriving in Italy with a crack mercenary army of twenty thousand men and twenty war elephants. Outfought by a military force of a kind they had never before faced, the Romans lost at least seven thousand troops in a preliminary battle; Pyrrhus lost about three thousand. Refusing Pyrrhus's offer of peace on his terms, the Romans were then defeated again in battle, losing another sixty-five hundred men to Pyrrhus's thirty-five hundred. Yet while he lost far fewer soldiers, Pyrrhus's capacity to replace them did not begin to match Rome's recruitment efforts. After the second battle, Pyrrhus abandoned Italy for an attempt to seize

Sicily from the Carthaginians, reportedly saying, "If we are victorious in one more battle with the Romans, we shall be utterly ruined."[3]

In 275, however, Pyrrhus came back for more. This time the Romans fought him to a draw, and Pyrrhus left Italy for good. The Romans' willingness to sacrifice their lives for their community, combined with Rome's large citizen population and Italian allies, allowed them to absorb terrible losses and still win out in the end. Moreover, the Romans had learned how to deal with a "modern" army. In the aftermath of the war, Rome forced the Greek cities of southern Italy into alliance. The Romans now controlled almost all of Italy.

The Carthage Challenge

Rome's next challenge was even greater: a long and arduous war with Carthage, up to that time the greatest naval power of the western Mediterranean. Like Rome, Carthage was a dynamic, expansive city-state with a republican government. Located on the coast of modern Tunisia, Carthage controlled much of northern Africa, and held outposts in Spain, Sicily, Sardinia, and Corsica. Rome had a long and mostly peaceful prior history with Carthage, but after the war with Pyrrhus, Rome's expansion into southern Italy, along with the Carthaginians' determination to expand in Sicily, created a volatile situation. In 264 BCE, a dispute brought matters to a head; Roman armies crossed to Sicily, defeating Carthaginian armies in a series of battles. But the Romans could not win the war without engaging the superior Carthaginian navy. The Romans had limited experience in war at sea, but they built and staffed a great fleet of oared warships virtually from scratch. The losses on both sides were staggering; tens of thousands of marines and rowers died in naval battles and storms. Both sides were nearly bankrupted by the costs of building and rebuilding fleets as well as carrying out and enduring sieges. Once again, though, the numbers and motivation of Rome's citizen-soldiers, and loyalty of semicitizens and allies, led to final victory.

In the aftermath of this First Punic War, the Carthaginians paid immense monetary reparations, and the Romans took over the rich island of Sicily—Rome's first overseas province. Soon after, the Romans opportunistically seized Sardinia and Corsica, taking the decisive first steps toward building a Mediterranean empire. New public offices were created to manage the provinces. Taxes imposed on the provincials became a major source of private and public enrichment. Meanwhile, the Carthaginians expanded their holdings in Spain. The Romans took notice. In 219, the dynamic Carthaginian general Hannibal attacked the Spanish town of Saguntum, with which Rome had opportunistically made an alliance. The Romans declared war, and Hannibal was ready to take them on. The Second Punic War had begun.

Since Carthage now lacked a navy, the Romans imagined the conflict would be fought in Spain and North Africa. But Hannibal moved first. Dramatically crossing the Italian Alps with his army, he allied with Gallic tribes and occupied northern Italy. The Romans found themselves fighting for survival on their home ground. Hannibal quickly won three great battles; tens of thousands of Roman soldiers were slaughtered. Rome named a dictator, Fabius Maximus, who sought to wear Hannibal down by avoiding battle while preventing Hannibal's army from looting. With the war in Italy stalemated, Rome went on the offensive in Sicily and Spain. Losing supporters in Italy, and with Carthage's African homeland threatened, Hannibal abandoned Italy. Roman general Scipio pursued Hannibal to North Africa, winning a decisive battle and gaining for himself the honorific name "Africanus." Carthage surrendered again, and again paid immense reparations. The Roman approach to expansive citizenship and alliances, resulting in the capacity to bear horrific setbacks and massive losses, had again proved resilient.

Conquerors of "Almost the Whole Inhabited World"

The Second Punic War had exacted a heavy toll on Romans and their Italian allies. There was much work to do. Cities that had betrayed Rome were punished by the expropriation of territory, which became "public lands" collectively owned by the republic. The proper distribution of that windfall, in ways that would sustain the strong cooperative bonds between the wealthy and ordinary Romans, might have seemed the first order of business. Instead, the Senate urged another war—this time against King Philip V of Macedon, who was suspected of colluding with King Antiochus III, the Macedonian grandee of western Asia. They were accused of interfering with Greek cities that had allied with Rome during the war against Hannibal. The Assembly of Centuries duly voted for war.

Within a half century and with only limited Roman casualties, Philip and Antiochus along with their successor kings had been crushed. Mainland Greece and Spain were added as Roman provinces; hundreds of thousands of war captives were transported to Italy as slaves. Vast quantities of loot were plundered from the wealthy cities of Greece and western Asia. Spain, now another Roman province and the site of ongoing military operations against highland tribes, provided mineral wealth—and more slaves. The slaves were bought up wholesale by wealthy Romans and put to work on the public lands—which in the meantime had been grabbed up by the wealthiest Romans. Pressure on the civic bargain increased.

But there was always another foreign war to fight; belligerent senators urged yet another war against Carthage, proclaiming, "Carthage must be destroyed." The war was quick and brutal; the great North African city ceased to exist after 146 BCE. There were still external threats to be managed. Yet the threat to Rome's very existence, the traditional fear of annihilation that had haunted the republic since its founding, was gone. This was the moment to which Polybius called attention at the beginning of his history, when he claimed that in just fifty-three years, the long half century following the Second Punic War, Rome had conquered nearly the whole of the inhabited world.

Taking Stock

The republic now faced a reckoning. The material benefits from a half century of highly profitable war making were both immense and unequally divided. Senators and equestrians—wealthy Romans whose families had not (or not yet) gained public offices—were doing extraordinarily well. From being merely rich, the Roman elite became vastly rich—at a scale unheard of in the earlier republic. But most ordinary Romans were faring relatively poorly: public welfare was not tracking imperial expansion. This had serious implications for Rome's social order and put the civic bargain under immense strain. The core of Rome's citizen army had long been small-scale farmers—those who owned enough land to support a family, but not a lot more. Heads of families, on the model of virtuous Cincinnatus, left their farms to fight as soldiers when the community needed their service; they returned to their farms when the campaign was over. Rome's citizen-soldiers were supported by Italian allies—people who, like ordinary Romans, were only part-time soldiers. They were farmers when they were not called on to fight.

The early and middle republican political bargains had been predicated on a sequence of existential threats. Those threats had required Rome to scale up by taking the demands of the Plebeians seriously, expanding its citizen population, and building strong alliances. The political bargains between Romans and their allies, and the civic bargain among Roman citizens, were sustained by a mutual sense that elite and ordinary Romans alike shared in a common project and all were willingly sacrificing for a common good. The ideal of res publica had meant that although some were better off than others, no one was shirking, and everyone was dedicated to a common cause. That cause—the flourishing of a self-governing, bossless civic community—had seemed worthy of sacrifice.

But during the long, hard fighting against Hannibal in Italy, many Romans and allies had lost their farms. Moreover, during the later phases of the Second Punic War and conflicts that followed, military operations were fought far from the Italian homeland—in Spain, North Africa, Greece, and western Asia. Men called up for these campaigns were often kept away from their farms for years on end. Unlike their wealthy fellow citizens, they did not have a ready supply of slave labor to make up the difference. As family farms were lost, bought up or confiscated by the ever-richer and ever-more-powerful elite, Rome became a sharply more unequal society. The middle republican civic bargain, along with the education in civic virtues that had sustained it, came to seem outmoded. It was not yet clear, though, what could take their place.

The civic bargain that had sustained Rome through the mid-second century BCE had been driven by the bargaining strength of nonelite Romans: the capacity of great numbers of ordinary Romans to make changes that elite Romans initially opposed. The credible threat of secession and the intercession of tribunes meant that even the most selfish elites were brought to the bargaining table and saw the need to compromise. There was a wide, if sometimes grudging, recognition that the compromises were positive sum: both sides did better inside the bargain than outside it. Bargaining was facilitated because fellow citizens were civic friends who bargained hard but also in good faith. All of that drove parochial altruism, the sense of being members in a shared community of fate. Norms and institutions that reified the value of res publica deepened civic friendship. Civic education—sharing in religious ritual and military service, and retelling stories about virtuous citizens of the past—underpinned constitutional stability and made possible the immense sacrifices that led to Rome's victories in the Pyrrhic and Punic Wars.

Striking political bargains enabled Rome's growth to greatness. It had required the emergence of talented leaders who were willing and able to rally masses of ordinary citizens and allies to achieve the necessary level of sustained collective action. The leaders of the Plebeians were both hardheaded and diplomatic enough to drive bargains with the elites of the day. While other high officials occasionally took on that leadership role, the leaders of the ordinary Romans had most often been the ten tribunes, elected annually by the Assembly of Tribes. But the role of tribunes had changed with the consolidation of the noble senatorial order, and then the huge material benefits that came from being on the right side of the increasingly vast gulf between rich and poor. By the end of the Third Punic War in 146 BCE, the tribunes were usually members of the wealthy elite, which meant that they had less stake in defending the interests of the relatively poor.

Patrons and Clients

The constitutional system that Polybius so admired was now a smoothly working machine—but it produced benefits (high offices, cheap slaves, vast loot, and free access to public land) for relatively few Romans. Increasingly it pushed the costs (long campaigns abroad, lost income, and broken families) onto relatively poor Romans and Rome's Italian allies. Fewer and fewer Romans, whether rich or poor, could claim to be the Cincinnatus-type of yeoman farmer who was long imagined as the bedrock of Roman society. More and more ordinary Romans found that their primary identity was not that of "citizens of Rome" but rather "clients" who were dependent on handouts from their rich and powerful "patrons."

Systemized patronage tended to strengthen the hold of the senatorial nobility on the levers of power. Clients were expected to vote for their patrons in elections, and the richest Romans had the largest numbers of clients. Patrons, in turn, looked after the interests of their clients. In some ways, then, they took over the role of the tribunes. The big difference was that individual patrons had no interest in bargaining on behalf of the masses of ordinary Romans; indeed, it was quite the opposite. Large-scale patronage privatized and fractured the broader political balancing of earlier times. It also changed the nature of citizenship. Some of the citizen-clients were former slaves and descendants of slaves. Among the innovations of Roman citizenship policy was granting citizenship to freed slaves and their offspring. So as the citizen body grew, its composition steadily changed too.

With the absence of existential threats, or leaders willing to push for a new civic bargain, wealthy elites now seemed secure. Rome, now operating as a network of patrons and clients, might have settled into being a complacent oligarchy, with the Senate ruling as a junta over millions of subjects, some of them masquerading as citizens. But any appearance of stability was belied by the ongoing, often-ferocious competition among the leading nobles for honors and influence. And it was threatened by the sense of betrayal on the part of many ordinary Romans who still cherished the ideals of res publica. Agitation arising from the

improper influence of patrons over the votes of their clients led to legislation in the early 130s BCE that established the secret, written ballot
for voting in elections and legislative assemblies. It was only the start of
a new era of confrontation.

Citizen-on-Citizen Violence:
The Gracchus Brothers' Failed New Bargain

The civic bargain of the Middle Republic was rent by violent conflicts that
erupted when two scions of a noble senatorial family took it on themselves to rally ordinary Romans in demanding a return to the bargaining
table. According to ancient biographical sources, Tiberius Gracchus, the
elder of the two, toured Italy in the mid-130s BCE. He was dismayed to
find that small citizen farms had been replaced by vast agricultural enterprises, owned by the rich and worked by gangs of slaves. Elected tribune
in 133 BCE, Tiberius circumvented the usual consultation of the Senate in
passing a bill calling for strict limits on the amount of Rome's public land
that could be managed by any one Roman. The bill called for distributing
the surplus land to displaced rural citizens. When Tiberius's opponents
co-opted another tribune to veto his legislation, Tiberius passed another
bill to have this new rival removed from office on the grounds that he was
thwarting the wishes of the people of Rome. The bargain Tiberius sought
to drive was democratic in its blunt assertion of the ultimate power of the
assembled people of Rome to decide policy.

Tiberius further enraged the elite by bypassing the Senate's traditional authority over foreign and financial policy. The ruler of western
Anatolia had recently willed his entire kingdom to Rome. Tiberius
passed a bill appropriating the revenues from this new "province of
Asia" to fund his program providing small farms for the poor. His opponents deployed the "*rex* word"—claiming that Tiberius intended to
make himself king. They threatened legal action as soon as his year as
tribune ended. Tiberius countered by breaking with precedent and
standing for a second term as tribune. At this point, after a rancorous
meeting of the Senate, a group of noble senators burst out of the Senate
house, rallied their clients, and fell on Tiberius and his supporters;

Tiberius himself and scores of others were beaten to death. Many more of his supporters were then tried and executed as "public enemies" by a hastily summoned senatorial court. The deadly practice of treating ideological opponents as enemies who must be destroyed rather than as civic friends with whom one negotiates in good faith was now added to the armory of Roman domestic politics.

By choosing fighting over bargaining, senators had won the battle. But the strife had only just started: the next century would see frequent repetition of the ugly spectacle of citizen blood flowing freely in the civic forum. The next skirmish began in 123 BCE after Tiberius's brother, Gaius Gracchus, was elected tribune. Gaius immediately expanded his brother's reform agenda. He adopted Tiberius's confrontational tactics while seeking to build a much bigger proreform coalition. Along with the distribution of public lands to poor citizens, Gaius sponsored legislation to create a new Roman colony in Africa on the ruins of Carthage. He turned over the taxation of the province of Asia and control of the law courts to the wealthy equestrians, potentially insulating them from legal difficulties arising from corrupt tax collection. Furthermore, he proposed a radical expansion of Roman citizenship in the allied towns of Italy.

The nobles pushed back, and the situation became increasingly unstable. After a client of a prominent senator was killed in a street fight, the Senate for the first time passed "the Ultimate Decree," advising the consuls that a state of emergency pertained and demanding that they protect the state. In essence, the Ultimate Decree identified some Romans as public enemies and urged the consuls to treat them as such. Perhaps imitating the Plebeian secessions of the early republican period, Gaius's supporters now occupied the Aventine, the southernmost of Rome's seven hills. Yet the attempt to resume bargaining based on shared citizenship failed; thousands of Gaius's supporters were slaughtered on the spot by senators and their supporters, or executed without trial.

Scaling Up Violence: Marius versus Sulla

The hard-liner senators had won another round and were wise enough not to press their advantage; they even proceeded with limited redistribution of public lands. Meanwhile, Roman armies marched on, adding new provinces in southern Gaul (modern-day France), and after a long war, crushing a "native revolt" in North Africa. The hero of that war was Marius, a "new man"—meaning that despite having no ancestors in high office, he had been elected consul. Marius inaugurated a highly consequential military reform by allowing landless Romans to enroll in the legions; the old "Cincinnatus ideal" of the part-time farmer-soldier was dead. Long campaigns far from Rome meant that soldiers became, in effect, clients of their commanding officers. This in turn created an incentive for ambitious Romans to gain and hold long-term commands. Marius employed his new-style army to good effect against serious external threats, pushing back attacks by Germanic tribes in northern Italy. Meanwhile, his lieutenants suppressed slave revolts in southern Italy and Sicily.

Widely popular due to his military success, Marius was repeatedly reelected consul. He initially worked closely with the senatorial nobility. But in 100 BCE, concerned about a payoff to his client-veterans, he joined forces with a tribune named Saturninus, who legislated land in North Africa for Marius's troops. Saturninus then took a page from the book of the Gracchi by introducing a new Italian land redistribution bill and demanding that all senators swear to support it. The hard-line senators resisted, riots broke out, and the Senate once again passed the Ultimate Decree. Marius, as consul, turned on Saturninus; once again citizen blood flowed in the forum.

Meanwhile there was trouble in Italy. The Italians, half of whom were Roman allies rather than citizens, had provided much of the labor that expanded the empire and enriched elite Romans. But they were cut out of the profits and subject to harsh treatment in military service. After proposals to extend citizenship to the Italians were repeatedly defeated, they saw that political bargaining was futile and prepared to fight. In 89 BCE, after savage battles and immense casualties on both sides, the Romans conceded the point: the residents of Italy were made Roman citizens. The city-state became a nation-state—but civic institutions had not kept up. The Italians were distributed into the existing centuries and only into certain tribes. The addition of millions of new citizens further diluted opportunities for meaningful participatory citizenship at the level of primary state institutions.

The top Roman general in the war against the allies, Cornelius Sulla, was elected consul in 88 BCE. He quickly left Rome to raise an army against a new threat in the province of Asia; a revolt led by an ambitious dynast, Mithradates of Pontus, had commenced with the murder of tens of thousands of Italians resident in the province. While Sulla was recruiting soldiers in Italy, a tribune sought to transfer the command against Mithradates to Marius. Sulla responded with a momentous step: he led his legionary army to Rome, quickly and violently capturing the city, driving out Marius and killing many others. When Sulla later left for the east, Marius's supporters retook the city, again with great violence. In 83 BCE, having pushed back Mithradates, Sulla returned to Italy at the head of his army.

Bargaining was not even attempted. Instead, a brutal civil war ensued, fought in Italy and across much of the empire, finally ending with Sulla's victory. It was followed by ferocious reprisals against the "public enemies" who had backed the other side. Sulla had himself declared dictator, but given that he ignored the traditional limits on tenure, in fact he made himself Rome's boss. He rewrote the constitution and confiscated land for his loyal soldiers. Sulla hoped new rules would forever break the power of tribunes, suppress the political role of the ordinary people of Rome, and ensure that hard-line senators ruled the empire without interference. Those hopes were not fulfilled.

The violent suppression of the Gracchi and their successors signaled that as a group, the senatorial nobles were unwilling to update Rome's civic bargain. Changes were, however, essential in light of the dramatic scale jump that resulted from Rome's rise to world power: Rome was no longer a city-state, but its institutional forms remained stuck. Rather than give up any significant part of the material advantages they had gained following the Second Punic War, and instead of bargaining with the ordinary people of Roman or the Italian allies, the Senate nobility chose, time and again, to fight. The system of clientage ensured that they had plenty of people willing to do the actual fighting and killing. The dilution of opportunities for meaningful participation by ordinary

Romans in state institutions, combined with the increasing cultural and linguistic diversity of the now-immense citizen body, made it more difficult for them to act cohesively.

The lack of cohesion among the ordinary Romans and lack of an existential external threat blocked the kind of secession that had forced political bargains in the early republican period. But there were serious cracks in the wall of senatorial authority; historian Robert Morstein-Marx lists at least thirty instances in the late republic in which legislation was passed despite the Senate's opposition.[4] The scale challenge Rome faced was now internal: How would the size and diversity of the Roman citizenship along with the ever-increasing territory controlled by Rome interact with fierce competitions among the nobles for election to office, honors, and prestige? The answer to that question sealed the fate of Sulla's new order—and then that of the republic itself.

Personal Bargains and Political Bargaining Failures

After Sulla's death in 78 BCE, his effort to restore stability through new rules was quickly undone by his ambitious lieutenants and their rivals. It's possible that some of the power seekers of the late republic were still moved by the citizen-centered values of res publica. Yet they saw clearly that power and wealth now flowed to those with the biggest armies of well-compensated client-soldiers. Concern for the common good was replaced with raw power politics. Competing leaders played a high-stakes game for control of the state, coupling promises of social reform with street violence in which citizens were regularly treated as enemies as opposed to civic friends. The game was played by highly talented men; losers were killed. The upshot was a society divided into coalitions led by power seekers. But Rome had seen numerous crises before. Could power politics create a new bargain—or would Rome devolve into open civil war?

The outstanding intellectual figure of the late republic, Marcus Tullius Cicero, stepped forward with a vision of a new civic bargain. A lawyer, orator, philosopher, and statesman, Cicero, like Marius, was a "new man." Although he was not a skilled general, Cicero saw clearly that the republic was in danger of falling prey to the rivalries of the power seekers. His own consulship, in 63 BCE, had been marred when a conspiracy led by a frustrated noble, Lucius Sergius Catilina (known to history as Catiline), provoked yet another Ultimate Decree by the Senate and more extrajudicial executions of citizens. Desperate to regain civic friendship among Romans, Cicero offered a vision for harmony between the senatorial nobility and the rest of Roman society. Like Solon of Athens, Cicero hoped to broker a grand, positive-sum bargain: a harmonious agreement by rich and poor, senators and equestrians, to live peacefully together. But he was no Solon; his talent was literary and philosophical, not political. Cicero's many literary works, written in elegant Latin prose and centered on the republican ideal, were a source of inspiration for America's founders, with as much influence on later democracy as Polybius's histories. Yet as a statesman in his own age, Cicero faced insurmountable problems. He lacked the means to force the power seekers to the bargaining table, and they were unpersuaded by philosophical arguments. Bypassing the orator-philosopher, they cut their own private deals—which paved the way for the rise of a boss and end of the republic. Power seekers in the ensuing civil war literally cut off Cicero's head.

Grasping for Power

A more consequent leader in the mix was Gnaeus Pompey, earlier nicknamed "Bloody Teenager" for his precocious, ferocious victories in Sulla's civil war. He shared the consulship in 70 BCE with Marcus Crassus, reputed to be the richest man in Rome. The two collaborated in dismantling Sulla's new institutional order.

But their relationship soon grew more complicated. Pompey left Italy to battle the pirates who had infested the eastern Mediterranean and lead the campaign against a resurgent Mithradates, the longtime nemesis of Rome. Triumphant in both efforts, Pompey returned to Italy in 62 BCE. He pressed the Senate to approve his reorganization of the eastern Roman provinces and lands for his veterans. Meanwhile, Crassus proposed his own sweetheart deal for wealthy tax collectors and hungered for a command that would gain him Pompey-style military glory. Before long, another power seeker was at the Senate door. Julius Caesar hoped to be voted a ceremonial triumph for military victories recently achieved in Spain. The Senate turned each of them down, driving the three rivals into each other's arms. This "First Triumvirate" was a private bargain between Pompey, Crassus, and Caesar, who now joined forces against their senatorial opponents. To seal the deal, Pompey married Caesar's daughter, Julia.

The three-man alliance paid off. Caesar was elected consul in 59 BCE and soon departed for a long-term command in Gaul, where he proved himself the greatest general of his age. Pompey got his diplomatic arrangements approved and founded new colonies to provide land for his soldiers. Crassus went on making money. Despite some strains, the deal was renewed in 55 BCE. Pompey and Crassus were again elected consuls; Caesar's command in Gaul was extended for five years. Crassus got a big payoff with the command against a new and dangerous external enemy—the seminomadic Parthians who had occupied Mesopotamia and threatened the rich Roman provinces of the east. Unfortunately for the First Triumvirate, in 54 BCE, Julia died. Crassus was killed in Mesopotamia in one of the greatest of all Roman military disasters. Meanwhile, rival political gangs were fighting nasty battles in the streets of Rome, making elections impossible. Pompey was named "consul without colleague" in 52 BCE—a short step from another boss-style dictatorship. He used his unique position to undermine Caesar's plan of stepping back into the consulship on conclusion of his Gaul campaign.

The End of the Republic

By 50 BCE, Caesar had crushed Gallic resistance and Gaul was a Roman province. Caesar had built a crack army and intensely loyal following among his veterans. Like every commander of this era, Caesar needed to reward his client-soldiers with grants of land. And that meant he needed the right legislation passed in the assemblies. In the Senate, Cicero desperately attempted negotiations that might avoid the looming crisis. A tribune, loyal to Caesar and known to history as Marc Antony, sought to broker a deal with Pompey. Instead, Caesar was declared a public enemy. Antony vetoed the declaration. When the Senate ignored the veto and passed the Ultimate Decree against Caesar, any hope for a peaceful new bargain was lost. Caesar crossed the Rubicon River with an army, leaving his assigned province and making clear his intention to contest the Ultimate Decree by fighting for what he regarded as his personal honor.

The rest is, as they say, history. Caesar defeated Pompey in the ensuing empire-wide civil war and was declared "dictator for life." He refused the title *rex*, but was boss in fact. His soldiers were paid off, but his plans for a campaign against the Parthians were cut short when he was assassinated on the Ides of March in 44 BCE by a coalition of former friends and enemies who struck in the name of "saving res publica."

Caesar's adopted son, Octavian, proved to be the kind of dealmaker whose partners always came up short. He built a Second Triumvirate with Antony and Lepidus, another prominent power seeker. The deal enabled each to exterminate his enemies; Cicero was one of the thousands of citizens killed without trial. The Second Triumvirate won the next civil war against the armies raised by Caesar's assassins. Antony left Rome to campaign, unsuccessfully, against the Parthians and allied with Cleopatra VII, the queen of Egypt. Having pushed aside Lepidus, Octavian declared war against Cleopatra and, by proxy, Antony. Victory in 31 BCE left Octavian the last power seeker standing. After the death of untold thousands of Romans in a century of periodic citizen versus citizen fighting, Octavian now declared the republic restored. But as everyone knew, Octavian had created the opposite. By becoming Rome's undisputed boss, he laid the foundations for centuries of one-man rule. Elections were suspended. The assemblies had no further reason to meet. The long Roman experiment with citizen self-government was terminated.

Postmortem and Looking Ahead

Through the subsequent long period of rule by emperors, Roman citizenship remained important as a legal status. Citizens enjoyed the full protection of Roman law. But they no longer participated in state governance.

The juridical conception of citizenship was paper-thin—little more than a right to a passport. Autocrats ever since have likewise falsely equated the legal title of citizen with membership in a democracy.

The Roman Empire, ruled by emperor-bosses, survived in the west for five hundred years after the fall of the republic, and for a thousand years after that, as Byzantium, in the Greek-speaking east. Yet it would be a long time before the practice of large-scale state self-government reemerged.

Scholars still debate whether Rome was ever a democracy. Some point out that the senatorial nobility had many of the features of oligarchy. Other historians, though, argue persuasively that the republic was indeed more self-governing than not. The nobles never had absolute control, and many bills were passed without the Senate's approval. Roman elections were fiercely contested. Candidates had to appeal to a wide constituency—as attested by a political manual (*Commentariolum Petititionis*, meaning "little handbook on electioneering") addressed to Cicero by his brother Quintus.

What is clear is that the Roman Republic survived as long as it did due to a series of political bargains struck between elite and nonelite Romans, and based on civic friendship as shared membership in a common enterprise. Other political bargains were struck between allies and would-be citizens. From the early third through the mid-second century BCE, a civic bargain provided a platform for Roman security and welfare. The republic faltered and finally failed when political bargaining across an increasingly large and diverse population was replaced by private dealmaking among power seekers. When those with the power to break the system pursued their private interests at the expense of the common good, when some of those with a seat at the table chose to fight rather than negotiate, the civic bargain was lost and the democratic republic of Rome slid into the rule of a boss.

What If?

One might nonetheless ask, What if certain key bargains had been sustained? What if Julia had not died young and Crassus had been victorious in Parthia? What if Cicero had persuaded his colleagues in the

Senate to negotiate with Caesar? But the issues faced by Rome were deep and determined by the relentless logic of scale. The Romans successfully answered the dilemma that had stumped the Athenians: how to scale up citizenship so that a citizen-centered city-state was able to take on the biggest and best-organized states of the age. The radical growth of the numbers of citizens, though, their increasingly wide geographic dispersion, along with their growing diversity in terms of wealth and social identity, proved to be a problem that the resources of Roman civic education were inadequate to address.

Rome created an institutional order that, in Polybius's account, balanced the powers of government such that each powerful office was checked by the others, and no individual or faction was able to dominate. Yet greater scale meant vastly larger armies. With the growth of inequality and the end of the era of soldier-farmers, the soldiers of those armies were ever more dependent on their commanders for basic welfare. The imperative of paying off soldier-clients and reluctance on the part of the senatorial nobility to compromise gave ambitious Roman leaders less room to make bargains as well as more reason to take their chances on fighting.

For their part, ordinary Roman citizens, ever further removed from the practices of meaningful, participatory self-government, had less reason to regard one another as civic friends, and more willingness to fight and kill fellow citizens when called on to do so. As scale grew and trust-building social networks also frayed, former civic friends were politically portrayed as dangerous enemies. When the rules no longer protected citizens from being executed without trial as public enemies, trusting fellow citizens was irrational; the civic ideals that underpinned friendship looked increasingly hollow. Ethical arguments had little purchase. Political participation devolved into partisan violence. Extermination was easier than negotiation. Democracy, under those conditions, became impossible.

Monarchy, Bosses, and Future History

After Octavian, the most ruthless and successful civil warrior of them all, finally killed the last of his enemies, he revived the name republic as a thin facade for the brute fact of his position as boss. Cynical manipulation it may have been, but it pointed to a distant future in which constitutional monarchy would be a reality. The long history of Roman rule under the emperors built "living as a subject" into the normative expectations of the people of Europe. The rise of Christianity opened the way for a new variant on the old theme of monarchs who ruled through their special relationship with a divine order. After the fall of Rome, as Europe transitioned to feudalism and the rule of local warlords, the memory of the rule of a strong, divinely ordained monarch remained as a model and ideal. The next long stretch of Western political history would revolve around the questions of who is boss, over what domains, and with what capacity to compel obedience.

Yet the enduring imperatives of security and welfare also meant that those styling themselves as bosses, whether kings, nobles, or local warlords, found that they had to make their own bargains with one another as well as the ordinary people from whom their revenues and military capacity derived. Christianity provided not only a religious justification for kingship but also the resources for contesting the legitimacy of monarchical authority over conscience and forms of worship. With the revival of classical learning in the Renaissance and later Enlightenment, local and regional bosses once again had to compete with the memory of the civic bargains and civic friendship that had once enabled bossless self-government in Greece and Rome.

4

BRITAIN

The Royal Bargains That Made Parliament Sovereign

They met on a summer's day in 1215, at Runnymede by the Thames River. In the meadow where ancient Anglo-Saxon kings once gathered councils of elders, a more ominous meeting now formed. Armed and angry English magnates, flanked by similarly resentful church leaders, were confronting their abusive king, John. The barons were fed up with King John's financial corruption—selling favors, arrogantly seizing indebted lands, levying arbitrary fines, and extorting money from widows. Clergy were irritated about the king's encroachment on sacred property. These challengers understood the privileges of royalty—but it was time to set some boundaries.

The scowling king was just as furious at the men facing him. Didn't they understand? He needed cash to keep campaigning for lost family lands in France. His English subjects were supposed to pay up, not push back. Still, John had agreed to come to this meeting so as to hear the complaints of these barons and clergy. He, like them, wanted to end a brutal civil war waged over the controversies that had brought them to this meadow. Critical questions hung in the air: Could English subjects somehow limit the king's authority? Should the monarch temper his high-handed demands—and if so, how?

Magna Carta

For five long days, the men traded proposals and counterproposals. The king grudgingly listened to the charges thrown at him. His subjects got back their own earful; His Highness wasn't used to justifying his actions.

Yet finally, a compromise was agreed on, as set down in a "great charter" in the king's name—Magna Carta. Exhausted, all swore oaths to uphold it: sixty-three clauses detailing limits on the king's power but also confirming the duties of subjects. Most famous were the promises of the king to moderate certain aspects of his royal reign, guarantee due process in resolving conflicts, tax only by prior agreement, and respect the rule of law.

Since then, Magna Carta's reputation as a monument of freedom has grown to mythical proportions. Today, magistrates reverently quote it in courtrooms, and parts of it remain verbatim in British common law. Popular lore holds it actually "invented democracy" for the English-speaking peoples. Putting the "invention" question aside for now, the episode of a medieval monarch confronted by his subjects is part of the familiar story of Britain's rise as a self-governing nation. Standard accounts tell how the ruling power of medieval kings steadily yielded to challengers: first to an independent (but mostly aristocratic) Parliament, which codified legal rights and imposed a system of "consent" on royal decision-making, and then over time, Parliament's power increased as its challenges became more political and occasionally violent. Along the way, its membership became less elite. The story ends with today's popularly elected and policy-dominant House of Commons, complemented by the largely ceremonial House of Lords and symbolic monarchy.

Such narratives are not fundamentally wrong, but the assumptions behind them can be misleading—that self-governance is only won through conflict, battles, and the progressive victory of "the masses" (or at least lesser elites) over autocratic rulers. The real story of British democracy is more complicated. It should begin with a deeper understanding of what the predemocratic governance of the nation was, and why that set the course for democratizing change.

The Hybrid Platform of Governance

"Britain was historically ruled by kings." At first glance, this is a true statement—but with a major asterisk. From earliest times, English kings buttressed their authority with the support and allegiance of other sources of power: the economic and military backing of regional aristocratic nobles, and sacred endorsement of the Catholic Church. That support was not guaranteed, and it could waiver under differing conditions; though monarchs were preeminent leaders, their power was always somewhat contingent. So we can say that early Britain was indeed "ruled by kings," but it was *governed* in partnership with others. Conceptually, this governance was a "hybrid platform"—a hub of authority combining three different sources of power, joining both central and distributed relationships (king and nobles), and secular and sacred sources of legitimacy (nonreligious leaders sanctified by religious leaders).

The balance of power among members of the platform was not static. If a king was a strong leader, monarchical authority might be dominant; in other times, nobles challenged weaker kings. The influence and power of the church also shifted based on the strength of religious movements and papal demands. Members of the platform had to monitor their relative strength and prerogatives as well as be ready to confront other members, either to protect their share of authority or offer assurances or resources to preserve the stability of governance. Members of the platform sometimes fought with one another, but many other times they bargained and compromised so they could operate effectively under the mantle of the monarch.

Both fights and negotiations brought new influences and members to the platform. Nobles bolstered their hand against the king with the support of members of the gentry eager for more say in decisions. Kings went over the heads of nobles with policies or programs that benefited popular constituencies. Church leaders mustered support from popular religious movements or drew on the influence of Rome. Bargains among platform members might avoid war or follow a victory in battle to consolidate a transfer of power. But whatever the stimulus, the bargaining frequently involved mustering less elite people to support a leader's cause, thereby expanding the governing platform. Bargaining was thus a vehicle by which governance over time became more popular and progressively "democratic." Democratizing bargains that expanded the governing platform often proved more successful in the longer term— by effecting change that created a public common good: more security for the community or more fiscal responsibility for the monarch in spending collected taxes.

Magna Carta is one such example. The magnates' deal with King John guaranteed not just more individual rights and protections for the English people (who were indirectly represented in the negotiations) but also bound the nobles to adhering to the same standards in their local domains. New freedoms were coupled with certain new equalities and duties—a linkage that would be fundamental to later democracy. As it turned out, soon after Runnymede, King John welched on his oath, and the bargain collapsed. But a generation later, Magna Carta was being used as a template to structure negotiations about relative rights and prerogatives between monarchs and their parliaments. Magna Carta didn't "invent" British democracy, but its influence helped push forward the conditions for it.

The story of British democratic evolution was long, but it was not smooth or predictable—it was instead akin to the kind of biological evolution scientists call "punctuated." Little or no progress was made during certain periods; one step forward sometimes collapsed into two steps back. Yet at other times, rapid and even disruptive transformation occurred. Such evolution was at least partly the result of the human dynamics of the hybrid platform along with the diversity of players who participated in governing. Throughout British history, we observe push and pull among power holders—king, nobles, and church—sometimes competing, but at other times working together to stabilize the collective leadership and minimize disruptions that would be disastrous for all.

Fluctuations in the governing balance of power are consistent with the history of a people that observers find paradoxical—a nation that both reveres tradition and readily adopts new ideas when needed; that today rules itself democratically and still maintains the symbolism of monarchy;

that has a deep tradition of law and no written constitution. But those who find it peculiar must also acknowledge that this parliamentary system has spawned and shaped a host of other such democracies around the world.

Our account of the rise of the British system is structured around six major bargains between rulers and ruled, spanning more than fifteen centuries of history. These bargains track the nation's cumulative achievement of the seven essential conditions. Some of them were explicit agreements of a particular moment, like Magna Carta, while others were more implicit and general, such as the gradual evolution of the system and rights of common law. The first five of them were "political bargains"—agreements between competing constituencies for political power, but that also created some public good that strengthened the broader community and made progress toward the conditions for later democracy. The sixth was the final civic bargain—fulfilling all seven conditions and symbolized when a significant majority of Britons had become full citizens, or royal subjects now only in name, eligible to vote for representatives in the people's House of Commons.

The Anglo-Saxon Bargain of Security and Welfare (410–1066)

Our list of essential democratic conditions begins with people free to live with no boss. That was on nobody's mind in early fifth century Britannia, the western province of the Roman Empire, far-flung but very much obliged to the dictates and military control of the Roman emperor. When in 410 Honorius called his imperial legions back to Italy, the abandoned local peoples quickly experienced full-blown bosslessness—and it was absolutely terrifying. The society of Britannia, stripped of Roman protection, soon suffered repeated incursions from nearby Celtic tribes and overseas raiders. Violence among local chieftains added to the chaos. The former province fragmented into an insecure patchwork of loosely connected Anglo-Saxon communities, blended from native Britons and generations of German and Scandinavian invaders, traders, and settlers. Freedom from the Romans brought only misery.

Slowly, Britain's people did start to regain some social order and security—but of the type that street gangs provide when they take control of unpoliced neighborhoods in modern cities. Regional and tribal strongmen arose—using violence and fear to enforce folk custom obedience, and rewarding their armed peacekeepers with the spoils they looted from neighbors. Safety was uncertain and temporary; warriors flocked to the next chieftain if the current tough guy failed to deliver. For most people, life was harsh, farming was episodic at best, and social order was guaranteed only by ephemeral allegiances and brief victories in family feuds.

The scale challenge was manifest: How could local inhabitants develop enough collective capacity to defend themselves so that they could survive and make a living? If the marauders didn't kill you, their looting left you starving. Britons had to find some way to regain security and basic welfare. Those conditions are essential to a democracy, and indeed any community or state. As we'll see, the medieval English approach to restoring order would be foundational for Britain's eventual self-governance.

Collective Power and Shared Responsibility

To ensure greater security and welfare, this society had to move beyond the street gang approach. Leaders slowly developed a solution that anticipated the more formalized feudal system of later times: a combined economic, social, and military organizational model that created more defensive capacity for all. The solution first grew out of the street gang model: scattered, vulnerable people offering their loyalty, resources, and fighting capacity to the more successful local kings in exchange for protection. Shrewd kings took the system to the next level by sharing leadership with networks of allies and even rivals, allocating privileges and prerogatives to their partners. Bypassing zero-sum fights, these consolidator kings "bought in" more partners with grants of conquered lands and a stake in a more stable enterprise that yielded more agricultural wealth—to the benefit of all. Thus was launched the first part of the hybrid platform of governance—the alliance of kings and regional nobles that would later be joined by the church. The platform began to form around a lattice of bargains among collaborating partners.

As part of the deal with nobles, these kings accepted some compromise in their power, granting their partners significant autonomy and control over the local working population. Bigger and better motivated hierarchies started to form—based less on fear, and more on mutual economic and political advantage. Working arrangements with the king became a bargain of bargains down the line: regional nobles allocated portions of their granted lands to farmers, who then became similarly obligated, serving under their lords in war and helping to pay their debts to the king. The bargain of bargains stipulated new, more specific accountabilities. Obligations were set up and down the hierarchy, with local managers hired to ensure a consistent provision of food and soldiery from their noble partners, and then in turn their dependents. Kings paid for arms and armor; retainers were trained for battle on command.

The addition of the church as a third partner to the platform significantly boosted power and security. Church support publicly sanctified the rule of what eventually became a single monarch for the nation. Catholic missionaries had been converting Anglo-Saxon society since the sixth century by building monasteries and parish churches along with proselytizing networks. As faith spread, so did the enthusiasm of kings and nobles for further alliance. Monarchs granted tax-free land and other privileges to parish churches and monasteries. In return, kings received religious legitimacy, monastic skills for royal administration, and community-building Christian followership. Nobles' regional leadership was similarly strengthened by church endorsement.

Social Bonding

A hybrid platform of governance was not unique to England (varying versions appear elsewhere in medieval Europe), but the customs and institutions that developed in Anglo-Saxon society were particularly suited to bargaining and agreement among the partners. The platform forged a strong bond among all critical leaders, based on clear mutual benefits that were showcased in public rituals. It therefore strengthened bonds with and for the broader community, enabling progress toward the essential condition of security and welfare. It was also a visible signal of the importance of another essential condition: common good compromise, with each partner giving up something to achieve more security for all, thereby preserving the collective ability to flourish. The bargain was a prototype for the mutually beneficial compromises of later self-governance.

This shared governance approach reduced earlier social fragmentation and the ethos of "every family for itself." Villages grew and prospered around the local magnate's manor house and its fields as well as a central parish church. What was different about the English version of shared governance was that the later Anglo-Saxon kings took pains to celebrate their alliances in periodic councils and local assembly meetings, often witnessed by or even including various lesser members of society. Community assemblies and courts, and periodic royal visits, commingled nobles, clerics, and even some more lowly people; kings' advisory councils included not only secular magnates but also senior church leaders. Coronations became unifying festivals, reinforcing the three-way partnership and providing a protocivic communal education for all. As they were crowned, divinely anointed monarchs swore ritual oaths before church, nobles, and other subjects to preserve peace, prevent injustice, and secure God's mercy for the whole community. The socially consolidating bargain built deeper allegiances and commitments, enabling England to survive repeated invasions of Vikings and others toward the end of this era.

The Platform's Future

The hybrid platform had both strengths and weaknesses, and the tradeoffs between those is instructive for the development of later British democracy. With its strengths, the platform foreshadowed how future leaders could increase their power by protecting the community, thus enabling it to flourish under their rule, and how power might grow by more inclusion and even participation of the community in decision-making. At the same time, the sharing of power among members of the platform made it vulnerable to disruption. Powerful people frequently disagree about who's really in charge in any ambiguous situation, and whether costs and benefits are being fairly allocated. Such questions became central, as we'll see, to the later formation of Parliament and its rise to prominence as a decision-making partner to the king. Parliament too would later struggle with these questions as its increasing political prominence led to partisan jockeying for popular support. Anglo-Saxon monarchs who wielded shared power sowed the seeds for governance that became progressively more horizontal over time.

The Medieval Bargain of Law and Individual Rights, 1066–1216

In 1066, the Anglo-Saxon bargain of security and welfare was temporarily broken when William the Conqueror invaded England, and after his victory at the Battle of Hastings, seized power for himself and his French Norman followers. The new king quickly restored the bargain under harsher terms for the subjected population—"the Norman yoke" of later English tradition. But two generations later, partly in reaction to the stricter Norman authority, two of William's successors created another bargain that furthered democratic evolution. The medieval bargain of law and individual rights established new freedoms and new protections, including equal access to justice, entitlement to due process, community participation in judicial decisions, and the principle of "no man is above the law." These became major down payments toward the eventual achievement of two other essential democratic conditions: the rights and responsibilities of citizenship, and citizen-led institutions. The political bargain was built on two subsidiary bargains: common law and Magna Carta.

Domestic Order and Scale

The Norman renewal of the security and welfare bargain was dealt with a pitiless hand. William and his conspiring lieutenants killed or drove from their lands most English lords—and then imposed their version of the hybrid governing platform with an alliance of French loyalist nobles and the Catholic Church. The king built new fortifications across the land. He tightened the demands for resources and military service owed to his magnates, strengthening aristocratic privilege and vertical hierarchies. The obligations of vassals to their lords, more ritualized and structured by elaborate rules of land tenure and personal relationships, now organized society in a feudal system that toughened the earlier model of Anglo-Saxon social and political organization.

The defense against invaders was now stronger than ever—but it had a cost. Domestic order, because of the new discipline and complexity of land tenure it created, remained fragile. William's immediate successors were plagued by repeated attempts on their thrones. In 1153, William's grandson, Henry II, deftly resolved a civil war among battling factions—and for that was named king. As he began his reign, he knew he had to restore more permanent stability. Yet as an ambitious young man, he was also eager to expand his royal realm—particularly to re-unify the English and cross–English Channel French domains that his grandfather had once held. The strategy he developed allowed him to achieve both objectives—and not wholly accidentally, a democratizing third outcome too. With his development of the common law and broader infrastructure supporting it, Henry II laid critical foundations for Britain's self-governing future.

The constraints Henry faced highlight the impact of a "win-win" strategy. Stabilizing society required resolving conflicts over issues and obligations of land control. As king, he might have doubled down to end civil strife with even more Norman-style repression. But Henry wanted to lead a war over in France—requiring long and expensive campaigns—and not be held back in England, battling local discord over property rights, status, and privileges. So he instituted a firmly administered but also impersonal framework of new courts and codified procedures for judgments, thereby introducing a more systematic legal approach to conflict resolution. Henry gambled that such a royal-supported system, especially if integrated with older traditions of local participation and initiative, would stabilize society and free him up for overseas campaigning. In addition, he saw that if it was properly—yet fairly—designed, it could generate substantial new revenues to help pay for that.

His gamble paid off. As the common law began to take hold, it provided enough domestic tranquility that the king could focus on building a broader "Angevin Empire" spanning much of the British Isles and France. And it formalized, in a practical way, the rule of law that came to define British governance.

The Common Law

English common law evolved over hundreds of years, but Henry's reforms were a formative launch. His initiatives improved customary legal practices, innovated others, and codified informal rules of social conduct. His reforms built on earlier Anglo-Saxon law codes and local courts, but were an important change in creating a more standardized and professional legal system.

Unlike statute-based Roman law, in which judges followed legislative enactments, English common law was distinctive for its basis in precedents: judges adhered to principles set by decisions made by magistrates in previous cases. The law was also comprehensive, unlike earlier Anglo-Saxon codes; it eventually extended to all places and all freemen in the English kingdom—and even in some cases, unfree serfs. A major innovation of Henry's work was the combination of central discipline with local accountability and initiative, reflecting well-negotiated partnerships across the hybrid platform. Though his monarchy sometimes dispensed justice directly in royal courts and directives (writs), more often it simply ensured that standardized procedures and precedents were applied uniformly and promptly by local magistrates, across all shires (regional administrative divisions first devised in Anglo-Saxon times) and villages.

This combined central-and-local approach led to greater fairness and regularity of application. Older, overlapping local and regional courts were rationalized, and a new corpus of law, especially about land and tenure, was gradually built. Local sheriffs were tasked with ensuring equitable processes across the realm, both for trials and penalties—and collecting royal fees. King's justices circulated across the realm to investigate offenses and convene trials neglected by local magistrates. Royal officials responded to claims in local communities, intervened where issues remained unresolved, and proactively issued writs in disputes over land and public order. The Crown court became the standard venue for serious crimes and appeals. Royal justice was further professionalized by written records, standardized penalties, the employment of specialized experts, and handbooks of case-based rules and judgments.

More Justice across Society

The participation of nobles and freemen in local courts and procedures made the common law vital and relevant at multiple levels of society. Royal writs triggered legal procedures, but calls for righting local wrongs were also invited bottom-up. Central to local engagement and accountability were "juries of peers," an early acknowledgment of legal equality advanced by Henry and then elaborated by later reformers. Peer juries had various forms and purposes—to make accusations and answer inquiries as well as making judgments; as peer juries grew in importance, their judicial integrity increased, eventually replacing folk customs such as oath swearing, trial by combat, and divination by ordeals.

The common law bargain transformed social and political life. It achieved greater order for subjects in exchange for more revenues for and quality control by a king who nonetheless still respected local initiative. The gives and gets of this bargain altered, without overthrowing, the balance of power across society. Enhanced land law and rationalized court venues established new precedents, clarifying conflicting obligations and resolving disputes. These changes strengthened the property rights of gentry (lesser nobles) and protected poor tenants—but the common law also affirmed noble privilege against usurpation by tenants. Similarly, clearer land law signaled royal approval for the nonviolent resolution of disputes over tenure as well as feudal obligations between nobles and gentry.

Henry also compromised to preserve certain property prerogatives for some critically influential aristocrats. Moreover, new land laws clarified boundaries between sacred and secular holdings, but the church gained some legal advantage too. Henry tried—but failed—to transfer cases of clerical wrongdoing to secular courts. His abortive quarrel with Rome in the case of Thomas Becket (later murdered by knights loyal to the king) forced the monarch to affirm autonomous jurisdiction for ecclesiastical courts. The king retreated, preserving the peace and regaining the support of Rome.

The common law bargain was imperfect, like all bargains, but the leader who launched it understood the value of trading off among interests to preserve the hybrid platform of governance. With these compromises, the reforms became an overall win-win for the king, kingdom, and community, once more highlighting the power of good faith bargaining essential to later democracy. The new system reduced the king's exposure to the threat of disorder while generating more money for royal campaigns that expanded the domain of his rule. But it also paid off for many others, by strengthening the common good of the social order via more fair and predictable resolution of disputes across all levels of society. Equally critical for future democracy, it institutionalized the idea that people across the land had certain rights of due process, and certain obligations to participate in the practices and decisions of justice.

The common law made further progress toward essential conditions for democracy: the additional development of specific rights and responsibilities of (future) citizens, more inclusive civic participation in the institutions for adjudicating those, and the value of compromise among multiple parties to make progress for all.

Magna Carta Again

We now return to Magna Carta, appreciating its democratizing significance in the context of the new common law. Agreed to in 1215, Magna Carta was a bargain struck some twenty years after the death of Henry II. The arrogant monarch John of the Runnymede story was a son of that same king, yet had learned little from his father about working with powerful partners. As we saw earlier, John's corruption and over-reach prompted an attempt at a bargain that became influential ever after.

The formation of the common law system and the stimulus for Magna Carta are a historical tableau of differing approaches to royal rule that nonetheless resulted in complementary kinds of progress toward future self-governance. Henry instituted the codification and systems supporting the common law so that he could fund his military ventures. His son abused that system and its principles, again to pay for his wars in France. Henry's reforms were largely successful, and partly for that, many historians regard him as one of England's most formidable kings. Few historians contest the claim that John was among the worst. Henry shaped his society around a new system of justice along with an expectation of more far-reaching rights and protections among his sub-jects. John's abusive rule prompted a reaction that ultimately affirmed those same democratizing ideas, stimulating a charter that set standards for future generations.

Magna Carta's essence was the granting (or reaffirmation) of specific liberties and personal rights for nobles, church leaders, and then more widely, "all free men of our kingdom."[1] It limited the king's authority to set policies and financial assessments for the entire community. It in-cluded both benefits for the king and some curbs—restoring the bal-ance of the hybrid platform that countered centralized authority with that of other stakeholders. It thus also reaffirmed the principle of good faith compromise.

The sixty-three-clause agreement outlined solutions to specific griev-ances. Some were quotidian (for example, standardizing weights and measures). Others protected against royal abuses: in judicial adminis-tration and the disposition of inheritances; against loss of the "ancient liberties" of towns and boroughs (especially London); in protections for the church (for instance, about lands, taxes, and inheritances); and in demands for scutage (taxes paid in lieu of military service). Several clauses protected the property rights of local lords against overreaching royal officials.

Other terms addressed lesser members of society, including merchants, knights, and widows, and even peasants and serfs. Most famous
are the universal rights of Clause 39 (still operative today) that "no free
man shall be seized or imprisoned or stripped of his rights or possessions, or outlawed or exiled or deprived of his standing in any way . . .
except by lawful judgment of his equals [per the common law]." Clause
40 curbed royal extortions: "to no one will we [the king] sell, [or] to no
one deny or delay right or justice." Clause 20 decreed that punishment
of freemen, merchants, and peasants must be proportional to the
level of offense, and imposed "except by the assessment on oath of repu-
table men of the neighborhood"—in juries, increasingly acknowledged
by the common law. Clause 52 restored property seized from anyone
without "lawful judgment."

The king in turn received some implicit guarantees. The charter
reinforced rights of taxation, with no mention about limiting its reasonable collection. Similarly, there was no mention of restraining the
royal-enforced common law. Barons and clergy tacitly accepted the
limits the charter placed on their local authority. The agreement also
signaled that arrogance on all sides must be curbed. Clause 60 specified that whatever freedoms and justice the king agreed to for their
subjects, nobles too must guarantee for their dependents, and so on
down the ladder of power. The deal similarly acknowledged that royal
courts must correct judgments that unfairly benefit landlords. And it
recognized the church as a partner in hybrid governance. Bishops,
abbots, and the archbishop of Canterbury (who contributed to drafting the initial grievances) helped forge the agreement at Runnymede.
Thus we see the charter protecting the clerisy from unjust taxation,
usurpation of monasteries' patronage, and revisions of church property law.

Like all good bargains, this one provided for accountability: Clause
61 appointed twenty-five barons to enforce the settlement by right of
seizure of royal property, if needed. The entire community was to swear
oaths supporting that—making everyone a stakeholder in the new deal.
It was a bold attempt to create community-wide pressure for restraint

of the king—but clearly ahead of its time, as John soon went back to civil war. Nonetheless, the specification of accountability was a potent democratizing idea, whose significance grew in future years.

Assessing the Bargain's Legacy

The bargain of law comprised of Magna Carta and common law together was less revolutionary than sometimes claimed: neither envisioned a world without a boss, where monarchs, aristocrats, and church leaders did not exercise significant power. This bargain regulated but did not upend existing hierarchies; it only somewhat improved the welfare of the unfree population, which was still the great majority of English feudal society.

Still, the overall bargain advanced the nation toward future self-governance and the achievement of its essential conditions. It put fundamental rights and freedoms, dignity for future citizens, and more civic institutions on the table. It demonstrated the give-and-take of compromises in seeking a larger benefit for all. Such conditions would be further developed in the political bargains that lay ahead.

The Bargain of Institutionalized Parliament, 1216–1509

Previous bargains of security and welfare, and then law and individual rights, demonstrate how the hybrid platform of English governance emerged to address critical challenges of scale. In the first, monarch, nobles, and church negotiated and compromised with one another to secure the ability of the nation to survive and flourish. In the second, the same stakeholders compromised to advance social order and resolve conflicts peacefully with a new legal system. Over the next centuries, a new bargain rebalanced the hybrid platform by creating a more representative and institutionalized Parliament. Building on the principles of Magna Carta, it further constrained the policy-making power of the monarch, especially to levy taxation to support external wars. A major compromise of the bargain was the admission of new participants in parliamentary decision-making over the monarch's pursuit of greater national scale.

The concept of a parliament advising but also sharing power with the monarch has deep historical roots. From earliest times, kings had turned to personal councillors for help and advice. In addition, many kings convened regional assemblies to gain the agreement of the community on decisions about war and property. Such early assemblies were arenas of local justice as well, later evolving into regional and Crown courts of the common law. But the most obvious forerunners of today's Parliament were the large national councils of the later Anglo-Saxon kings. Those assemblies (sometimes called the *witan*, meaning "king's wise men") gathered powerful nobles and church leaders to develop shared policies and build allegiance to common causes with kings during the tenth century. After 1066, Norman kings continued those national councils, albeit with a more hierarchical approach—summoning a smaller group of major landholders and clerics as vassals to serve their feudal lord.

During the thirteenth century, changing economic and social conditions began to erode land-based feudal hierarchies. Open-field farming commercialized agriculture, and the wool industry and trade boomed. Some peasants found new opportunities and occupations in towns whose population grew. Deaths from the fourteenth-century Black Plague further strained vassal-lord relationships as the surviving field workers and gentry wielded more market power for their services. The countryside was periodically torn by popular uprisings, sparked by demands for better governance and lower taxes, and growing anger at the aloof and pecuniary Catholic Church. Medieval assumptions of social subservience weakened.

Meanwhile, king after king pursued greater scale through military conquest, especially in France in the Hundred Years' War (1337–1453) and dynastic War of the Roses (1455–85). Chronic warfare continued with Wales, Scotland, Ireland, and Spain. New military technologies—the longbow and cannons—shifted tactics away from mounted knights toward mercenary infantry. More royal warfare demanded more taxation from subjects who increasingly chafed at the burdens.

Forging a New Parliamentary Bargain

Intensifying royal financial needs clashed with a more commercial, less feudally subservient society. Tensions among leaders of the hybrid platform as well as in relationships with gentry and freemen became more fraught about taxation, but also about land, judicial administration, and extravagant royal campaigning. Landed magnates maneuvered politically to build support from broader constituencies. Before long there were some new faces at the bargaining table.

Demands arose for a council more capable of holding the monarch accountable for rising tax burdens. Eventually a new bargain took shape: expanding England's hybrid governance by adding more voices and formal control to the process of royal decision-making. In exchange, kings were allowed to collect more taxes and gain popular support for their overseas wars. The deal ultimately reformed the royal council in three ways: it become more broadly representative, gained a greater say in legislation, and had greater political independence. The changes further advanced the development of future citizen rights and citizen-led institutions.

During this time, the more inclusive (and usually challenging) royal councils started to be called *parlements* ("speaking occasions"). Sources also link the institution to representing the "community of English people." Membership was expanded from feudal magnates and church prelates to include certain elected delegates from across the kingdom. The bargain of a more widely representative and fully institutionalized Parliament offered greater public legitimacy for royal decisions in exchange for more public say in what those decisions would be.

The transformation began in the mid-thirteenth century during a dispute between nobles and Henry III over membership in his council. Troubles started when the king's brother, seeking to legitimize tax increases for invading Sicily, invited selected knights (members of the lesser noble gentry) from the shires to join the elite membership of nobles and senior clerics. Controversy erupted as major magnates challenged the move, demanding a *parliamenz* to reassert their traditional oversight of royal spending. A standoff ensued with the king, forcing the nobles into full-scale rebellion. Their leader, Simon de Montfort, then decided to fight fire with fire—summoning his own, even more expanded parliament to oversee royal levies and spending, now including two knights from each shire and two burgesses from major townships. The strategy failed, as did the rebellion. The king killed and mutilated Montfort for his insolence. But what also died was the old "magnates-only" membership model of the king's council. Subsequent monarchs and nobles grasped the political value of broader and regular representation, especially for taxation decisions. In 1295, Edward I, seeking public support for expensive wars against Scotland and Wales, convened the first legally elected, less elite Parliament. Appointed barons and elite clergy were complemented by 292 of these members ("commoners," signaling the representation of "communities"). Edward's initiative affirmed a new constitutional principle too, reflecting a more inclusive strategy to build capacity at scale: "that which touches all shall be approved by all"—for example, heavier taxation for war should be agreed on by all affected subjects.[2] By the early fourteenth century, parliaments were being systematically convened, including elected knights and burgesses.

Parliamentary size has fluctuated through history but has generally trended toward becoming bigger and more representative. After 1341, Parliament was reorganized into two separate Houses, the Lords (monarch-appointed "peers" of nobles and clerics), and the (more broadly elected) Commons. The modern Parliament of today—with almost 800 peers and some 650 commoners is smaller than certain earlier periods, but gone forever are the intimate gatherings of "wise men" favored by the first Anglo-Saxon kings.

Power of the Purse

Growth in size accompanied an expansion of legislative power. A partly mythical tradition held that English lawmaking had always been shared between kings and their subjects. Such was factually realized during thirteenth- and fourteenth-century taxation controversies, when individuals and communities began to petition kings and their Parliaments for relief. The petitions became sources of national legislation, eventually following elaborate procedures of negotiation between the monarch, lords, and commoners. Later, commoners submitted their own petitions about taxation as part of the evolving legislative process—thus sharpening the gives and gets of the hybrid governance shared by monarch and parliamentary representatives.

The status and scope of Commons lawmaking continued to grow. In 1414, Henry V agreed that the king and lords should not alter any legislative bill submitted by the Commons, and that no bill should become an act (statute) without the Commons' approval. By the end of the fifteenth century, legislation could only be enacted "by authority of Parliament."

Taxation gradually became a special privilege of the Commons. From the fourteenth century on, the lower house had dominant authority for movable property assessments and custom duties; it institutionalized its prerogative to expand kings' taxation requests into broader vetting of the policies requiring the new money. Parliament's financial control tightened further thereafter. In 1401, the Commons decreed that "granting supply" (funding royal requests) would now require the monarch first to address specific grievances. In 1407, Henry IV acknowledged that all taxation must originate in the Commons—a norm still in place today.

Political Consciousness and Parliamentary Power

The larger, more inclusive, and legislatively empowered Parliament soon developed more formal identity and political consciousness. Shared opposition to rising taxation emboldened members to confront their king. The feudal *duty to serve* monarchs evolved into the *right to challenge them*—in pursuit of the same "common good" that the monarch invoked. Parliament thus became an institution to question what that common good should be, and how the benefits and costs of achieving it should be shared.

Other reforms—the establishment of representatives' plenipotentiary authority, more sophisticated review and voting procedures, and regular meetings at Westminster—added to parliamentary self-confidence. That confidence translated into political action. In 1327, the body removed Edward II, responding to public anger over his military failures and financial mismanagement. His son, Edward III, ruled more successfully, but in 1341 Parliament imposed limits on his treasury-draining war campaigns. In 1367, Parliament further challenged him, electing the first-ever speaker of the house, who attacked Edward for corruption—thereby establishing the right of parliamentary impeachment. Edward's successor, Richard II, tangled with his Parliaments too: in 1399, the king was forced to resign, yielding to mounting attacks on his poor leadership and tyrannical behavior.

During the fourteenth and fifteenth centuries, parliaments were involved in deposing five kings and influenced the accession of three others (Henry IV, Richard III, and Henry VII). By 1600, the representative Parliament had become a major power in England's hybrid governance. A key influencer in the making and unmaking of English kings, Parliament was increasingly a self-conscious and frequently effective limit on the king as boss.

The new parliamentary bargain was another step toward greater self-governance amid continued efforts by English kings to grow the scale of the nation. As the medieval period ended, all-important decisions of the realm—its defense, potential expansion, laws and justice, and who would pay for it all—were more formally shared between monarchs and their parliaments of chosen lords and elected commoners.

But how "democratic" was this new parliamentary bargain? It did not end royal rule. Strong and politically astute rulers like Edward I, Henry VII, and Henry VIII forged productive win-win partnerships for bargaining with their parliaments. Such monarchs could bend parliaments to their will, drawing support from their court staff, royal resources, and loyal nobles and prelates. The king formally summoned parliaments and normally retained great influence over them, including the right to dissolve or "prorogue" (suspend meetings).

The larger, more inclusive parliaments of this era were also still relatively elite and remained so for centuries to come. In the fourteenth century, even the "new" members were mostly local leaders of note, knights who owned major tracts of land, and burgesses selected by urban oligarchs. Three hundred years later, almost half of all commoners still traced descent from titled families.

But the rise of authority by progressively more representative parliaments was advancing the essential condition of citizen-led institutions. From the late thirteenth century on, royal decision-making and freedom of action, especially for all-important taxation, were more constrained by a somewhat-broader segment of the free population. Kings had to work hard to maintain political allegiances—not just nobles and church leaders, but now a growing body of representatives of the wider free population. The new representatives also enjoyed more individual rights and protections enforced in the courts. Lord-vassal tenurial relationships were transitioning to political representation, explicitly linked to geographic communities.

This era saw other "democratizing" changes and forward motion toward future citizen rights. Shire elections became more competitive. Though eligibility to vote for Commons' members was restricted in 1430 by a forty-shilling property requirement, subsequent inflation expanded the franchise, adding more artisan and farmer voters. In 1451, the electorate comprised only about 15,000 people; by 1689, it encompassed 240,000 people, or about 20 percent of adult males. In 1715, the electorate was 300,000 people, or some 23 percent of the male population. While elitist by Athenian or American standards, English electoral representation was broadening.

Moreover, the new parliamentary bargain stimulated other, indirect democratization. From the late thirteenth century on, the rights of individuals and communities to petition kings and Parliament became a new norm. Moreover, kings began to publicly proclaim parliamentary acts in an effort to build more popular support for royal initiatives. Proclamations sparked discussion (and sometimes collaborative opposition, especially about taxation) across local communities.

The rise of parliamentary representation molded other aspects of civic life and the expectations of future citizen life too. Since Anglo-Saxon times, knights and lesser freemen had participated in the local judicial administration and tax collection as "royal servants." As the common law evolved, many others also served on local juries. Shire and village assemblies along with the civil and religious duties of parishes further shaped an ethos of shared and representative governance. Democracy still lay far in the future, but was becoming a little less distant.

The Bargain of Parliamentary Monarchy, 1509–1707

In the centuries following, Parliament's authority grew stronger. By the start of the eighteenth century, wars, controversies, and socioeconomic change called for a new governing bargain: parliamentary monarchy. It would undergird the development of the British Empire, modern United Kingdom, and civic bargain of the twentieth century.

Parliamentary monarchy reconfigured the governing platform, replacing its partners' frequently ambiguous relationships with more structured legal roles and responsibilities: a more empowered Parliament, more formally constrained king, and revised sanctifying endorsement by a new church offering a pluralistically limited state religion. The bargain also tacitly acknowledged a more direct influence on decision-making by enfranchised electors and political activism by the nonvoting population.

This bargain emerged through a process of learning and adaptation from often-agonizing revisions of smaller political bargains along the way. All of these required imperfect compromises that periodically erupted into fighting. Eventually, however, they made for an overall bargain that carried the nation forward. It was a difficult journey to reach this agreement, navigated in an era of intricate diplomacy, foreign and civil warfare, economic revolution, and religious persecutions. But the complexity is critical to understanding why the bargain eventually took hold—and why it furthered the system's progress in fulfilling essential conditions, moving closer to no-boss, citizen-led institutions, and civic freedoms and responsibilities forged through compromise.

Crises of Identity

England in the sixteenth and seventeenth centuries faced scale challenges comparable to many we know today: a more populous nation (up

60 percent between 1500 and 1650) of greater diversity (religions, professions, and economic classes) struggling with governance amid massive social changes and international pressures. The nation had to steer a course, keeping enough coherence to survive in a more threatening world—competing with larger and more ambitious nation-states, all jostling for power, territory, and commercial opportunity. The England of this early modern period was breaking free from medieval political structures and beliefs, with more people asking for more say in their futures. What kind of nation would theirs be, and what would it mean to belong to it? Like many democratic (or would-be democratic) nations today, this state was struggling with multiple crises of identity.

The sixteenth-century European Reformation and Henry VIII's Anglican rejection of papal authority (1533) fractured Catholic religion in England. Rival (mostly Protestant) denominations were soon sparring over doctrine, rituals, and church organization. Core concepts of community, rooted in English parish life, ruptured. Conflicts over religious identity forced politicizing questions: Who are we? Who's not one of us? and How tolerant should we be of others? Persecutions against supposed heretics became common. Regional and cross-border religious conflicts only worsened the confusion, both within England and in wars with neighboring Scotland (largely Protestant Presbyterian) and Ireland (largely Catholic). Questions of loyalty and freedom added to the stakes; the Celtic nations often allied with continental powers based on shared religion against England. English leaders pondered trading national identity for more security: Should the Celtic peoples be brought into our realm for the sake of future safety? At what cost? And what would a country divided by differing faiths mean for our own sense of who we are?

Debates about borders, religion, and community were further magnified by the powerful European rivals that flirted with Scottish and Irish alliances of their own: Catholic Spain, France, the Holy Roman Empire, and the Protestant Dutch Republic. The religious identity of foes regularly informed the strategic calculus among maneuvering countries: Should we build more cross–English Channel alliances buttressed by denominational agreement? Or should we subjugate others whose beliefs threaten our own? Dodging from defense to offense, English leaders scrambled to build national solidarity, fight religious battles, and compete in burgeoning overseas trade and colonization. Thus more questions of identity and scale arose: How independent should England be? Should the country build national autonomy or pursue commercial integration? Could it do both?

Conflicts over identity were further stoked by rapidly spreading information, the result of the fifteenth-century printing press revolution. This created another scale challenge: The flow of new ideas sparked popular passions and revolutionary movements. By the seventeenth century, newspapers, political tracts, and religious pamphlets were reaching more and new readers. Ideas about governance and freedom penned by poet John Milton, philosophers Thomas Hobbes and John Locke, and others sharpened controversies. Public discourse flourished in coffeehouses and other new social venues in growing cities. More people had more opportunities to get riled up about what they believed in—and many wanted to do something about it. This was an age of crowd-supported clashes between kings and parliaments, of conspiracies, urban mobs, and rural armed movements.

In the divided and invasion-threatened nation, public decision-making became more complicated. Kings and their increasingly independent, larger, and politically divided parliaments had to find enough common ground to forge policy, pay for it, and build enough support to make it stick while managing the roar of popular disapproval if they misjudged. In the sixteenth and seventeenth centuries, kings and their parliaments faced not only each other but also crowds and fiery public opinion. More money, and hence taxation, was needed for defense and campaigns against the growing French and Spanish Empires. The purse-holding Commons, selected by a larger and more economically diverse set of electors, was plagued by its own political divisions too. Parliamentary elections of this era were more frequently contested. The same policy debates similarly splintered the House of Lords.

Such fissures triggered questions of monarchical versus parliamentary rule, animating this era's civil wars and (as historians call it) the Revolution of 1688. By the end of the seventeenth century, formal political parties (Whigs versus Tories) developed, transitioning national controversies toward less violent (but no less contentious) partisan battles of wills and beliefs.

The Break with Rome

The parliamentary monarchy bargain had early origins in the religious revolution of Henry VIII. Quarreling with the pope over his right to divorce, the Tudor king famously broke with Catholic Rome during the 1530s, triggering religious conflict for centuries to come. Enacting reforms with a compliant Parliament, he declared himself head of a new Anglican faith and plundered the English Catholic Church of tax revenues and monastic lands.

Henry's religious revolution spawned a governance revolution. The king's invention of English Protestantism fractured the traditional hybrid platform. Abandoning Catholic sanctification, he bet his monarchy on a new version of the historical bargain: the king would rule by means of his hefty charisma, a well-managed Parliament, and newfangled Anglicanism. The bet succeeded, but only just. The backlash was swift— with a thirty-thousand-strong rebellion in 1536, when "Pilgrims of Grace" demanded restoration of the Catholic faith for the nation. Henry quashed the revolt but was thereafter forced to maneuver politically, supporting Anglicanism but also affirming strategic public acceptance of certain Catholic rituals. The traditional faith of the community would not be as quickly undone as the self-confident king had first believed.

Subsequent Tudors inherited Henry's gamble, seeking more social cohesion sometimes via more religious tolerance and sometimes via more repression. Edward VI (1547–53) pursued aggressive Protestant reforms by "ordinances which the majority obeyed very grudgingly."[3] Before long he too faced a Catholic uprising (1549). Queen Mary (1553–58), known as "Bloody Mary," tacked opposite. After a Catholic marriage with the Spanish royal heir, she pursued "unification" with violent evangelical persecutions that saw neighbor denouncing neighbor and gruesome public burnings. These were later chronicled in the popular Book of Martyrs (1563), which further inflamed religious conflict.

Queen Elizabeth (1558–1603) steered a shrewd middle course. Her religious enactments (1558 and 1563) "looked Catholic while sounding Protestant."[4] But the nation remained divided, amplified by faith-related threats from Scotland and Spain. In 1569, Elizabeth battled a northern Catholic rebellion, and a decade later, clandestine Jesuit initiatives that threatened her authority. The target of multiple plots, she issued an unusual "Bond of Association" in 1584 seeking pledges of loyalty and protection against rival (and Catholic) Mary Queen of Scots; hundreds of officeholders, gentry, and clerics signed. Ultimately Elizabeth unified the nation, combining managerial skill with potent symbolism: navigating alliances and threats from overseas powers, and publicly celebrating victories against a Spanish invasion in 1587 and then her signature triumph over their armada in 1588.

Stumbling Stuart Kings

Elizabeth's successful reign was followed by the troubled rule of the seventeenth-century Stuart kings. The political conflicts they triggered would eventually lead to the new bargain of parliamentary monarchy. James I (1603–25) and his son, Charles I (1625–49), were more absolutist and less politically skilled than Elizabeth. Both were severely tested by religious factionalism, the complexity of foreign policy controversies, and Parliament's cantankerous wrangling over funding for diplomacy and war. These kings also labored against new and dramatic challenges of scale: a society now buffeted by increasing political extremism, more public activism, and vying financial interests competing for New World wealth.

James first stumbled in his leadership when he attempted unpopular English unification with his native Scotland (1603). When he next tried to strengthen the Anglican Church, the Catholic Gunpowder Plot (1605) almost killed him. He clashed repeatedly with his parliaments over royal debt, taxation, and governance, jousting regularly with Commons' Magna Carta–invoking jurist Sir Edward Coke. The king, frustrated by such challenging legalism, periodically refused to convene

Parliament. He wondered aloud in 1614 why "[his] ancestors should ever have permitted such an institution to come into existence."[5]

James's son, Charles I, similarly faced mounting parliamentary backlash against his foreign and funding initiatives. Both the council and country more broadly were splitting into adversarial protopolitical parties. On one side, there was a "country" faction antagonistic to the king—wary of France, Spain, and Catholicism; on the other, there was a proroyal "court faction," opposed to Presbyterian Scotland and High Church Anglicans, but willing to deal with Irish Catholics and those aligned against Protestant Dutch mercantilism. Issues of governance became a focus of both public and parliamentary bargaining between the factions.

In 1628, those questions intensified when Parliament rebuked Charles with a challenging declaration, the Petition of Right. This document was on the surface an attempted compromise by the council, conceding certain powers to the king in exchange for his guarantees to limit absolutism. (It also later influenced America's Bill of Rights.) But demands for due process, no taxation without Commons' approval, and prohibition of royal standing armies enraged the king. Charles abruptly dissolved Parliament in 1629, launching an eleven-year hiatus. Critics publicly derided his "tyranny."

Conflict between the king and Parliament steadily worsened: over a royal end run to impose "ship money" taxation on coastal cities (1635); over war declared against Scotland sparked by the imposition of Anglican prayers; and over policy about Catholic rebellion in Ireland. In 1641, a furious Commons recast the Petition of Right as "the Grand Remonstrance," acerbically reproaching His Majesty and asserting even stronger parliamentary prerogatives: regular convenings along with control over taxation and church, courts, and military. The vote on the remonstrance split the House 159–148, echoing cries of angry proroyal and procommons mobs gathering across London. In January 1642, the frustrated monarch led a band of supporters against his antagonists as they sat in Parliament. The coup failed, and Charles assembled troops to reclaim his royal dignity. Civil war soon erupted.

Civil Wars

Causes of the English Civil Wars (plural, for its three phases, 1642–51) have been long debated, but the complex identity crisis of religion, foreign policy, commerce, class, and governance are all part of the story. The wars' tolls, however, are uncontested. Battles and disease killed over two hundred thousand—more by population percentage than English losses in World War I. Also catastrophic were the aggravated social and political divisions, relations rubbed raw with Scotland and Ireland, and the opportunities the dissension opened for hostile rival states.

Conflicts and battles were costly, but the warring constituencies periodically tried to bargain with one another. Through eleven years of discord, opponents wrestled to find a deal, balancing the difficult choices of any embittered and divided community: Should they accept more fighting in the hopes of later triumph? Surrender and concede to rule by the other side's boss? Or find a compromise that avoids both—achieving a peaceful arrangement and maybe even one that would allow ordinary people to rule themselves? The English Civil Wars failed to achieve the latter. Yet the on-and-off negotiations, trials and experiments, and subsequent revolution finally pushed England toward a more popular governing platform: a parliamentary monarchy.

Attempted Bargains

Before the fighting began, a parliamentary contingent proposed "Nineteen Propositions" to the king—accepting peace if the king conceded more control over the church, ministers, and armies. Charles countered vaguely, affirming simply support for a "mixed government." Soon thereafter, parliamentary "Roundheads" struck a military and political bargain with the Scots, securing twenty-one thousand troops in exchange for a promise to create some future (ill-defined) parliamentary-Presbyterian government. Scottish forces were decisive at Marston Moor in the first major Roundhead victory, when the parliamentarians under Lieutenant General Oliver Cromwell triumphed over the royal Cavaliers (1644). Cromwell leveraged the momentum to develop a more professional "New Model Army," whose subsequent victories forced Charles's surrender in 1646. The Scots, though, were not repaid with any special Presbyterian authority in Westminster. Meanwhile, the conquering New Model Army, encamped outside London, was demanding back pay and more say in parliamentary decision-making.

Fear of lawlessness stimulated a longing for some stabilizing change. Partisan propaganda flowed from all sides, and London was roiled by activist mobs and competing movements, religious and ideological: Quakers, Baptists, Levelers (agrarian communists), Diggers (social egalitarians), and splinter initiatives from the New Model Army. As each maneuvered for influence, a froth of new ideas arose, some pioneering, some delusional, and all pushing for rethinking governance and identity. In 1647, the New Model Army hosted the "Putney Debates," which surfaced revolutionary notions about universal suffrage and parliamentary reform. More concrete proposals were also aired, including a new governing bargain ("Heads of Proposal"), suggesting Charles compromise about Anglicanism and certain royal powers as a framework for peace. All of these offered possible but uncertain prospects for future democracy.

Charles rejected such proposals and bargained with the Scots in the aftermath of Cromwell's broken promise. If Scotland would help restore his monarchy, he would elevate Presbyterianism and preferential power for Scottish nobles. A moderate parliamentary faction counteroffered to restore the king, with the familiar demand that he concede some authority over the church and army. Charles refused and bet once more on military force, emboldened by the Scots, who now joined the king's march into England. Thus began the brief second English Civil War. Cromwell's forces thrashed the invaders, and then captured and imprisoned Charles (1648).

Kings and Would-be Kings

In January 1649, Charles was tried for treason by the "Rump Parliament"—a subset of radicals who remained after Cromwell and the New Model Army had purged moderates and royalists from the body.

The king challenged this court's legitimacy, albeit to no avail; he was convicted and beheaded to the groans of the assembled crowd. The nation remained divided about governance, though most people still yearned for some form of kingship.

Undeterred, the Rump Parliament swiftly proclaimed a nonmonarchical republic in which "the commons in parliament assembled, being chosen by and representing the people, have the supreme power of the nation."[6] The harsh democratizing mandate was more coup than bargain: censorship was imposed, the House of Lords was abolished, and national decision-making was transferred to a forty-one-person council led by Cromwell and the Rump Parliament. The new republican leader soon resumed his military exploits—brutalizing rebellious Ireland, punishing the Scots for embracing Charles's son as king, and then defeating the young man's army and driving him to France (1651). This third English Civil War also failed to restore any stable governance for England.

Cromwell fared no better after the victory. He faced major challenges—first, like the one that confronts many revolutionaries, was the question of how to rule when much of the nation does not support the regime. Second, there was the issue of how to manage a complex governing platform, unified only by one man's personality, and also how to accommodate the demands of the hovering New Model Army. The republican government repeatedly stalemated, quarreling over money, religion, war with the Dutch, and its own decision-making powers. Public calls for its dissolution grew louder until Cromwell shut the government down, blasting members as "whoremasters and drunkards."[7]

Cromwell next attempted a different approach to republican government: an army-supported Parliament of "godly members" from "independent" (but Cromwell-friendly) congregationalist churches. This again was no bargain at all; the new group fractured with infighting, and its members implored Cromwell to seize control. Refusing pure military government, Cromwell attempted a final new constitutional bargain, documented in "the Instrument of Governance" (1653). This charter outlined a mixed government of a Lord Protector (a label intended to avoid naming a new king-like figure), Parliament, and council. Rejecting offers to become "king," Cromwell accepted the Lord Protector role. As such, he was soon threatened by a royalist conspiracy. In fear and frustration, Cromwell made himself into an absolutist boss—wielding an oppressive military and Puritan rule in twelve districts across the nation. His death in 1658, and the flailing attempt of his son to succeed him, encouraged the army to reassert full control. Who would now govern the nation?

Uneasy Restoration

That question was center stage when the army reassembled the Rump Parliament to end Cromwell's protectorate (1659). After some further political floundering, a potential new solution arose. George Monck, Cromwell's practical governor in Scotland, stepped forward with an unusual lack of self-interest. Marching with troops to London, and sidestepping an opportunity to make himself dictator, Monck proposed a return to more traditional governance. With an army at his back, he "suggested" a resumption of parliamentary control to be (somehow) combined with kingship and committed to tempering the still-roaring religious conflict too.

Monck knew a good bargain required authorized negotiation. Dismissing the radical Rump Parliament, he recalled the Long Parliament of 1640 and encouraged it to initiate elections for a new "Convention Parliament"—whose purpose would be to negotiate the restoration of Charles II. Well-intentioned bargainers were chosen and worked productively on a politically conciliatory but shrewdly vague agreement. Charles announced the deal in the Declaration of Breda (1660): he would return as king and grant amnesty for most civil war veterans, back pay for the army, reinstatement of a "free Parliament," and toleration for those of "tender consciences" (that is, differing faiths). Church bells pealed and crowds cheered as Charles II was unanimously restored as king (1660).

Charles tried to bind wounds by proposing a more inclusive Anglicanism, but the new Cavalier-dominated Parliament was less forgiving. It ordered the public humiliation of the regicides' bodies and renounced the religious toleration of the Breda agreement. Political conflicts over governance raged anew. The identity crises remained: the nexus of foreign wars, commercial competition, religious factionalism, and fighting over fiscal control and separation of powers—all were burningly unresolved. England's commercial and military struggles with rival nations continued apace, with ever higher stakes. Beneath the policy debates, the more fundamental questions of governance remained: Who was empowered to make the critical decisions facing England, and who would be authorized to raise the money to pay for them?

Thoughts of a renewed parliamentary-monarchical bargain vanished when the Dutch burned the English fleet in 1667. Seeking revenge, Charles courted alliance with Catholic France and was eagerly welcomed as partner by the Dutch-hating Louis XIV. The deal, however, soon pitted Charles against Parliament. Monarchical authority was now criticized as "treason"; the working relationship worsened over fears of "papist plots" and suspicion of Charles's Catholic-leaning brother, James.

Tories and Whigs

Charles's anger continued to rage. When Parliament prohibited Catholics from holding office, he furiously dissolved it. Rough-and-tumble politics escalated, and structured parliamentary parties formed. Royalist and French sympathizers were now branded "Tories," (a slang translation for "Irish Catholic bandits"), and pro-Dutch, Protestant-leaning enthusiasts became "Whigs" ("Scottish cattle drivers"). The parties rallied around competing visions for England's economic future. Whigs backed opportunities for England's rising manufacturing sector and seagoing commercialism. Tories represented older land-based wealth, which they preferred to grow through military campaigns abroad. Though their agendas and identities would change over time, these parties would continue to shape parliamentary politics for centuries to come.

After 1681, Charles simply ignored Parliament. Instead of requesting further funding from the body, he merely subsisted on French subsidies and ruled as a boss. The nation was now further than ever from a good working partnership between the king and the people's representatives. And it was increasingly divided over religion as well as economic visions for the future.

Inglorious Revolution

Charles's successor, James II (1685–88), calmed neither political storms nor religious controversies. In his first year as king, he brutally suppressed a revolt led by the Protestant duke of Monmouth, who had invaded England with promises of annual parliaments and greater religious toleration. The king also enraged his parliaments by demanding funds for an army of Irish Catholics and seeking more Catholic involvement in the government. Religious suspicions were further antagonized when James's Catholic wife gave birth to a plausible "popist" heir. Meanwhile, Whig-aligned interests attacked James's French-style bureaucratization, which they feared would throttle the financial dynamism of the commercializing age. Whig leaders, supported by some Tories, Anglicans, and "nonconformist" Protestants, sought help for "regime change." They found their man in Dutch stadtholder William of Orange, whose Protestant wife, Mary, was also the prime heir to the English throne.

In 1688, William crossed the English Channel with a huge army and overwhelmed English defenders. When James fled to France, William was welcomed by (stage-managed) cheering crowds en route to London. There he started negotiation with a new Whig-dominated Convention Parliament, organized by his advocates. Elaborate bargaining ensued about the legality of William's invasion and what sort of government to put in place. Negotiations proceeded delicately, with all parties aware that much of the still-divided country believed James remained the legitimate ruler. Renewed civil war certainly loomed—which by now, nobody wanted. In Parliament, the lords were split between restoring James or making William and Mary temporary regents. In the House of Commons, the Whigs, eager to avoid perceptions of a military coup, proposed a clever narrative: James had "abdicated" and thereby had broken his contract with the people. Thus Parliament had a "duty to fill the position." When negotiations stalled, William called the question by threatening to sail home. Consensus quickly emerged around the "good enough" Whig position. Fear of disorder had forced the compromise of a new governing agreement.

A new Declaration of Rights was quickly drafted, with principles acceptable to a majority. Its language was opportunistically vague, allowing enough Whigs and moderate Tories to agree—about rights of petition, free elections, and consent for taxation, all aimed at limiting the absolutism of a boss. The bargain was buttressed by public choreography so William would not seem to be crowned by unilateral parliamentary command. At his coronation in April 1689, William proclaimed that he and Mary had come to England simply "to preserve [its] religion, laws, and liberties."[8] Attendees closed their eyes and smiled.

Detailing the governing specifics of this Revolution of 1688 fell to a still-divided Parliament. While William was off warring with France and Ireland, a bargain of parliamentary monarchy was forged by multiple negotiated bills, some at odds with William's preferences—but through his agents back in London, the practical king let most differences pass. Secure in his position, William accepted the greater good of stability and conceded various ruling prerogatives to the people's representatives. In so doing, he moved English kingship toward a more symbolic and less boss-like governing role. His compromise rebalanced the hybrid platform, away from autocracy and toward more popular rule.

A series of enactments filled out the bargain of parliamentary monarchy. The Toleration Act (1689) created a compromise over freedom of worship, recognizing most Protestant dissenters, although still excluding Catholics. The Bill of Rights (1689) affirmed the liberties of Magna Carta and the Petition of Right. It outlined a monarchy working with, but now subservient to, the will of Parliament—foreclosing royal suspensions of legislation, peacetime armies, and unilateral tax levies. It also guaranteed freedom of elections and speech, and specified future royal succession, excluding James and his son, and future Catholic rulers. The Triennial Act (1694) mandated elections every three years. In 1694, adapting Dutch innovations in monetizing public debt, Parliament established the Bank of England, which became a critical support for the growth of England's subsequent commercial, financial, and military power. The 1701 Act of Settlement further tightened rules of royal succession, affirming that the choice of future kings belonged to both monarch and Parliament.

In 1707, William's successor, Queen Anne (1702–14), established the Kingdom of Great Britain, uniting England with Scotland and adding elected representatives of the latter to Parliament. Scotland's vote for the union avoided the fate of Wales, which was forcibly conquered in the thirteenth century and then legally incorporated into England during the sixteenth century. Ireland, long divided in loyalties, was forced down a more bumpy and violent road. After centuries of rebellions against English rulers and settlers, it too joined Great Britain, first (after 1707) as a colony under the British Crown and later with parliamentary representation under the Acts of Union (1801). Ireland's political status has shifted many times since then and remains a source of bitter controversy even today.

Nonetheless, the addition of Ireland, Scotland, and Wales to the nation opened the door for a dramatic increase in scale. What would soon be called "Great Britain" was now to be governed under the bargain of parliamentary monarchy.

Reflections on the Bargain

In tradition, the Revolution of 1688 stands as a triumph of English moderation: the nation, after two centuries of turmoil and war, achieved the stability of limited monarchy and reasonable Protestantism. The settlement following 1688 is similarly portrayed as a "glorious" and even "bloodless" achievement of mixed rule, buttressed by a sensible religious tolerance.

Stabilization would indeed be critical to the nation's future success, but as we'll see, Parliament soon became its own threat to that. The glorious 1688 tradition underappreciates the complexity that the new bargain had to overcome—not just questions of religion and royal versus parliamentary rights, but also the continuing intrusions of foreign policy, competing economic visions, and deeper questions of national identity. As seen in other political bargains, conflicts about how the platform would function are difficult to separate from the foreign and domestic policies that were forcing the change, or from the constituencies that stood to win or lose from a new model.

The divisiveness that preceded the bargain continued well after it was agreed. Partisan conflicts in the reformed Parliament were bitter; in the broader public, thousands of competing petitions were drafted, and oaths were sworn to support opposing sides in the controversies over governance. Local armies formed, and mob violence periodically erupted, some in support of William and others opposing. The Revolution of 1688 was far from bloodless. Yet the bargain did fend off the chaos of full-blown lawlessness or major civil war and avoided the rule of an absolute boss. The elected body became sovereign in most important matters and thereafter grew in legal authority. But kings did not disappear, and parliamentary representation was not yet democracy. Members were still chosen by less than a quarter of adult males. Religious tolerance was limited, favoring less absolute but still dominant Anglicanism.

Nonetheless, parliamentary monarchy ultimately took hold because it was an effective compromise—not a flawless solution, but rather an agreement that created a new "institutionalized disunity." Conflicts over authority, freedoms, and religious tolerance continued, but were pragmatically accommodated within a framework of governance that recognized differing beliefs, political agendas, and identities. Institutionalized disunity is inherent to self-government at scale—and for that reason, we might consider how this bargain advanced the nation toward full democracy.

The agreements and compromises integrated two competing strands of English political culture: from Whig values, popular restraint on absolute rule, honoring individual rights and supremacy of the law; and from Tory values, rejection of zealotry, respect for authority and tradition, and stern disapproval of rebellion based simply on disagreement with a current government or political foe. Institutionalized disunity has its dangers, however. Its underlying paradoxes and tensions are inherently volatile. Bargains that institutionalize disunity, whether democratic or protodemocratic, must be maintained and continuously renewed. The question now facing the nation was whether the historical tensions concerning governance, between Whig and Tory worldviews, and among an increasingly political public, could be managed and tamed in the years to come.

The next bargain, as it evolved, provided an answer of "yes." With this bargain, we'll see still further progress toward self-governance—marked by new steps toward an expanded franchise, new civic friendship, and more purpose-driven civic education.

The Bargain of Civic Solidarity, 1708–1914

The immediate democratizing advances of the parliamentary monarchy bargain were promising but still limited. Structurally, the 1688 settlement had tipped decision-making authority firmly to the elected representative body, yet had not fundamentally changed how members would be elected or how "representative" it would actually be; the percentage of adult males entitled to vote for the still largely elite House of Commons was small (and for women was zero). And none of that would change any time soon. Culturally and politically, the nation was still divided, and its collective identity was further complicated as Scotland and Ireland were drawn into the union.

Nonetheless, out of the turbulence and economic change of the eighteenth century and then during the nineteenth, countervailing trends emerged, including victories against France and Britain's further development of its growing empire. Together these helped form a more unified national identity, which helped strengthen civic friendship and stimulated the development of patriotic and protocivic education. In parallel and not accidentally, the voting franchise was expanded during these years. By the end of the era, the nation was primed for a full civic bargain, with most of the seven essential conditions near fulfillment.

The agreements that anticipated that final stage of democracy together formed a "bargain of civic solidarity." Like the previous bargain, this one too emerged from complex and interconnected socioeconomic and political changes, along with the accompanying leadership responses.

To appreciate the dynamics of this next phase, let's once again consider challenges of scale.

Stabilizing Great Britain

The first scale challenge for Britain's leaders was to stabilize the governance of a larger and more prosperous nation—domestically, as the union took shape after 1707, and overseas, as the growing network of overseas colonies grew into a more formal empire. Second was making the right social and economic policies, as money flowed into the nation from imperial commerce and trade. Additional wealth came from innovations of the Industrial Revolution and expanded production. The British workforce increased with threefold population growth between 1700 and 1850. Yet Britain's new financial might had its own liabilities. The nation was now becoming an even greater prize for foreign conquest. New riches also increased inequality and social conflict— dilemmas well-known to the imperial democracies of ancient Athens and Rome. How was Britain to manage both the ambitions and burdens of empire?

Finally, this era witnessed more of the "dangerous ideas" that had begun to spread in the post–printing press world of the sixteenth century: about freedom, social equality, and revolutionary change. Publications, pamphlets, and coffeehouse conversations animated public and private political discussions with ideas of contemporary radicals like Thomas Paine as well as earlier theorists like Locke. London and other cities became hubs of discussion about the reforms and natural liberties of the American and French Revolutions. Such things were exactly what political conservatives had feared, and they argued strongly against them.

Stabilization, Corruption, and Critics

After 1689, many Britons still longed to return to absolutist Stuart rule, and Catholic France stepped forward to help their cause. French money and forces supported James and his descendants, who made repeated

"Jacobite" attempts to reclaim the throne. Mobs in London added to the pressure, rioting against Protestants and the "illegitimate" Hanoverian kings who succeeded William. But the parliamentary monarchy stood firm. The revised platform of governance was clearly succeeding, guided by whichever political party controlled the House of Commons, even as the Hanoverian kings either withdrew from politics (George I and II) or worked productively with Parliament (George III). Though policy making was intensely partisan, the British people united to beat France as well as sustain imperial and economic growth. Meanwhile, however, the elected legislature was becoming more closed, elitist, and self-dealing.

In 1720, the Whigs mobilized behind the silver-tongued and venal Robert ("Robin") Walpole. Walpole had risen to power as chancellor of the exchequer, engineering a national budget bailout after the "South Sea bubble" crisis, which not accidentally enriched himself and his supporters. As prime minister, Walpole methodically built a twenty-year Whig oligarchy, trading favors for key programs, further secured by patronage schemes, government payroll manipulation, and electoral district gamesmanship. He bribed newspapers to deflect his many public critics.

Walpole's party also benefited from a parliamentary election system that had become even less representative than before. When Scottish members of Parliament (MPs) joined Parliament (1707), the percentage of enfranchised adult males sank from about a quarter in 1700 to a sixth by 1800. Moreover, about a quarter of all electoral districts had become "rotten boroughs," small, low-population locales controlled by landowning families that nonetheless elected MPs. Nonelite representation became progressively "virtual."

Walpole fell from power in 1742, but parliamentary patronage and electoral manipulation endured. So did the de facto elite oligarchy: most MPs were landed gentry, while the rising commercial cities remained underrepresented. The medieval forty-shilling property requirement continued to slow any franchise expansion. Balloting was not secret. MPs were often elected unopposed by voters reluctant "to challenge M'Lord." Some cynically accepted the system for what it was and saw little need for any kind of "civic friendship." Others, like economist Edmund Burke, defended "virtual representation of the whole": Parliament was not a "congress of ambassadors [representing] different interests [but rather] a deliberative assembly of one nation."[9]

Trends for Change

British governance was praised by outside observers for its commitment to commerce and science. But domestic critics, who regarded the oligarchy as an illegitimate boss, demanded change. They sought wider representation, more respect for natural rights, and reform of "tyrannical rule." The Whigs' self-dealing politics fueled an opposing movement to renew public virtue and patriotism. George III and parliamentary leader William Pitt, the Earl of Chatham, rallied to such ideas, embracing British patriotism to justify imperial campaigns against the French in Canada and India (1756–63). The call to virtue, though, energized domestic critics of elitism and corruption too. Crowds rallied around popularizing politicians like John Wilkes—no saint in his personal ethics, but a beloved public crusader for a more open and accountable Parliament.

The controversy over governance intensified in the last quarter of the century, as revolution brewed in America. Parliament split over questions of colonial rule, with some MPs advocating for more American-style self-determination; others retorted that colonies of the Crown already had fair (again, because of virtual) parliamentary representation, just like all other Britons who still lacked the vote. Stormy debates prompted related questions about British identity at home and abroad. Steep tax increases to pay for the American war catalyzed a Whig "Association Movement" that pushed (unsuccessfully) for parliamentary reform, annual elections, greater manhood suffrage, and a secret ballot.

The shock of defeat by the Americans in 1783 only increased tensions, with some MPs blaming British ambivalence about suppressing "fellow Englishmen with the same ancient liberties as us." Radical reformers demanded more American-style freedom by restructuring parliamentary elections and the voting franchise. The 1789 French Revolution became another lightning rod. Readers of Paine's radical *Rights of Man* (1791) pressed for Gallic-style reform in Westminster. Opposing Loyalist and Radical societies squared off on the dangers or blessings of *liberté et égalité*, while others urged compromise. Passions ran high; in 1791, a dinner in a Birmingham hotel celebrating Bastille Day sparked three days of rioting.

Despite all the political controversies, an opposing trend emerged during the eighteenth century: a broad and diverse yet still discernible cultural movement toward "politeness." Its form and significance is much debated by scholars, but older interpretations about its affirmation of elite privilege have given way to an opposite understanding. In manners, speech, dress, education, and memberships of the growing network of social and political clubs, we can see enthusiasm for boundary-blurring values of openness, "moderation, mutual tolerance, and the overriding importance of social comity."[10] Contemporary sources suggest that the agreeableness promoted by the politeness movement made working together more effective and meritorious. This movement was, by our terms, an incipient version of civic friendship. And it was fully in accord with rising momentum for a more self-governing society.

Reform and Reaction

As the nineteenth century opened, controversies over governance were temporarily overshadowed by the looming security threat of postrevolutionary France. Peasant armies had rallied around Napoléon, the sort of "liberating" dictator that British moderates had feared, and the Corsican general was now marching to topple other established monarchies across Europe. Britain embarked on years of inconclusive military alliances and campaigns against Napoléon and his own autocratic ambitions. Finally, in 1815, the Duke of Wellington's victory at Waterloo ended the threat. But ensuing jubilation soon devolved into domestic strife. Agricultural failure and falling postwar production prompted rural and anti-industrial riots, and then major food shortages. Politically charged debates erupted over tariffs and free trade, and anti-Catholic sentiment resurfaced.

Activists meanwhile demanded more democratic representation in Parliament. In 1817, a petition for increasing male suffrage collected 750,000 signatures—but was flatly rejected by the House of Commons. In 1819, a follow-on protest in Manchester's St. Peter's Field was broken up by volunteer cavalry sent to restore order; they killed a dozen protesters and wounded hundreds of others. After this "Peterloo Massacre," the Tory government cracked down further, passing the "Six Acts" to toughen laws on seditious dissent. But the pressure for reform continued, finally forcing a quarreling commons into legislative compromise, the Great Reform Act of 1832. The act reduced the number of patronage-enabling rotten boroughs and reassigned seats to underrepresented industrial centers; urban freeholders were enfranchised under a new property requirement; and Scotland and Wales gained voters and MPs. The measures raised the nation's franchise back up to 18 percent of adult males.

Historians disagree about the democratic significance of the reform. Nevertheless, the act created in Great Britain one of the largest body of voters in Europe. It also likely enhanced Parliament's ability "to provide for the common defense" by enfranchising "new money" traders and manufacturers who recognized the need to address rising costs and raise additional labor forces to protect Britain's new commercial might.

Democratizing momentum soon slowed, however. The 1832 Act was a high-water mark of electoral reform for the next thirty years. In 1838, a "People's Chartist" movement collected millions of petition signatures, demanding fairer electoral districts, universal male suffrage, a secret ballot, and an end to property requirements for MPs. The proposal failed in Parliament, and the movement faded. Public attention shifted toward other reform priorities (tariffs, food prices, poor laws, and child labor). The emigration of millions of men, who traveled abroad in search of new opportunities during this era, may also have bled off the bottom-up pressure for more popular governance.

National Identity

On the other hand, during this same period, British national identity—a sense of belonging to the United Kingdom, beyond the individual "nationhoods" of its constituent parts (England, Wales, Scotland, and Ireland)—accelerated after the French Revolution and consolidated during the Napoleonic Wars. Contemporary art, journalism, and public discourse celebrated British exceptionalism, emphasizing the contrast with the French enemy. By the early nineteenth century, popular culture was rife with images and rhetoric depicting powerful "John Bull" and British lion characters dominating effete and decadent French foes. British identity was also strengthened by tangible (or imagined) distinctions between the British themselves and the peoples of different races in their growing overseas empire—reflected in cartoons, parliamentary speeches, and public images of colonial subjects.

As the nation focused its energies outward—fighting enemies and ruling colonies—traditional internal ethnic and social distinctions at home blurred. Religious sectarianism faded; an expanding list of "dissenting" Protestant faiths (including fast-growing Methodism) were more tolerated, loosening the grip of Anglicanism. Catholics still suffered discrimination but were allowed to serve in government by the Emancipation Act of 1829. Religion slowly became "a more private choice, less a matter of public identity."[11]

Other social differences eroded through both conscious and unconscious mixing across the British population. Some of this began during the defense against Napoléon, as the army intentionally reorganized to integrate people from different parts of the kingdom and different social classes. Irish and Scottish volunteers earned the respect of English comrades in both the military forces and then later the administration of the empire. Meanwhile, the rising value of land due to agricultural fragmentation stimulated estate-preserving intermarriages between English, Scottish, and Irish families. More integrated commerce across the new United Kingdom furthered cross-boundary integration as many internal taxes were dropped. New explorations about the nature of government, freedom, law, commerce, and virtue by thinkers of the flourishing Scottish Enlightenment increasingly influenced English education.

Class differences were also diluted by new commercial and leisure practices. A London-based movement to promote a more generic "received pronunciation" of English language reduced the hierarchy of accent in daily business. Civil service and imperial administration positions were filled by meritocratic exams instead of birth. Victorian era sports—horse racing, rowing, boxing, and cricket—became popular across all classes. Men of the middle classes also mingled with elite patrons in hundreds of clubs, promoting a blend of commercial and patriotic values among members. Society remained male-dominated, but women began taking on professional and public roles. A burgeoning literature questioned traditional gender inequalities. Women staffed many Victorian era civic and charitable organizations. Women's suffrage, first explored by eighteenth-century writers, grew into an active political movement, and was accelerated by the 1832 reforms and Chartist movement.

The growth of a British national identity and blurring of social boundaries opened the way for further progress in civic friendship as people increasingly saw themselves as part of a larger "imagined community."[12] Unifying trends emerged or grew stronger. First was a shared belief in progress. Enlightenment ideas of bettering society, leading humankind toward more freedom and prosperity, now seemed validated by repeated British military successes, advances in science and technology, an expanding economy, and a more effective system of governance. Military victories and a growing empire were easy to feel good about. As British power and influence spread, Britons cheered successes abroad, including the defeat of the Sikhs in India (1846), triumph over Russia in Crimea (1856), and British field marshal H. H. Kitchener's avenging victories in the Sudan (1898). Optimism stiffened upper lips against setbacks, such as the disaster of Afghanistan in 1842 and Indian mutiny in 1857. British power on land and sea were celebrated in songs, poems, adventure stories, and labels of commercial products.

Meanwhile, gleaming steam railroads were connecting the nation, and prosperous urban centers boasted distinguished municipal buildings, new infrastructure, and charitable organizations to care for the poor. Both political parties agreed that government costs must be kept down, but both also enacted new measures for housing, sanitation, and welfare.

Civic Education

Political progress was promoted in national histories that shaped contemporary education. Works by historians Thomas Babington Macaulay and Thomas Carlyle as well as Bishop William Stubbs emphasized exceptional British struggles against tyranny and the successful achievement of a representative political system stabilized by prudent monarchs. School texts touted Britain's leadership in European civilization. Classroom maps colored bright red flaunted Britannia's unprecedented territorial reach and influence across the world. Both schools and universities developed curricula highlighting character-building leadership and public service through the study of heroes and lessons of ancient empires. British progress was associated with personal excellence, merging politeness with principles of open commerce, social dignity based on both mercy and self-reliance, and the striving after respectability. Such values further developed beliefs among many that the British governance system was a unifying key to its success.

The monarchy played its part in the patriotic parade, which became its own form of public education. George III self-consciously and visibly promoted British heritage and majesty. Queen Victoria's public jubilees were celebrated and widely attended across the empire. A Great (Royal) Exhibition in 1851 joined thousands of exhibitors and spectators in London's Crystal Palace, showcasing the hope and greatness of British commercial, technological, and political achievement. As one historian underscored, "The sheer psychological gratification [of] the Empire's importance [among British people] can never be exaggerated."[13]

Moral Purpose

A growing sense of moral purpose animated the education and celebration of a proud nation. The British also came to believe, and taught rising generations, that the empire was a force for bringing greater good to the world. Conservative and liberal leaders alike trumpeted the nation's higher calling. In 1848, British Tory statesman Lord Palmerston proclaimed that "without any vainglorious boast . . . we stand at the head of a moral, social and political civilization. Our task is to lead the way and direct the march of other nations."[14] Liberal prime minister William Gladstone similarly affirmed noble progress a few decades later: Britain had become, he said, "the center of the moral, social, and political power of the world."[15] Other leaders joined the chorus, stressing the historical distinctiveness of the British people, whose empire was now the "triumph of a moral idea," rooted in the "sympathy, common thought, and feeling between those . . . of a common race and . . . common history to look back upon."[16] In his best-selling volume *The Expansion of England*, contemporary historian John Seeley portrayed the extension of this triumphant system to the rest of the world as Britain's ultimate goal.

The national sense of moral purpose took a major leap forward when Parliament passed, and the public celebrated, laws aimed at ending slavery (1807 and 1833), and the contrast with slavery-condoning America was soon proclaimed as proof of British superiority. Britain's increasing belief in moral purpose was further exemplified in the enforcement of the ban on slave trading in the British colonies; initiatives to bring "proper laws, practices and tools of civilization" to colonial peoples; the encouragement of limited self-governance made in agreements with several of its colonies; attempts to spread the English systems of education; and missionary efforts to bring Christianity to India, Africa, and other "nonbeliever" territories.

Contrary views were aired, emphasizing the profit motive of British imperialism and its occasional cruelty (for example, in vengeance wreaked by British troops on mutineers of the 1857 rebellion). Historians today vigorously debate the costs and sins versus benefits and accomplishments of empire, with no end in sight. But in its day, the empire was widely regarded by millions of British people as a project that successfully combined material progress and moral improvement, providing the ruling nation with a sense of shared purpose and historical destiny.

That sense of shared imperial purpose coincided with a renewed push for a broader franchise at home. In 1867, Conservative leader Benjamin Disraeli outflanked political rivals by passing the "Representation of the People Act," after which 30 percent of adult males had the vote. A few years later, women gained the right to vote in local elections, and in 1872, the secret ballot was finally institutionalized. In 1883, the Corrupt Practices Act curbed manipulative partisan public spending. In 1884, Gladstone's Liberals passed their own (Third) Reform Act, which unified the property requirements between country and borough districts, enabling voting by two-thirds of all adult men. New momentum was building for a fully inclusive democracy, nudged ahead by decades of growing British pride and accomplishments, rising patriotism, greater civic friendship bonded by a shared moral purpose, and popularizing reforms in Parliament.

The Civic Bargain, 1914–28

Early in the twentieth century, imperial Great Britain faced a new, existential challenge of scale: the collapse of the European "balance of power" on which its continental security had depended. After years of intricate diplomacy with France, Russia, and other continental nations, Britain went to war in 1914 against Germany and its allies to preserve its empire and secure lasting peace (it was hoped) in Europe. Civic friendship, manifest in a willingness to sacrifice for the common good, was apparent in the national response to the crisis. When the fighting began, Lord Kitchener appealed for 100,000 soldier volunteers; more than 700,000 answered the call. With no conscription system and horrifying battlefield losses mounting, new recruits were vital. By the end of 1915, 2.5 million men had joined up, or a third of the eligible population, from all segments of society. Many of those who would later be killed were from the upper and middle classes, including peers and many sons of MPs. Women also volunteered for civilian and military roles, including 100,000 who served in uniform, and many were killed in action. Volunteers from the empire totaled over 2 million, mostly from the "white dominions" (Canada, Australia, and New Zealand). Rapidly mounting battlefield losses did force the institution of a draft in 1916, but the compelled obligation did not markedly change the class composition of the forces.

The war severely tested the resilience of the nation. One-fourth of all British infantry were wounded, and one in eight was killed.[17] The particularly strong spirit and collective commitment of the British troops in battle have been explained by (inter alia) their belief in the rightness of the cause, the trust they held for their institutions, camaraderie and esprit de corps, and strong support and encouragement from home.[18] Civic solidarity carried over into the trenches and bridged to the home front.

Duty and Sacrifice Rewarded

It was in this context that a full British civic bargain finally emerged. In 1916, at an all-party parliamentary speaker's conference, MPs agreed that those serving the country now deserved the vote (not coincidentally, wartime sacrifices suffered by other European nations similarly triggered legislation for universal male suffrage). In Britain, the franchise was initially proposed for all males age twenty-one and older, and women over age thirty. In 1918, under the Liberal government of David Lloyd George, the Representation of the People Act made the proposal official, adding another 12.9 million men (mostly without property) and 8.4 million women to the citizen rolls.

Even this measure, however, entailed compromise. The bill was partly motivated by the need to ensure adequate participation at the polls after the great losses of the war.[19] Moreover, the age thresholds failed to recognize voting rights for the many men younger than twenty-one then serving in the trenches, nor was the privilege extended to younger women who were also serving in various ways. The enfranchisement of women was initially contested, with the final deal struck only due to the ongoing pressure of the suffragette movement. Yet the Sex Disqualification Removal Act of the same year also opened jury service, magistracies, and legal practice for women.[20] The right to vote in parliamentary elections was extended to all adult women ten years later. Today a substantial and diverse majority of the UK population governs itself via the widely franchised body of voters who elect their representative government.

The final civic bargain came late in the history of this nation, reflecting the lengthy development of the hybrid platform of governance and a journey through several intermediate bargains across many centuries. The "punctuated equilibrium" of the evolution saw starts and stops in progress, but a clear overall trajectory of fulfilling all essential conditions for democracy by the twentieth century: no boss (but for some ceremonial vestiges in the surviving monarch); a commitment to preserving security and welfare, launched and restored faithfully (if sometimes episodically) since Anglo-Saxon times; a progressively defined citizenship, with rights and responsibilities forged through ongoing acts of Parliament, treaties, and common law judgments; a parliamentary and judicial system led by citizens; and a historic tradition of civic friendship and education, particularly strong during the imperial period, yet still enduring in different forms today.

British democracy was long in arriving, but history certainly teaches us that it didn't come out of nowhere.

5

UNITED STATES

Painful Compromises in Search of a More Perfect Union

In the hot summer of 1787, a group of men, known to history as America's founding fathers, gathered in Philadelphia to discuss how the citizens of a young country could govern themselves without a boss. They had been appointed by twelve of the thirteen states of the recently proclaimed United States to revise the failing Articles of Confederation, an earlier attempt to create a workable government for the new country. What they did instead was write the document that was later ratified by votes in each of the states as the US Constitution. The Constitution is an immensely important civic bargain—a prominent landmark in the long prior and subsequent history of democratic political development. The political history of America is one of bargains, complicated by scale, facilitated by civic friendship, and threatened by civic discord. Those bargains enabled the country to adapt in the face of a series of daunting scale challenges. But bargaining also resulted in fundamental injustices, which remained—and in some cases, still remain—to be rectified.

The basic facts of American political history are well-known. The era of British colonization was followed by a successful War of Independence that led to the ratification of the new Constitution for the newly proclaimed United States. The next seventy-five years saw a dramatic increase in the size of the country at the expense of Indigenous populations, the development of formal political parties, and increasing tensions

between the northern and southern, slave economy states. A bloody
civil war ended slavery. Former slaves were granted civic rights and
thereby became legal citizens of the nation. But in the southern states,
Jim Crow rules quickly suppressed participatory citizenship for most
Black people. Meanwhile, the economy expanded, the country grew
rapidly as new states were added, immigration from Europe and Asia
increased, and colonies were established overseas. In the twentieth
century, women and ethnic minorities were finally granted national citizenship, and America fought two world wars, survived a worldwide
economic depression, expanded social services, and by midcentury,
became a dominant player on the world stage.

A long struggle to establish true civic participation for Black people
resulting in national legislation that ended the formal rules of the Jim
Crow era failed to eliminate race-based disparities in income, wealth,
and educational achievement. In the late twentieth and early twenty-
first centuries, America fought futile overseas wars and abandoned the
military draft. Legally mandated civil rights expanded with formal
protections against discrimination based on race, gender, and sexual
orientation. In the twenty-first century, the country became increasingly politically polarized along cultural lines while trust in government declined, eventuating in the violence at the US Capitol on January 6, 2021.

This chapter focuses on America's foundational civic bargain: the
Constitution. The Constitution was designed to ensure security and
welfare by specifying the duties of representatives on the assumption
that citizens would attend to the common interest in electing them. It
was revised to guarantee freedom and equality. It remained imperfect
in respect to justice and failed to prevent the Civil War. By attending to
how this fundamental bargain was made and amended—by asking
"who was at the table and who was not" as well as "what was on the
agenda, when, and what was not"—we will better understand the role
of civic friendship and the challenges of scale in the historical development of American democracy. And we will better comprehend the dilemmas that Americans face in the twenty-first century.

A Forgotten Founder

On June 5, 1787, Pierce Butler, a delegate to the Philadelphia Convention from South Carolina, objected to a proposal aimed at establishing a federal judiciary. According to James Madison's notes, Butler claimed that "the people will not bear such innovations. The States will revolt at such encroachments. Supposing such an establishment to be useful, we must not venture on it. We must follow the example of Solon who gave the Athenians not the best Govt. he could devise; but the best they [would] receive."[1] Butler's comment and its historical context exemplify the bargaining that created America's republican democracy.

Like many of the men gathered in Philadelphia that year, Butler was well versed in Greek and Roman history, and believed it had much to teach those who sought to write fundamental rules for a new nation. The line he cited from Plutarch's *Life of Solon* (see chapter 2) had alluded to the inability of nonboss lawmakers to establish rules that are, in their view, "best" when the citizens will not readily "receive" them. Butler raised the specter of civil conflict: the citizens of the several states might "revolt." So even supposing that the innovation would be "useful," the delegates "must not venture on it." As Butler clearly hinted, the alternative to a positive-sum bargain struck by civic friends was a fight between enemies.

It was not entirely clear in summer 1787 who would or could be included in "the people." Some delegates were not sure that a single union was necessary; Butler's own sketchy notes include a draft proposal that "the Security of equal liberty and general welfare will be best preserved and continued by forming the states into three Republiks distinct in their Governments but United by a Common League Offensive and Defensive."[2] Were that proposal to have been approved, instead of one United States, there would have been three independent countries with different legal systems. That would have taken some of the hard problems off the table. But it would have compromised security by reducing scale: foreign rivals would have been quick to play the three minirepublics against one another.

The American founders disagreed on many things—and those disagreements led to the hard bargaining that resulted in the Constitution presented to the states for ratification. As the proposal mentioned by Butler shows, though, the founders agreed on the value of equal liberty—at least for white men. They were also agreed on the goals of security and welfare, which is presumably why the "three republics" proposal was never brought to the floor. Most of the founders, although not all of them (Alexander Hamilton, who urged that the executive office be held for life, was an outlier), agreed on the fundamental democratic goal of no boss. In the debate over the powers of the federal executive, Butler alluded to Roman and British history in warning that an executive officer with an absolute veto would become "a Catiline or a Cromwell." He was citing the Roman aristocrat who tried to seize control of the republic after he was defeated in an election for consul in 63 BCE (chapter 3), and the British revolutionary commander who after the execution of King Charles I, took for himself the bossy title of Lord Protector in the mid-seventeenth century (chapter 4).[3]

Butler is largely forgotten today. According to historian John Fiske, he was one of "the rank and file of thoroughly respectable, commonplace men, unfitted for shining in the work of the meeting, but admirably competent to proclaim its results and get their friends and neighbors to adopt them."[4] Butler was a slave owner who saw his role at the convention as defending the interests of southern slave owners; the proposal to create three republics was surely aimed at legally entrenching slavery. Butler introduces us to some key themes in the history of American democracy. As in each of our previous cases, liberty and equality, along with security, welfare, and no boss, are prominent among the shared goals of the democratic community. Revised bargains and sustained civic friendship, expressed as respect for and recognition of the dignity of fellow citizens in the face of scale challenges, are the drivers of democratic development. But America is distinctive because the need to shoehorn racial slavery into a system of fundamental law, predicated on natural liberty and equality, overshadowed every political bargain of the young republic. That misfit led to enmity among former civic friends, and finally to abandoning bargaining in favor of fighting a devastating civil war.

American Exceptionalism and an Imperfect Bargain

The founders who struck the original American civic bargain appealed to sophisticated political theories and comparative history. They were intensely aware of the long history of self-government in Athens and Rome as well as parliamentary government in Britain. Moreover, they drew on 250 years of experience and experiments with local and regional self-government in the New World. Unlike our previous cases, America lacked a history of homegrown monarchs or control by a hereditary class of aristocrats. Although before the revolution, Americans were formally subjects of the British king, there was no deep political tradition of subservience to royal authority. There was no social habit of deference to aristocrats that had to be overcome before the people could govern themselves, nor formal guilds or royal monopolies to constrain innovation. American exceptionalism meant that the negotiations that led to the Constitution and its ratification were parts of a self-conscious attempt to create a political bargain that would be strong and yet dynamically adaptive. Rather than the hypothetical thought experiments of seventeenth- and eighteenth-century social contract theorists, the American founders wrote a real contract—one that would have to be affirmed by the positive votes of their fellow citizens.

Because of the entrenched interests of slave owners, the original American founding bargain fell far short of being "best"—in the sense of being true to the principles of liberty, equality, and justice eloquently enunciated in the Declaration of Independence of 1776. Yet the founders knew that an imperfect bargain was vastly preferable to no bargain at all. Without a formal agreement uniting the states under a workable government, there could be no single, strong country, capable of growing in population, territory, and wealth, and able to defend itself against rivals. If the contract was not ratified by the citizens—so that the Constitution could be said to be authored and authorized by "We the People"—the new government would not be legitimate. It would not command the loyalty of enough people to survive the struggles to come. In brief, the Constitution reflected both the brilliant insight of men like Madison who were outstandingly suited for "shining in the work of the meeting" and the strategic compromises required to get the likes of Butler on board—men who were "admirably competent" at the work of proclaiming the results and persuading their friends and neighbors to accept them.

In the Beginning

After the rediscovery of the New World in the late fifteenth century, European states moved to claim and exploit its riches. But only the English established permanent settlements. In contrast to the Spanish, Portuguese, French, and Dutch, English migrants to the New World were mostly farmers and craftsmen, and they were accompanied by their wives. The English plan was, from the start, to establish lasting communities, not just frontier outposts for trade and missionary work. The English created self-sufficient villages that later developed into a network of towns and cities. Moreover, the English settlements were largely self-governing. As we have seen (chapter 4), the seventeenth-century kings of England struggled to maintain their authority: English royal power was too weak to govern the new colonies directly.

The earliest English settlements in the lands later divided into the original thirteen states were small, vulnerable, and largely on their own in terms of security and welfare. Lacking resort to third-party enforcers of rules or guarantors of their safety, the members of those communities had to cooperate closely with one another if they were to survive. Conditions in the new settlements were hard. If the agreements struck by the new settlers were not self-enforcing, they would fail—as early settlements sometimes did. The famous "Lost Colony" on Roanoke Island (Virginia) was founded in 1587 but had disappeared by 1590.

Colonists in the settlements of what came to be called New England struck political bargains aimed at establishing local self-government. Those bargains were often sealed by formal, sworn compacts and facilitated by strong, shared values. Many of the new settlements were founded by religious dissenters. Puritans and Quakers were outside the mainstream of both Catholicism, with its hierarchical authority structure, and the Church of England, with the king at its head. The dissenters came to the New World intending to practice Christian faith according to their own lights. While communities based on shared, dissident religious belief led to parochialism and limited viewpoint diversity, they promoted civic friendship and enabled local self-government.

The Mayflower Compact of 1620 is a prime example of early self-governance. Before landing in the New World and establishing the Massachusetts Bay Colony, the Pilgrim signers agreed to "enact, constitute and frame, such just and equal Laws, Ordinances, Acts, Constitutions, and Offers" that would be necessary "for the general Good of the Colony; unto which we promise all due Submission and Obedience." The obedience they promised was *to one another*, not to any third-party boss, and their compact aimed at their own, collective "general Good."[5] While the colonists brought with them English ideas of private property and personal salvation, there could be no effective pursuit of individual interests without first securing their common interest in security and welfare. Those interests were gained without bosses. In 1636, the colonists in nearby Plymouth planned that all freemen would meet annually to make new binding rules. Two years later, they decided that electing deputies would be more efficient. This move toward representative rather than direct Athenian-style self-government allowed for scaling up. The new local governments were republican in employing representation and democratic in that they were aimed at self-government by citizens. The settlers of Narragansett Bay colony (now Portsmouth, Rhode Island) declared in 1641 that their public order would be "a DEMOCRACIE, or Popular Government."[6]

Collective self-government by citizens was facilitated in the New World not only by the shared values and devotion to the common interest of local communities but also by a remarkably wide franchise. In the seventeenth and eighteenth centuries, civic rights, including the right to vote for local representatives, were more widely distributed in the English colonies of the New World than anywhere in Europe. In early New England, local citizenship was officially predicated on church membership and property holding. But the colonists in any given settlement tended to be church members. And the ready availability of land, purchased or appropriated from native peoples, meant that most freemen could meet the property qualification. Moreover, even those whose property fell below the minimum were frequently granted de facto participation rights. In small settlements, dependent almost entirely on their own local resources for security and threatened by sometimes-hostile natives, the need for solidarity in the face of common threats trumped wealth-based status distinctions. Some 60 to 80 percent of adult male residents in New England towns were able to vote in colony-wide elections in the first years of settlement. Although those numbers declined in later decades due to more rigorous requirements for church membership and rising wealth inequality, as many as 75 percent of adult males could vote in Massachusetts by the early eighteenth century. As we have seen (chapter 4), the situation was quite different in the United Kingdom, where in the eighteenth century, adult male franchise fell as low as 17 percent.[7]

In the period before the revolution, colonial Americans voted on a range of matters and at different levels. Town meetings were typically directly democratic, with open discussion of matters of local concern and direct voting by those holding the franchise. Although the British government appointed a governor for each of the colonies, in practice the governor's powers were limited by both advisory councils, often elected by the enfranchised residents of the colony, and colony-level assemblies, whose members were elected by the residents and claimed the right to legislate. Royal governors sometimes sought to appoint their own councils and veto the rules made by the assemblies. But governors were frequently stymied by their erstwhile subjects and ill supported by the distant British government. Colonists voted on town charters, elected representatives, and ultimately wrote and ratified their own state constitutions. The colonists gained valuable experience, educating themselves through the practice of exercising their powers as citizens. They did so by both voting directly on local matters and voting for representatives who were expected to promote the interests of their constituents. Some assembly representatives were given formal instructions by the electorate and expected to carry out those instructions to the letter. More often, representatives were trusted to exercise their own judgment in the interests of those they represented.

Scaling Up

As discussed earlier (chapter 4), the mid-seventeenth century saw a protracted civil war in England. During that time the American colonies were relatively free to develop on their own. With the restoration of the monarchy, the British government sought to impose stricter control. In 1684, King Charles II proclaimed the Dominion of New England, reasserting the authority of English law, ending the independent status of Massachusetts, disbanding all colonial assemblies, and raising taxes. Those measures provoked outrage and outright resistance. After the bargain of parliamentary monarchy of 1689, the British government relented. Colonial self-government was largely restored. With that restoration came changes that reduced the tendency to insular local parochialism.

Massachusetts received a new charter in 1691 that restored an elected General Court (colonial legislature) and local town autonomy. Yet it also eliminated the rule that only members of Puritan churches could vote—although Catholics and persons "vicious in life" were still excluded. In Pennsylvania, a democratic government emerged through and in resistance to the bold political initiatives of the colony's founder and first governor, William Penn, who sought to establish government on the Quaker ideals of equality and "brotherly love"—with himself as boss. In 1701, Pennsylvania's General Assembly passed a new "Charter of Liberties" that eliminated both the governor's council and his veto. The Pennsylvania colony was opened to Europeans from many nations and different religious denominations. The pluralistic commitments of the residents led to the emergence of factions and frequent conflicts, but over time, to a habit of building coalitions, making deals, and compromising to gain positive-sum outcomes as well. As a result, Pennsylvanians became accustomed to the bargaining required by self-government at scale.

The situation was different in Virginia and the other southern English colonies, where the agricultural regime favored cash crops. In the early seventeenth century, the first African slaves were imported to North America. The soaring price of tobacco and limited numbers of indentured white servants drove increased demand for labor. That demand was met by the growing transatlantic slave trade and a radical rise in the number of enslaved Africans put to work in the southern colonies. With the growth of slave labor, race became a defining feature of the social order. White immigrants who worked off their indentures were granted voting rights and persuaded to align their interests with slave-owning landowners along the lines of racial identity. The few free Black people were denied the franchise. The implicit bargain among rich and poor southern whites sustained what came to be understood as their common interest in defining freedom and civic membership in explicitly racial terms. Meanwhile, slavery remained relatively uncommon in New England, where much of the produce of farms was consumed locally. The difference in the economic and labor systems of the northern and southern English colonies was already laying the groundwork for the constitutional bargain struck in 1787—a bargain that made deep compromises with the values of freedom, equality, and dignity.

The English colonies in the New World, both north and south, grew steadily in population. The free population more than doubled between 1710 and 1740, and redoubled by 1770. The slave population grew more rapidly still. By the mid-eighteenth century there were roughly two million residents in the British mainland colonies, compared with some sixty thousand in the French colonies. Self-government grew apace, with colonial assemblies taking ever more control of regional affairs. The power of royal governors was likewise increasingly constrained as the distant British government repeatedly failed to enforce its commands.

Meanwhile, hostilities broke out between France and England—the Seven Years' War of 1756–63. In the New World, both sides enlisted native allies, but given their demographic disadvantage, the French were constrained to rely heavily on native fighters. France fought at another disadvantage: the French government was hard put to borrow the money needed to prosecute the war. The autocratic French monarchy was regarded by potential lenders as all too likely to default on its loans. But in Britain, Parliament, which had controlled state finances since 1689, included among its representatives many whose interests were intertwined with those who had money to lend. Loans to the British government were seen as safe, meaning that the British could readily float massive loans allowing them to finance warfare on two continents.

A treaty of 1763 effectively ended France's colonial presence in North America; the English now laid claim to all territory east of the Mississippi—opening the vast Ohio territory to colonial expansion. Moreover, the military threat to English settlements from Indigenous confederations was considerably reduced. Ironically, the decisive British military victory, by reducing large-scale military threats, further reduced the American colonies' dependence on the king. Local self-government and self-reliance could now more readily be scaled up, and ambitions for regional independence grew apace. After the war, British prime minister George Grenville sought to crack down on the colonies by enforcing trade regulations: he asserted that the colonists should help pay off the loans that had facilitated the British victory and secured their own safety. But Grenville found that the king's North American subjects saw the situation differently. The thinking of the Americans was affected by their long experience with local self-government, the disappearance of the system-level threat of the French and their native allies, and the new ideas arising from the eighteenth-century European Enlightenment.

Enlightenment Culture and Democratic Ideas

The history of democracy in America is closely connected to bold new ideas about ethics and politics, moral philosophy, religion, and history. The impact increases when ideas are more readily, widely, and rapidly communicated across the population, so literacy is a key accelerator. In part because reading the Bible was an essential aspect of Puritan culture, literacy was widespread in America, among women as well as men, from the seventeenth century onward. It is estimated that at the outbreak of the American Revolution in 1776, around 80 percent of men and

50 percent of women in New England were literate.[8] In the 1800s, perhaps one in four Americans remained illiterate. Meanwhile, even the illiterate engaged with a wider world of ideas. This was due to the habit of reading newspapers and pamphlets out loud in coffeehouses and other public venues—an example of civic education at the most local level. As we have seen (chapter 4), similar habits helped foment the English Civil Wars in the seventeenth century.

New ideas fueled the private and public debates over the fundamentals of self-government—both moral principles and the practical conditions necessary for a people to rule themselves. Some of those high moral principles were ultimately expressed in the Declaration of Independence and, imperfectly, written into the Constitution. An interest in ideas was not limited to men; women, including, for example, Abigail Adams, the brilliant and strong-willed wife of founder and later president, John Adams, formed reading circles in which they taught and learned from one another by discussing books and ideas.

The American founders who gathered in Philadelphia in 1787 were avid readers and writers of books and pamphlets. They eagerly acquired books from Europe, and local American printing presses reprinted European editions and original works by American authors. The founders were not limited to English-language literature; most were fluent in French, many in Latin, and some in ancient Greek. They were all committed to the basic notions that education was essential for active citizenship and ideas were of central importance to the enterprise of creating a constitution. They were influenced by new directions in political philosophy and their study of earlier history—especially the Greek, Roman, and British histories surveyed in our three previous case studies. In seeking to establish a novel form of polity, the American founders were able to survey early experiments in collective self-government. In assessing the potential value of bold new theories of government, they had reference to a rich body of historical evidence for the successes and failures of earlier regimes. Their goal was to combine philosophy with history, build on historical successes, and avoid the mistakes that led to the failure of democratic republics of the past.

Influential books highly relevant to the development of American ideas about self-government famously included major works of political philosophy, prominently Locke's late seventeenth-century *Second Treatise of Government*, which advocated a "Right of resisting" an unjust sovereign ruler and argued for a natural right to life, liberty, and property.[9] Locke's ideas were reworked by Thomas Jefferson in the writing of the Declaration of Independence. The Baron de Montesquieu's *Spirit of the Laws* (1748) offered a full theory of republicanism based on the principles of political equality, representation, and separation of governmental powers. Madison and other founders adapted Montesquieu's framework when thinking through the relationship between the legislative, judicial, and executive branches of government.

American readers were steeped in the history of earlier experiments with republican and democratic government. Montesquieu authored an influential work on the history of Rome, *Considerations on the Causes of the Romans' Greatness and Decline*, which introduced the genre of "philosophical history." His thesis was that Rome's republican greatness was predicated on a virtuous commitment to civic life; the decline set in when that commitment waned. The founders assumed that a virtuous commitment by citizens to fulfilling a duty to seek common interests was a necessary, if insufficient, part of every republican government. They also read the works of the classical era historians, biographers, and theorists that bore directly on the successes and failures of Athenian democracy and the Roman Republic, including works by Thucydides, Polybius, Cicero, and Plutarch.

Among the lessons that the founders took away from their reading in the history of self-government was that virtue coexisted with self-interest. They recognized that the strategic pursuit of self-interest was a persistent feature of human moral psychology. They knew that if unchecked, self-interest would doom any attempt to create and sustain a self-enforcing government "by the people." But in their historical and philosophical reading, they also learned that self-interest could be tempered by the active promotion of civic virtue. Formal institutions and civic education could help build strong norms of public-spirited commitment to seeking the common good, a passionate love of country, and a consequent willingness to sacrifice when necessary to preserve the community. The founders were deeply aware of the tension between the freedom of individuals to pursue their own conception of the good and the virtuous commitment by moral equals to the common good of their shared community.

Through their reading of history and political philosophy, the founders were convinced that both political freedom and equality were imperatives for democratic government, but they came to understand that there were trade-offs between those values too. They learned that sustaining self-government required the cultivation of norms that defended the dignity of each citizen, and that civic norms exceeded mere obedience to formal laws; dignity meant showing respect to one's fellow citizens, even to those with whom one strongly disagreed. And dignity was incompatible with paternalistic infantilization and groveling subservience.

And finally, through their reading of philosophy and history, the founders learned to think deeply and seriously about the problem of scale—the difficulty of sustaining participatory government while the community grew bigger, more diverse, and wealthier. Indeed, many of the philosophers and historians they read claimed that a successful democratic republic was only possible at a small scale. This led to a serious question: Must the United States remain small, agrarian, and isolated? Or could it become a large, powerful, commercial state capable of rivaling the greatest states of Europe?

Crises of Representation and the Failure of a Political Bargain

By the mid-eighteenth century, the American colonists' long experience with local and regional institutions of self-government had convinced them that the ancient Athenian approach of making public policy in an assembly open to all citizens was unworkable: Self-government beyond the level of the town meeting must be based on some form of representation. The growing commitment to republican ideals meant that representatives would be chosen in election, and that while limited to free males, the franchise would be wide by contemporary British standards. There was some uncertainty, though, concerning the correct relationship between the citizen-electors and those they elected to represent them: To what extent ought the choices and actions of an elected representative—say, a member of a state assembly or indeed a constitutional convention—be determined by the preferences and interests of the citizens who had chosen him?

As we have seen, in some cases, citizens gave their representatives formal, written instructions and expected them to stick to these directions. But it was increasingly clear that the "loyal delegate" model was unworkable in practice; circumstances changed quickly, while communication between the representative and electors was slow in a pre-electronic age. Moreover, Enlightenment values included a respect for reasoned and impassioned argument, debate, and deliberation. Civic assemblies and conventions were not merely occasions for voting based on interests but instead for listening to arguments, and forming and adjusting preferences accordingly. And finally, the representative was legitimately concerned not only with the local interests of those who had elected him but also with the wider interests of a colony, state, or entire country. The question of the degree to which good representatives hew to the clearly expressed views of their constituents or form independent judgments based on their own research and interchange with other representatives has never been definitively resolved; in eighteenth-century Britain, MPs debated the same questions. Yet as the habit of electors issuing written instructions faded away, representatives were assumed to retain some independence of judgment. Accountability was retrospective; voters dissatisfied with a representative could vote in someone else the next time.

In the dozen years following 1763 and the British victory over France, the question of representation became increasingly fraught between Americans and the British government. In the aftermath of the war, the British, who had borrowed heavily to finance the war, expected the Americans to help pay off the debt. The British also intended to maintain a large, costly standing army in America; this would keep well-connected British officers gainfully employed. Parliament duly imposed a series of new taxes on the Americans. These culminated in 1765 with the Stamp Act, which required that printed materials, including newspapers and legal documents, be produced only with paper carrying a British revenue stamp. The colonists protested vociferously, complaining that they were being taxed without the benefit of political representation; "no taxation without representation" soon became a revolutionary slogan. The British maintained that the Americans were indeed represented, as were all subjects of the British Crown, in a virtual sense by the British Parliament. Likewise, most British subjects living in the United Kingdom, while denied the franchise because they could not meet the high property qualification, were virtually represented by MPs duly elected by the few British men who enjoyed voting rights.

The American colonists were having none of it. They contended that the only legitimate taxing authorities in the British colonies were the colonial assemblies, elected by the voting citizens of each colony. Committees of Correspondence, connecting groups from New England to the mid-Atlantic, sprung up to protest the newly enforced taxes. Demonstrations by bodies of men styling themselves "Sons of Liberty" hung tax collectors in effigy. These protests were augmented by newspaper editorials and violent attacks on the property of British officials. A Stamp Act Congress with delegates from nine colonies was held in New York City in October 1765 to draw up a formal petition of protest. The result was the Declaration of Rights and Grievances, arguing that Americans possessed all the rights of the English, and that lacking voting rights in the British Parliament, the Americans lacked responsibility for taxes imposed by any authority other than their own colonial assemblies. Some leading British politicians, including Burke, supported the American case.

The unenforceable Stamp Act was revoked early in the next year, but it was just a prelude to an escalating series of British attempts to assert the authority of Parliament to legislate for the American colonies. These included the new taxes imposed by the Townshend Acts of 1767. Acts of retaliatory violence also increased, including the Boston Massacre of 1770 in which British soldiers guarding a customhouse against a protesting crowd killed or wounded a dozen Americans. Americans pushed back with larger-scale protests and more destruction of property, including the famous Boston Tea Party of 1773, to which Parliament responded with the punitive so-called Intolerable Acts of 1774. The Stamp Act Congress was likewise a prelude to a series of continental congresses, attended by delegates from the thirteen colonies. The First Continental Congress was called in response to the Intolerable Acts and resulted only in more formal petitions for redress. The Second Continental Congress was called immediately after an attempt by British troops to seize an arms cache in Massachusetts sparked the Battles of Lexington and Concord in April 1775. The Second Continental Congress became a de facto national government. On June 7, 1776, delegates to the Congress from all thirteen colonies resolved "that these United Colonies are, and of right ought to be, free and independent States, that they are absolved from all allegiance to the British Crown, and that all political connection between them and the State of Great Britain is, and ought to be, totally dissolved."[10] A commission of five men was established to draft a more detailed statement. A month later, on July 4, 1776, fifty-six delegates signed the Declaration of Independence from Britain.

The Declaration of Independence marked the final failure of the complex web of political bargains that had been struck between the government of Britain and residents of the English colonies in the New World. The core of those bargains was an exchange: colonists gave their obedience to the king, and legitimately established laws and policies emanating from his government, in exchange for welfare in the form of advantageous trade with the home country and security in the form of military defense as well as domestic tranquility. The bargain was beneficial to the colonists so long as their security and welfare were secured, and so long as the burdens of being the subjects of a distant boss were not too odious. The bargain was beneficial to the British so long as the benefits of colonialism—economic advantages and prestige relative to European rivals—exceeded the costs of maintaining security.

The colonists, however, were in many ways self-reliant and locally self-governing from the beginning. Meanwhile, the circulation of republican/democratic ideas made subservience to a distant boss seem less and less palatable. Although openly renouncing loyalty to the British

Crown was a big step, with the end of bargaining and a new willingness to fight, it became increasingly thinkable. On the British side, after the end of the war with France, the bargain was increasingly costly given the violent response of the colonists to the attempts to impose taxes. In the background, and increasingly in the foreground, was the question of legitimate authority, wrapped up in opposing conceptions of representation. The Americans felt that their rights as English subjects were violated when they were denied their own elected representatives in Parliament. The British government asserted that the Americans were already represented—virtually—just as were millions of Crown subjects living in the United Kingdom.

The breakdown of the bargain was hastened by problems of scale. In the mid-seventeenth century, the total white population in the English colonies was around fifty thousand persons, while the population of England was about six million. By the time of the Declaration of Independence, the population of England was about eight million, and there were about two million whites and a half-million African slaves in America. The ratio of colonists to British residents thus went from something like 1:120 to around 1:4 or 1:3 (depending on whether slaves are included in the count). In brief, the American population, while still far smaller than that of Britain, was increasing much more rapidly, and there was every reason to believe that the trend would continue.[11] Both in terms of numbers and wealth as well as economic clout, the relationship between the home country and its colonies had changed dramatically in favor of the Americans.

At the same time, local and regional bargains, resulting in effective forms of self-government, and facilitated by civic friendship and education along with increased communication and bold acts of resistance, bound the white residents of each of the colonies closer together. Economic differences and value disputes persisted, especially on the matter of slavery. Yet most of the colonists, north and south, shared more with one another than they did with the British government. The Committees of Correspondence and series of congresses demonstrated the potential for collective action among the disparate colonies. Courting danger by actively opposing the British established deeper forms of trust and demonstrated the credibility of costly commitments to the cause of independence. The belief grew stronger that Americans were indeed civic friends who shared a core of republican values and were willing to fight for them, even in the face of some personal enmity and deep disagreements.

In sum, from the point of view of many Americans, by the early 1770s, the time had come to either renegotiate or abandon the political bargain with their home country. When the British government refused to compromise on the grounds that the Americans had no legitimate complaints about the current terms, the view held by many Americans of the existing political bargain shifted from a positive-sum, win-win, and integrative one to zero-sum. At that point, the option of fighting appeared preferable to continued cooperation under the old terms. And so the War of Independence was engaged.

Justifications and High Ideals in the Declaration of Independence

The unanimously adopted Declaration of Independence, signed by fifty-six delegates to the Second Continental Congress, is a bill of particulars listing the reasons that the colonists were unable to keep the old bargain in light of multiple violations of its terms by a king who had become a tyrant. Among other lapses, the British government failed to provide security, interfered with naturalization and immigration, and ignored the rule of English law. The declaration is also a lofty statement of high principles and enduring values. It was authored in the first instance by Jefferson, but as political philosopher Danielle Allen has shown, it is best understood as a collective effort. It is a statement of the central and inviolable value of freedom. As Allen eloquently demonstrates, though, it is just as deeply concerned with political and moral equality.[12]

Building on Locke, Montesquieu, and other seventeenth- and eighteenth-century intellectuals, the Declaration was premised on a conception of natural, prepolitical rights that could not be abrogated by the will of a sovereign. By reference to "the Laws of Nature and of Nature's God," the declaration famously asserted that it is a self-evident truth that "all Men are created equal," and that the purpose of government is to secure certain "unalienable Rights, among them Life, Liberty, and the Pursuit of Happiness."[13]

Government in turn derived its "just Powers from the Consent of the Governed," and when government failed to secure its rightful ends, "it is the Right of the People to alter or to abolish it, and to institute new Government." Furthermore, when an existing government "evinces a Design to reduce them under absolute Despotism, it is their Right, it is their Duty, to throw off such Government." In other words, when the existing political bargain is unilaterally violated by a sovereign, those formerly bound by it are free to strike a new bargain among themselves. The bill of particulars concludes, "We must, therefore . . . hold them, as we hold the rest of Mankind, Enemies in War, in Peace, Friends." The British were thus no longer assumed to be connected to Americans by special bonds of friendship; they were just as likely to be Americans' enemies as all other peoples of the earth. The Declaration ends with an oath-like assertion of mutual self-binding: "we mutually pledge to each other our Lives, our fortunes, and our sacred Honor."[14]

Implicit in grounding the justification for renouncing the existing political bargain with the king on the high moral ground of natural equality, the right to liberty, and the pursuit of happiness was the idea that the bargain that would be struck among the Americans themselves would be a just bargain. It would respect the values of freedom, equality, and dignity as well as the natural rights that were the equal possession of "Mankind." The question that the founders gathered in Philadelphia in 1787 had to answer was whether a sustainable new bargain could be hammered out that would be true to those high ideals. The answer was no, for reasons that we have already foreshadowed—most saliently, the presence of a half-million or more enslaved people along with the economic and cultural system that had been built on the assumption of their continued enslavement.

A Long War and a First Constitutional Bargain

The American War of Independence lasted seven long years. It was finally won by grit and determination on the American side, the financial and military aid from French supporters, and the disinclination on the part of the British government to expend the people and treasure necessary to sustain a costly enterprise of colonial exploitation. The war dragged on in part because failures of coordination among the thirteen semi-independent states of the newly declared union severely impeded their collective performance. In some ways, the war was not so much won by the Americans as lost by the British. But the end result of a new beginning was unmistakable.

The government of the new country was to be based on a new and formal bargain among the states. The individual states had been experimenting with constitution writing for decades, so the first order of business after declaring independence was preparing a constitution for the self-proclaimed new nation. America's first attempt, the Articles of Confederation and Perpetual Union, was finally approved by delegates in November 1777 after over a year of discussion by the Second Continental Congress. It was another three and a half years before all thirteen states ratified the Articles, in March 1781. Maryland delayed final ratification for two years over the question of management of the planned expansion into the Ohio territory to the west; the challenge of increasing the scale of the new country loomed large from the start. In the meantime, the Continental Congress used the Articles as a framework when attempting to raise money and conscript soldiers to carry on the war with Britain, engage in foreign diplomacy with other powers, and deal with territorial disputes with Native Americans.

Problems quickly became apparent. While the first of the thirteen articles officially named the new country "United States of America," the union was more aspirational than real. Lofty aspirations were apparent in the third and fourth articles: the states were to "enter into a firm league of friendship with each other," whose purpose was "to secure and perpetuate mutual friendship and intercourse among the people of the different States in this union."[15] Both the premise and aim of the union was therefore a kind of civic friendship. The problem was that assertions of friendliness were not enough to create a workable government.

The second article defined the limits of the new national government, noting that "each state retains its sovereignty, freedom, and independence, and every power, jurisdiction, and right, which is not by this Confederation expressly delegated." The powers delegated to the national government were largely limited to foreign policy. Each of the thirteen states had one vote in all matters; no declaration of war, treaty, or alliance could be made without the agreement of at least nine states. In practice, even getting a quorum of delegates from that many states for a meeting of Congress proved daunting. Congress had no authority to regulate international trade or commerce between states. Nor did it have the power to levy taxes. It was limited to requesting allocations of funds raised by taxes set by the individual state legislatures, and those requests were often ignored. The new national government did take on a large war debt, but had no means of repaying it. It issued paper currency, but the unsecured paper proved essentially without value, "not worth a continental dollar." Finally, the Articles were declared to be "perpetual," able to be altered only by approval of Congress and subsequent ratification by all thirteen state legislatures.[16] In sum, the first attempt at a civic bargain struck by the new country was at once unworkable and unalterable.

The weakness of the new government was evident in the constant problems faced by the Continental Army: getting soldiers into the field, and supplying and paying those who did show up. Because the national government could not require states to contribute soldiers or funds, on several occasions during the winters, the army faced starvation and came close to disbanding. Even after the war was finally won, the Treaty of Paris, ending hostilities with Britain, could not be ratified for months because too few delegates showed up for Congress to gain the required nine-state quorum. Given the constraints on Congress's powers, there was little incentive to serve as a delegate. The leading figures of the revolution either retired from public life, like George Washington, returned to state-level political offices, or like Franklin, served as diplomats abroad.

After the war, the economic problems were exacerbated. Soldiers returning to their farms were owed back pay, but Congress, unable to raise funds on its own, could not pay them. The farmers were assessed taxes by state legislatures, and some states demanded that they pay in hard currency—rather than in-kind or in useless continental dollars. Those incapable of paying their taxes faced foreclosure on their tangible assets, usually meaning their land. As farmers became more desperate, the situation became volatile, especially in Massachusetts, which refused to allow taxes to be paid in debased paper. Protesters marched against local courthouses, seeking to close down judicial hearings and thereby stop foreclosures. The government of Massachusetts responded by suspending the right of habeas corpus, enabling protesters to be jailed indefinitely without trial. That led to heightened antiboss rhetoric; rebel leaders advocated smashing the "tyrannical" government of Massachusetts. The protests culminated in an open rebellion in 1787. Under the leadership of Daniel Shays, a Revolutionary War veteran, some four thousand "Shaysites" formed a local militia and attempted to seize the national armory in Springfield, Massachusetts.

The national Congress, hamstrung by the Articles, was unable to raise troops to oppose the rebels. Shays's Rebellion was finally suppressed by a private militia, raised by a veteran Continental Army general and privately financed by Massachusetts merchants. In the aftermath, Massachusetts reduced the tax on farmers, but this in turn precipitated a crisis in the state's finances. Jefferson, writing from distant Paris, where he was American ambassador, remained sanguine, opining that "the tree of liberty must be refreshed from time to time with the blood of patriots and tyrants."[17] Others worried that the new country was degenerating into lawlessness. Jefferson himself was concerned that the lack of national funding made it impossible to fund an American navy, which in turn left merchant ships vulnerable to slave-hunting pirates operating from bases in North Africa.

Constitutional Convention, 1787

The political bargain was failing: internal and external security was compromised. Commerce within the country, and hence material well-being, was threatened by high internal tariffs. The difficulties of securing coordination among the states stymied the westward expansion on which the growth of the country depended. That was the context in which delegates from twelve states (Rhode Island declined the invitation) gathered in the statehouse in Philadelphia in summer 1787. The ostensible purpose of the convention was to amend the Articles. But the unanimity requirement of the "perpetual union" made that impossible without Rhode Island. Many of the delegates, including Madison of Virginia and Hamilton of New York—future coauthors of *The Federalist*—were in any event convinced that the Articles must be thrown out and replaced by a new constitutional bargain establishing a stronger central government. That required reimagining the union as a federated democratic republic.

The conventional wisdom, exemplified by the Articles and based on the experience of Greece and Rome, was that a republic must be small and sovereign, and thus that the American union must consist of an alliance among small, sovereign republics. Moreover, some remained convinced that the high level of civic virtue necessary to sustain a republic could only be fostered in an agrarian rather than a commercial society. Madison, Hamilton, and the other Federalists (as they came to be known) had to convince skeptical fellow delegates that a wealthy (and thus partly commercial) republic could be scaled up successfully. They needed a plausible plan for how to do that.

Ever present in the background was the question of slavery. Some of the delegates, cognizant of slavery's moral wickedness, wished to ban human bondage outright, or at least ensure that it would soon wither away. The emphasis of the Declaration of Independence on the moral equality of all persons and an inalienable, God-given right to liberty and the pursuit of happiness seemed to promise something of the kind, albeit its primary author was a slave owner. Delegates from some southern states were equally adamant that slavery remain a permanent, legally protected feature of their state's economic and social structure. Others equivocated, hopeful that the issue could be kept off the table. Because the Articles had been based on the complete sovereignty of each state— and hence the full authority of each state government to set the rules governing property and commerce—slavery was indeed off the table in 1777. Ten years later, it was clear to many delegates that full state sovereignty was unworkable. The topic of the legal status of slavery was no longer avoidable; decisions on slavery would be built into any revised bargain.

In addition to the widespread recognition that the Articles had failed, the Federalists had two things going for them. First, Washington, the immensely respected hero of the revolution, was in attendance. Washington was the unanimous choice as president of the convention—and an obvious choice for whatever constitutional executive office the delegates might ultimately agree on. Next, Madison had done his homework. He was a diligent and astute student of both political philosophy and history as well as a prolific and brilliant writer. His pamphlet "Vices of the Political System of the United States," published just a month before the convention opened, was a devastating indictment of the Articles. Madison also had a blueprint for a replacement constitution; called the "Virginia Plan," it quickly caught on as a framework. The delegates agreed that the national government would be federal: each state would retain a considerable authority, including determining the participation rights of citizens (who could vote and who could not) and setting local laws. But the states would have to give up sovereign powers in foreign policy, interstate commerce, and taxation. The national government would consist of legislative, executive, and judicial branches. Many specifics remained to be hammered out, but the Articles were now a dead letter.

Key features of Madison's Virginia Plan included the creation of a bicameral legislature (on the model of the British Parliament and most of the existing state constitutions) and proportional representation by population in one of the houses. But proportionate to *what* population? Northern delegates favored counting only freemen. The representatives from Georgia and the Carolinas urged counting all persons, including slaves—which would yield them more representatives. Northerners argued slaves should be assessed as taxable property; southerners disagreed since excluding slaves as property would reduce their federal tax burden.

The compromise was the infamous rule that "three-fifths" of the slave population would be included in determining the number of each state's representatives and the basis on which direct national taxes would be assessed. While the Constitution avoided the term *slaves* in favor of "all other Persons," slavery was decidedly on the table in 1787 and built into the bargain. In another compromise on slavery, a clause was added (on the motion of Butler of South Carolina, the quoter of Solon) to Article 4.[18] It required that "a person held to service or labor" who flees to another state was to be returned to that person's master in the state from which the freedom seeker had escaped; by this first version of the Fugitive Slave Law, the institution of slavery was, at least potentially, nationalized.[19]

In the "lower house" (the House of Representatives), the selection of legislative representatives would be directly by the enfranchised people of the state. Senators, in the "upper house," were elected indirectly by the legislature of each state (senators were directly elected only after 1912). In a key compromise demanded by the smaller states, the Senate preserved the Articles' principle of equal representation by state: two senators for each state, large or small. Yet each senator was to have an individual vote, honoring the principle of individual judgment.

The executive branch was hotly debated. It had to be strong enough to overcome the weaknesses of the Articles, but not so strong as to become a boss. The revolution had rejected the king, and with it, the British solution of a constitutional monarch. Athens had chosen most officials by lottery, but the Americans' widespread belief in the value of merit ruled that out. The Roman Republic had featured two consuls as executive officers; perhaps a committee of some sort might work? Finally, on repeated motions by James Wilson of Pennsylvania, and with the happy thought that Washington was available to fill the office, the delegates agreed on a single president, chosen for a four-year renewable term by an electoral college. Each state would send as many presidential electors as it had national representatives (House and Senate). The president could be removed by impeachment, in which both House and Senate would play a role. One other major hurdle was overcome when the delegates agreed that the judicial branch would be led by a "supreme tribunal" appointed by the Senate and serving for as long as the appointed justices chose, subject only to "good Behaviour."[20] The extent of the powers of this Supreme Court in respect to the other branches of government was subsequently determined through practice.

Then there was the question of implementation and revision. The new bargain must be amendable; the Articles' rule that the agreement was perpetual and required unanimous approval of the states had proved vacuous. The ultimate agreement was that amendments could be made by either a national convention (at the time of this book's writing that has not yet been tried) or congressional proposal subsequently ratified by three-quarters of the states. In America's history thus far, there have been twenty-seven amendments made.

The final draft of the Constitution included the stirring preamble, which assigns authorship of the bargain to "We the People of the United States," and asserts that its purpose was "to form a more perfect Union, establish Justice, ensure domestic Tranquility, provide for the common defense, promote the general Welfare, and secure the Blessings of Liberty to ourselves and our Posterity." It was signed in September 1787 by thirty-nine of the fifty-five delegates who had attended. Before it became the law of the land, the new bargain had to be ratified by conventions in two-thirds (nine out of thirteen) of the states. The delegates to those state conventions were to be popularly elected. The handful of elite and propertied men at the bargaining table in Philadelphia had all along been looking over their shoulders at a vastly larger constituency of free, mostly but not entirely white, men.

Debating Ratification

The nine-state minimum for ratification was achieved on June 21, 1788, when New Hampshire approved the new national bargain. But ratification had not been a foregone conclusion. Deep worries about the dangers of a powerful centralized government remained, ardently expressed in verbal and written arguments by those who became known as the Anti-Federalists. Moreover, neither New York nor Virginia was among the early ratifying states. If either of the biggest states held out, the prospects for the new bargain would be dim. The urgent need to make the case for the Constitution as America's defining civic bargain in New

York was taken up by Hamilton, Madison, and John Jay, who planned and wrote the eighty-five newspaper editorials later collected as *The Federalist*.[21] Designed to instruct a sometimes-recalcitrant citizenry in the thinking that lay behind the bargain struck in Philadelphia, the series is a preeminent example of self-conscious civic education.

The editorials were published anonymously under the name "Publius" in honor of the Roman general and republican founder Publius Valerius Poplicola. The most articulate and influential of the Anti-Federalists (probably Robert Yates of New York, who left the convention early in protest) wrote editorials under the pseudonym Brutus, the name of both the Roman republican founder who killed the last of Rome's early kings and his distant descendant, who helped to assassinate Julius Caesar. Greek and Roman history, along with Enlightenment political philosophy, was much in evidence in the ratification debates. Among the topics animating "the greatest non-violent verbal battle ever waged in America" were scale, civic virtue, and slavery.[22]

Brutus laid out the "small republic" argument, with reference to both the philosophy of Montesquieu and ancient history:

> A free republic cannot succeed over a country of such immense extent, containing such a number of inhabitants. . . . History furnishes no example of a free republic, any thing like the extent of the United States. The Grecian republics were of small extent; so also was that of the Romans. Both of these, it is true, in process of time, extended their conquests over large territories of country; and the consequence was, that their governments were changed from that of free governments to those of the most tyrannical that ever existed in the world.[23]

Brutus's point was clear: when a republic grew large, it led to tyranny. Political authority must reside in the small individual states rather than in the expansive union.

Writing as Publius, Madison countered in *Federalist* 10. He took on the questions of scale by reference to corruption through the emergence of political factions, each seeking its own narrow interests and thereby trampling on the common good. Although elsewhere in his writings Madison emphasized the necessity of civic virtue to a republic, in *Federalist* 10 he boldly rejected the notion that the new American republic would be primarily grounded in civic virtue or even civic friendship. He defined *faction* as "a number of citizens, whether amounting to a majority or a minority of the whole, who are united and actuated by some common impulse of passion, or of interest."

Madison agreed that factions threatened both the rights of other citizens and the common good. Distinctions among people, and especially wealth inequality, "kindle their unfriendly passions and excite their most violent conflicts." There were two possible "cures" for faction: eliminating either liberty or viewpoint diversity. Neither was acceptable in a free country, and therefore factions were both inevitable and invariably destructive in small, direct democracies: "Hence it is that such democracies have ever been spectacles of turbulence and contention; have ever been found incompatible with personal security or the rights of property; and have in general been as short in their lives as they have been violent in their deaths."

Madison then developed his famous distinction between republic and democracy (chapter 1)—one that had not featured in early American discussions of self-government and was not accepted by the Anti-Federalists. The key features of a republic were, he claimed, representation versus direct voting in a mass citizen assembly, and importantly, "the greater number of citizens and extent of territory." Bigger was better for a republic because it lessened the *danger* of faction: "extend the sphere, and you take in a greater variety of parties and interests; you make it less probable that a majority of the whole will have a common motive to invade the rights of other citizens." That is, scaling up eliminated the danger of a majority establishing itself as a boss over the others. Or or least due to coordination problems, it will be less likely that they would succeed in doing so. In sum, majority tyranny, a central concern of the Anti-Federalists, became less likely as the scale increased.

With this contention, Madison took the challenges of scale and civic virtue by the horns, boldly asserting that in the presumed absence of the deep ethical friendship that would arise from a shared commitment to virtue, scale itself would counter the dangers of self-interest and passion. In a related argument (*Federalist* 51), Madison defended the constitutional principle of separation of powers with the claim that "ambition must be made to counteract ambition"—that is, the selfish interests of the officials in each branch of government, an interest in maximizing their own power and influence, would ensure that they jealously guarded against any other branch growing too powerful. In framing a government for men as opposed to angels, he bluntly declared, "You must first enable the government to controul the governed; and in the next place, oblige it to controul itself." A strong central government would address the first requirement; human nature itself would take care of the second.

In his third letter, in which he maintained that representatives can represent only those who elect them, Brutus drew attention to the disconnect between the publicly proclaimed values of the new country and the proposed Constitution's embrace of slavery. He ripped the flimsy veil from the three-fifths compromise, which had assigned representatives by

> adding to the whole Number of free Persons, including those bound to Service for a Term of Years, and excluding Indians not taxed, three fifths of all other Persons. . . . What a strange and unnecessary accumulation of words are here used to conceal from the public eye what might have been expressed in the following concise manner. Representatives are to be proportioned among the states respectively, according to the number of freemen and slaves inhabiting them.

Brutus noted that the property of slave owners prominently included "their fellow men, who are held in bondage, in defiance of every idea of benevolence, justice, and religion, and contrary to all the principles of liberty, which have been publickly avowed in the late glorious revolution." He ironically suggested that the argument for including slaves in apportioning representatives could be extended to horses and oxen.

To the moral issue, Publius had no good response. Madison himself was a slave owner, as were many of the delegates to the Philadelphia conference. In *Federalist* 42, Madison deplored the "barbarism" of the

"unnatural [transatlantic] traffic" in "unfortunate Africans" and regret-
ted that the Constitution had put off any consideration of ending it until
1808. But in stating that "it is not difficult" to account for the delay, he
implicitly acknowledged the necessity of getting the southern states on
board. In *Federalist* 54, Madison offered a lawyerly rejoinder to the Anti-
Federalist arguments against the three-fifths compromise: while the
slave was regarded by the law as a "moral person," enslaved people were
also legal property. Counting slaves for the purposes of representation
was justified by a counterfactual: "if the laws were to restore the rights
which have been taken away, the negroes could no longer be refused an
equal share of representation with the other inhabitants." In this preg-
nant sentence, Madison seems to acknowledge that the natural right to
liberty and equality, celebrated in the Declaration of Independence, had
wrongly "been taken away" from enslaved persons while simultaneously
subordinating natural rights to human-made laws.

The law was not just about persons, Madison continued in *Federalist*
54; "government is instituted no less for protection of the property, than
of the persons of individuals." Charles Pinckney of South Carolina, Butler's fellow delegate at the Philadelphia convention, also emphasized
property rights in justifying his support of the constitutional bargain at
that state's ratification convention: "considering all circumstances, we
have made the best terms for the security of this species of property
[slaves] it was in our power to make."[24] The "power" Pinckney alluded
to was the southern states' ability to kill the bargain if they were forced
to give too much and get too little: if the two Carolinas and Georgia
joined Rhode Island in opposition, the nine-state supermajority necessary for ratification would have been put at risk: "union" would be out
of the question. The negotiated compromise at the heart of the constitutional bargain was therefore explicit—even while Pinckney employed
yet another delicate circumlocution in referring to enslaved persons.

With ratification by twelve states (and the coerced agreement of
Rhode Island), the Federalists won the great verbal battle: the Constitution was established as, and remains today, the United States' fundamental
civic bargain. That it was imperfect from the standpoint of justice as well
as the principles of liberty and equality was clear from the beginning.

Those imperfections, called out in Franklin's final speech in Philadelphia (referenced in our introduction), were necessitated by the power of the southern states to defeat the new bargain; Butler, Pinckney, and their fellow southern delegates in Philadelphia were committed to sustaining slavery, and accordingly, they argued long and hard. More important, everyone at the time knew that they had the power to impose their views: ratification of the bargain would fail if the Philadelphia delegates did not compromise with what some of them already recognized as an inherent evil.

The aspiration of the Constitution's preamble, for justice and "a more perfect Union," would be potentially addressed by amendment. Indeed, the Anti-Federalists achieved part of their goal when the Federalists were constrained to accept amendments making explicit the individual liberties of citizens and the limits on the powers of the federal government. Although he initially thought them irrelevant, Madison himself authored the ten amendments ratified in 1791 and known ever since as the Bill of Rights.

The question that would face the country in years to come was whether the bargain could be adequately renegotiated, thereby avoiding the collapse of the union and resort to violence. Of course, the final answer was "no": some seventy years after the ratification of the Constitution, Americans fought the Civil War, the bloodiest conflict in our history to date. That war ended slavery and enfranchised former slaves. But the aftermath of the Civil War allowed southern states to build systems that formalized indignity, restricted voting, and corroded civic friendship. All subsequent adjustments to the basic civic bargain have been hostage to that history. Americans live with the consequences today.

Scale and Political Parties

Between the later eighteenth century and outbreak of the Civil War in 1860, America fulfilled and exceeded the ambitions of the founders, who like Madison, had dreamed of the possibility of a great republic, capable of taking its place alongside the great powers of Europe.

Between the Louisiana Purchase, land grabs following one-sided conflicts with Native Americans, and other acquisitions, the territorial extent of the country increased 3.5 times over, from about 860,000 to 3 million square miles. Meanwhile, the population of the United States increased tenfold, to over 30 million. That included 500,000 free Black people, close to 4 million enslaved Black people, and some 340,000 Native Americans of whom only 1 in 10 was "taxed"—that is, regarded as a citizen. The Hispanic population was about 150,000; Asian and Pacific Islanders were about 35,000.[25]

Immigration from Europe boomed: between 1820 and 1830, almost 500,000 Europeans came to live in America; in the decade of the 1850s, the number of immigrants was about 2.5 million. Some of these were Irish laborers, fleeing famine and brutal conditions in the United Kingdom. Many others came from Germany and settled as farmers in the Midwest. Poles, Czechs, and Scandinavians also arrived in large numbers. By the beginning of the Civil War, twenty new states had been admitted to the union. The Thirty-Sixth Congress (1859–60) sat 66 senators and 238 members of the House. Both the scale and stakes of politics were greatly magnified.

In contrast to the small, ideologically and ethnically homogeneous communities in which colonial era traditions of local self-government had emerged, the country and its government had grown vastly larger and much more diverse. Madison's conviction that a bigger republic would be better able to handle the problem of factional self-interest was put to the test. The Constitution provided a framework. But how, without a boss to run things, could the people who made up the increasingly large and diverse citizen population strike the many local and national bargains that were necessary for the maintenance of security and prosperity (keeping in mind that many were poor and some were destitute)? The answer was the development of organized political parties. The two-dominant-party system that emerged within the constitutional frame structured public debates on policy and promoted decisive outcomes. Organized parties made representation more straightforward but also more coarse-grained by aggregating a range of domestic as well as foreign policy issues under the banner of the party's platform and articulated in speeches by party leaders. Civic education would come to be repackaged as partisanship.

At the time of ratification, none of the constitutional founders were members of a political party, nor were they advocates of organized factionalism. Washington, unanimously chosen by the Electoral College as the nation's first president in 1788 and reelected without opposition in 1792, was actively hostile to parties. During the eight years of the Washington administration, however, two developments led to the emergence of the Federalist and Republican Parties. The first was the formation of local societies, designated as Democratic or Republican (or both), which advocated for stronger forms of popular participation in government, and protested what they saw as bossy overreach and monarchical tendencies by the government. Meanwhile, Madison and Jefferson broke sharply with Adams, Washington's vice president, and Hamilton, a close associate of Washington, over various matters, notably the creation of a national bank. Elections for representatives to the House and Senate became more sharply partisan. Hamilton's supporters seized the title of Federalists. The Madison-Jefferson block labeled itself Republican and hewed more closely to the agenda of the Democratic-Republican societies.

Washington declined to stand for a third term, warning in his farewell address about the dangers of faction. In 1796, in America's first contested presidential election, Federalist Adams was narrowly elected president. Adams and the Federalist majority in Congress inflamed the fears and anger of the Republicans by passing a series of Alien and Sedition Acts, hardening the process of naturalization, and imprisoning those who criticized the president or Congress. After the hotly contested election of 1800 was narrowly decided in his favor, Republican Jefferson sought a conciliatory line. Speaking at his inauguration, he averred that now that the citizens had voted "according to the rules of the Constitution," all Americans would "of course arrange themselves under the will of the law, and unite in common efforts for the common good." After all, he concluded, "we are all Republicans: we are all Federalists."[26]

Jefferson sought to undo much of the legislation passed by the Federalists but found it hard going. Eighteen months after his inauguration, facing constant opposition from Federalists in Congress, he told an associate that he planned to "sink federalism into an abyss from which there shall be no resurrection for it." The slip from the language of unity and the common good to that of enmity and destruction foretold problems for the republic. Looking back at what he came to think of as the "revolution of 1800," Jefferson saw himself as a pragmatist; citing Solon the Athenian, he opined that "no more good must be attempted than the nation can bear." Here Jefferson employed the exact line from Plutarch's *Life of Solon* that Butler had quoted in 1787. While different in goals and talent, both men understood equally well that no political bargains can ever be a "first-best."[27] The gulf between Jefferson's high idealism in the Declaration and his Solonian pragmatism as president, between his inaugural optimism about unity for the common good and his grim wish for the destruction of his political opponents, captures the problem of scaling up self-government while sustaining civic friendship.

With the purchase of the Louisiana Territory from France, Jefferson doubled the size of America's territory. The Federalists complained that it was a waste of money, but the move was popular, and Jefferson was reelected in a landslide in 1804. As the Federalists found themselves on the wrong side of public policy debates, Republicans, who reconfigured themselves first as Democratic-Republicans and then as Democrats, controlled the presidency until 1841. Meanwhile, the tenor of American politics became more overtly democratic in the sense of directly reflecting popular opinion expressed by the voters in an ever-widening franchise. Yet it did not immediately become any more liberal in the sense of respecting the rights of all persons.

Jacksonian Democracy

The expansion of the country, accompanied by economic development and hardening moral attitudes, exacerbated the debate over slavery. In the northern states, slavery was slowly being eliminated; in the South, it was ever more deeply entrenched, economically and legally. Fierce political battles raged over the status of new territories and states, with northerners eager to keep them slave free, and southerners equally determined to expand the ambit of their special social system. With the close-run "Missouri Compromise" of 1820, which added Missouri as a slave state while banning slavery in the Louisiana Territory north of latitude 36° 30', the slave versus free state balance in the Senate was maintained. The political bargain held, keeping the peace and enabling continued growth. But the question of the status of millions of Black residents was kicked down the road.

In 1828, Andrew Jackson, renowned as a war hero, first against native peoples and then the British at the Battle of New Orleans in 1815, won the presidency at the head of the Democrats, now the first truly national political party. The election featured near-universal white male franchise and fierce partisanship. It was stoked by partisan newspapers, heavy electioneering, and clever strategic maneuvering. Jackson's presidency advanced democracy as self-government within the white population and brought men from outside the traditional New England and Virginia elites into national affairs. It also underlined the fact that Native Americans had been excluded from the constitutional table. Indigenous peoples were now treated as foreign powers, and a treaty between nations could be broken as soon as one side saw an advantage in doing so. The result was massive removals of Indigenous peoples from their traditional homelands. Tensions over slavery grew as moral arguments made by abolitionists gained traction in the North, resistance by enslaved people drew ferocious reprisals in the South, and technological and agronomic developments made cotton a viable cash crop outside the Deep South.

In 1831, French aristocrat Alexis de Tocqueville took a nine-month tour of the United States. His ostensible mission was to study American prisons, but the result of his trip was a much broader and enduringly influential interpretation of American politics and society: *Democracy in America* (2 volumes, 1835, 1840). Tocqueville saw that among white men, American democracy was in fact collective self-government: "the people [are] the real directing power; and although the form of government is representative, it is evident that the opinions, the prejudices, the interests, and even the passions of the community are hindered by no durable obstacles from exercising a perpetual influence on society."[28] He argued that equality was the animating value of democracy and that political equality led to (by European standards) a remarkable degree of social equality. He was struck by the important role of local associations and civil society as conduits of civic education, observing that it was in their local communities and voluntary associations that Americans learned to practice the skills of democratic citizenship.

Tocqueville saw all this as exemplary of a wider "democratic revolution," which he regarded as both the wave of the future and dangerous given the ever-present threat of majority tyranny. He traced the revolution back to the era of the Puritan founding and recognized that it was powered by (and helped to drive) the growth of an industrial and commercial society. Tocqueville's analysis of American democracy is justly famous, and he was in some ways remarkably prescient in his prognoses. While he was wrong to claim that a country lacking an aristocracy could never produce a world-class military, he correctly surmised that the issue of slavery would tear the nation apart. A short human generation after his visit, that is exactly what happened.

Sectionalism, Nationalism, and Scale

Congress banned the transatlantic slave trade in 1808 as soon as it was constitutionally able to do so; around the same time, slavery was abolished by Britain, first for the North Atlantic trade in 1807, and then throughout the British Empire in 1833. Yet the total number of American slaves was growing rapidly due to native births.[29] Neither of the two dominant political parties, the Jacksonian Democrats and the anti-Jacksonian Whigs, was eager to make slavery an issue in national politics. Opinions on the topic were only incompletely sorted geographically; neither party could afford to give up its northern or southern partisans. Moral abolitionists, Black and white, called for an immediate end to slavery. Yet even some northern opponents of slavery were unwilling to countenance Black people as full citizens; legislation in several northern states narrowed the definition of citizenship on racial lines. In Pennsylvania, thousands of free Black men were disenfranchised in 1838, when

a revised state constitution, ratified by the slenderest of majorities, in-
serted the word "white" before "freemen" in its definition of the citizen.[30] The question of whether civic friendship could ever extend across
racial lines was starkly posed, and Tocqueville's worry about majority
tyranny was vindicated, by this blunt use of majoritarian process to strip
fellow citizens of rights.

The movement for women's voting rights was jump-started at a convention in Seneca Falls, New York, in 1848. Elizabeth Cady Stanton, one
of the organizers, was the primary author of a Declaration of Senti-
ments, self-consciously modeled on the Declaration of Independence
and signed by a hundred attendees. It proclaimed that all men *and
women* were created equal and asserted the "sacred rights" of elective
franchise.[31] Among the active supporters of the convention's suffrage
resolution (which passed narrowly) was a Black man whose best-selling
autobiography, *Narrative of the Life of Frederick Douglass, an American
Slave* (1845), had given new life to the abolitionist movement by helping
to expose the lie that slaves were kindly treated by their masters.

Some politicians dreamed that a leap in scale might diffuse sectional
debates over slavery. The establishment of the Republic of Texas, after
the unexpected military victory of a Texas militia over the Mexican
army, stimulated nationalist visions of democratic America's "manifest
destiny." Negotiations with Britain next led to the incorporation of the
Oregon Territory. A war with Mexico, engineered by the ambitious
president James Polk, gained California and New Mexico. But Polk's
hope that belligerent nationalism would overshadow sectionalism was
dashed when the question of the status of the newly acquired territories
returned slavery to the center of national politics.

The complicated legislative Compromise of 1850 offered temporary
relief to both political parties but resolved nothing. Along with negotiated arrangements for limiting slavery in some of the new territories,
the legislation included a strengthened version of the Fugitive Slave
Law that had been embedded in the Constitution and reiterated in 1793.
Responding to the Underground Railroad, the informal network of
abolitionists that spirited freedom-seeking slaves out of the South, the
new law required ordinary citizens and local authorities to aid in slave

recovery. It mandated heavy penalties for abetting runaways and denied jury trial to fugitives. Abolitionism based on nonviolent moral suasion seemed increasingly dated. Douglass opined that "the only way to make the Fugitive Slave Law a dead letter is to make half-a-dozen or more dead kidnappers."[32]

To Civil War

The 1850 Compromise quickly unraveled over the status of the Kansas-Nebraska Territory, west of Missouri. Both pro- and antislavery settlers flooded into the territory and mounted competing territorial conventions aimed at petitioning for statehood. Rampant voting corruption by proslavery partisans was accompanied by killing and arson by large organized militias and small terror groups. "Bloody Kansas" was reprised inside the Capitol in 1856, when in retaliation for a fiery antislavery speech on the Senate floor, a southern representative savagely caned Charles Sumner of New York at his Senate desk. A year later, the Supreme Court issued a startlingly broad decision in the matter of an enslaved man, Dredd Scott. Scott's lawyers argued that since he had lived for a time in the free Wisconsin Territory, he was no longer legally enslaved.

The Supreme Court decided otherwise. The majority opinion, written by Chief Justice Roger Brooke Taney, offered a multipoint argument. First, residence in a free territory had no effect on an enslaved person's status. Next, asserting judicial supremacy over the legislative branch, Taney declared that the Missouri Compromise of 1820 was void because it violated the constitutionally protected property rights of slave owners. Finally, falsely maintaining that Black people had had no part in the ratification of the Constitution, Taney opined that free Black people had never been citizens of the United States and therefore could be denied both civic and civil rights. The court thus claimed the boss-like power to strip free Black people of their citizenship.[33]

Amid the escalating violence and in shocked response to the *Dredd Scott* decision, the Whig Party imploded. It was replaced by a new Republican Party (the name recycled from Jefferson's era), entirely northern and ideologically opposed to slavery. The opposing Democrats consolidated their hold on the South, but they were divided on how to defend slavery and "states' rights." When Lincoln, a Republican, was elected president in 1860, defeating three proslavery candidates, the southern response was quick and decisive. Before Lincoln's inauguration, South Carolina, soon followed by other southern states, held a constitutional convention and seceded from the union.

The breakaway states declared themselves to be the Confederate States of America; they eventually wrote and ratified their own constitution. Meanwhile, the Confederates began seizing US forts and property in the South. At his inauguration, Lincoln made it clear that he would not countenance the breakup of the union. A battle between Confederate and Union forces at Fort Sumter, guarding the harbor of Charlestown, South Carolina, opened hostilities. The war that followed was contested between the United and Confederate States of America. Each, by its own lights, was a democratic republic.

With the Civil War (1861–65), the imperfect civic bargain of the founders—hammered out in Philadelphia, sealed by ratification of the Constitution, and frequently revised yet still inadequate to the challenge of ending slavery—was finally broken. Vastly expanded scale, increasingly entrenched interests, and firm moral convictions rendered further negotiation nugatory. The founders had depended on the bonds of civic friendship along with the common interest in security and welfare to hold together a union in which regional interests diverged and passions ran high. But fellow citizens now saw one another only as deadly enemies. The fighting was horrendous. According to a recent estimate, upward of 750,000 American combatants died in the resulting war, more than in all the United States' external wars combined to date.[34]

In the course of the war, Lincoln's Emancipation Proclamation freed slaves in the Confederacy. Then after the war, between 1865 and 1870, a series of amendments to the Constitution established a revised civic bargain: Slavery and race-based restrictions on citizenship were formally ended. The Thirteenth Amendment abolished slavery "within the United States, or any place subject to their jurisdiction." The Fourteenth

Amendment made citizens of all those "born or naturalized in the United States," including former enslaved persons, and provided all citizens with "equal protection under the laws," thereby extending the liberties guaranteed in the Bill of Rights to the states. The Fifteenth Amendment prohibited states from disenfranchising voters "on account of race, color, or previous condition of servitude."

Reconstruction, Retrenchment, and Increasing Scale

Despite the resistance of President Johnson, who took office after Lincoln's assassination, from 1866, when the Republicans regained a dominant majority in Congress, until 1877, efforts were made to enforce this revised civic bargain. Those attempts faced fierce and frequently violent opposition by the Ku Klux Klan and other terrorist organizations. A major economic recession, followed by a contested presidential election in 1876 and a deal cut by political insiders, led to the withdrawal of federal troops from the former Confederate states and ended the period of Reconstruction. The way was left open for the imposition of Jim Crow rules in southern states, effectively reversing the effect of the recent amendments while stripping most southern Black people of both civic and civil rights.

The letter of federal law proved irrelevant to the ability of southern whites to impose a systematic regime of indignity on Black people; appeals to civic virtue did not dissuade them from treating those who opposed them as enemies, subject to every form of violence. As in Pennsylvania in 1838 and the *Dredd Scott* decision of 1857, the ratchet of participatory citizenship was reversed, violating a fundamental condition of the civic bargain. In "the Great Migration" of 1916 to 1970, some six million Black people voted with their feet, leaving the South for urban areas in the industrial North. In the old Confederacy, the Jim Crow regime continued in full force until weakened by consequential Supreme Court decisions in the mid-twentieth century as well as an organized and effective civil rights movement. The Twenty-Fourth Amendment, ratified in 1964, abolished poll taxes in federal elections. It was followed by the expansive Voting Rights Act of 1965.

Meanwhile, some nine million immigrants, primarily from southern and eastern Europe but many also from Asia, had arrived in the United States in the late nineteenth and early twentieth centuries. By 1920, America's population topped a hundred million; by 1970, it was over two hundred million. Debates raged over the kind of education that could inculcate the skills and virtues of citizenship. The goal was building what we are calling civic friendship among ethnically diverse residents, and committing them to assuming the duties as well as embracing the rights of democratic citizens. Did that require linguistic and cultural assimilation to some conception of "standard American" values? That question remains unresolved in the twenty-first century as rates of immigration have again spiked and immigrants to the United States are primarily from Latin America, Asia, and Africa. Recent research suggests, however, that forced assimilation was historically counterproductive in its primary goals of Americanizing immigrants from abroad.

The campaign for women's suffrage gained momentum in the later nineteenth century: women were granted voting rights in Wyoming in 1869, and in most other western states by 1914. The political leaders in western states had realized that attracting women was an imperative to local economic growth and that voting rights provided an incentive for women to migrate west. In 1920, the Nineteenth Amendment forbade states to deny the right to vote on the basis of sex. Native Americans were finally guaranteed voting rights in 1947, tardy redress for the first peoples of the continent whose native lands were largely confiscated through violent conquest by generation after generation of foreign settlers. People of Asian ancestry, including Japanese Americans, many of whom had suffered the misery and indignity of being forced out of their homes and herded into camps as suspected traitors during World War II, were ensured voting rights in 1952.

The most recent consequential amendment to the Constitution, extending voting rights to all citizens aged eighteen and above, was ratified in 1971 in the context of the increasingly unpopular Vietnam War. Conscription into state militias and the national armed forces, employed since colonial times and provided for in the Constitution as a duty of citizenship, ended two years later.

In the last fifty years, proposed revisions to the civic bargain have tended to focus on the matters of individual rights addressed in the Bill of Rights, and increasingly, the extension of rights to persons as members of groups, defined variously by race, ethnicity, nationality, immigration status, sex, gender, and sexual orientation. Yet the ferocity of recent conflicts over state-level rules governing voter identification, voting by mail, polling places, and vote certification—notably but certainly not exclusively in the states of the old Confederacy—is evidence that the basic question of "who *actually* has a place at the civic table" has not been fully resolved. Meanwhile, polarization and partisan gridlock have thwarted, at least for the time being, the possibility of constitutional amendment or the sort of comprehensive legislation represented by the Voting Rights Act. In lieu of those remedies, the Supreme Court has reasserted itself as a highly consequential branch of American government, establishing new rules on, for example, abortion, voting rights, and gun ownership. Other important rules are created by executive fiat and appointed administrators. In many ways, this represents an admission of failure concerning the original civic bargain: more bossiness now seems to many the only way to resolve conflicts in the current political climate.

Can America's constitutional civic bargain be renegotiated in the face of a toxic mix of misinformation, ideological rigidity, and the threat and fact of resort to violence? Is civic friendship again being replaced by the fatal enmity that led to the Civil War? What civic education might shore up the civic bargain and enable democracy to survive? These are the questions to which we turn in the remainder of this book.

6

PATTERNS IN DEMOCRATIC
BARGAINING AND SURVIVAL

The previous chapters explored democracy's development "in the wild" via four major historical cases, each framed as a series of negotiated agreements within a particular chronological, geographic, and cultural setting. Over time, those agreements (some successful, and others not) were reworked and revised, eventually resulting in a civic bargain that enabled collective self-government by citizens.

We now look back at those cases, probing for crosscutting insights about the development of democracy and the processes that pushed it forward, creating in each instance a system of self-government capable of surviving and thriving for an extensive period. What do the cases reveal about the role of bargaining and norms that make effective bargaining possible? What challenges did the sequence of political bargains, eventuating in a civic bargain, have to confront and overcome? How were those challenges met or exacerbated by scale, as state populations grew larger and more diverse, and as states that became democratic competed in a world of often-hostile rivals? When democracies survived or failed—why did that happen? What lessons might be gleaned for today's beleaguered systems of self-governance?

Case Summaries

Throughout this book, we have explained democracy as a negotiated system of collective self-governance, where citizens are a substantial and internally diverse subset of the population, and citizens are responsible only to one another for public decisions and conflict resolution. We outlined the seven essential conditions for getting and keeping democracy. There is no boss other than the citizens themselves. Adequate levels of security and welfare are achieved and sustained. Citizenship is defined as a right of active participation in collective self-governance, exercised within defined boundaries. Citizens lead the institutions of decision-making and conflict resolution, ensuring basic political freedoms and equality of civic standing. Citizens compromise in good faith as they negotiate the terms of their shared lives together, acknowledging the impossibility of legislating perfect justice. They treat one another as civic friends, engaged in a common enterprise, rather than as enemies to be destroyed. They create and sustain formal and informal ways of educating one another, generation by generation, in the material and ethical benefits of self-government as well as concerning the costs that must be paid in terms of civic responsibility. We posit that each of these is a necessary condition for democracy. But we are concerned with their copresence as opposed to their measurement. As our historical chapters have shown, the seven conditions are manifest in different forms and in varying degrees across ancient and modern states that fit our definition as self-governing democracies.

To appreciate the differing approaches to the seven conditions, let's reconsider the four cases. Ancient Athenians invented their democracy—the earliest well-documented state-level system of citizen self-government—creating an original civic bargain with an extensive free, male citizenship and citizen-centered institutions in about 508 BCE. This democratic government was predicated on a long, previous history of political bargaining among rich and poor Athenians. Operating as a relatively small citizen community of free, fighting-capable men, Athens's governance was highly participative, with an open assembly and courts along with elected and lottery-selected officials. Security and welfare were achieved through the expansion of the sphere of private initiative and effective collective action—including the exploitation of noncitizens, both at home and abroad. Citizens educated one another through the practice of self-government, and publicly committed themselves to one another and the common good through a variety of civic rituals. Although the Athenians did not extend the franchise after 508 BCE, they did revise their civic bargain to reduce the volatility of popular decision-making in the aftermath of a bloody civil war in 403 BCE. Athenian democracy lasted with only brief interruptions for some two centuries until the Macedonian conquest in 322 BCE. Although democracy was periodically revived thereafter, the Athenians never again enjoyed a long period of self-rule without a boss.

The Roman Republic was inaugurated when an unacceptably autocratic ruling king was replaced by a coalition of elite Romans, the Patricians, in 509 BCE. Political bargaining began in earnest in the early fifth century BCE, when the majority of its fighting men, the Plebeians, went on strike against Patrician domination. Following this first Plebeian secession of 494 BCE, a series of political bargains enabled the community to grow by conquering and incorporating neighboring states in Italy. The Roman civic bargain was finalized when Plebeians achieved civic equality in 287 BCE. Rome's democratic republic balanced the wealth and power of the rich with the labor of ordinary citizens, who participated in civic assemblies steered by elected officials. Military prowess, built on a shared commitment to civic virtues—learned in army service, through shared rituals, in tales of past exemplars, and summed up in the ideal of res publica—grew the Roman Republic into a Mediterranean-wide empire. As it expanded, the Roman state bound the conquered by threats of force, but for those who yielded or bargained, also with grants of social and legal privileges, and finally political participation rights, thereby dramatically expanding the citizenship. This larger republican democracy blended participatory civic governance in and around Rome with virtual representation across a vastly wider realm. Starting in the later second century, the civic bargain came under increasing strain as Romans treated one another as public enemies versus civic friends. It collapsed in a multigenerational civil war culminating in the late first century BCE. Res publica was replaced with the rule of an emperor, albeit one who claimed to have restored the ancestral regime.

In Britain, bossless collective self-government, across an extensive and socially diverse citizen body, emerged only in the early twentieth century, when the voting franchise for electing Parliament was extended, first to all adult men and shortly thereafter to the full adult population. Through its long prior history, the nation was ruled by a hybrid government platform, first combining monarch, nobles and church, and later adding an elected Parliament. The authority of the kings was always limited by the other participants in the platform; the king's power and the role of state religion diminished over time, while that of Parliament steadily grew. Yet only a small fraction of the adult male population was able to vote for elected MPs before the twentieth century. Nonetheless, British democracy was founded on a centuries-long development of the institutions, legal practices, and civic culture that enabled "His Majesty's subjects" to become the self-governing citizens of modern times.

The civic bargain that stabilized the nascent American democratic republic was sealed in 1788 with the ratification of the Constitution by nine of the original thirteen states. Voting citizens were initially taxpaying or landowning adult males, with requirements set variously by each state. The national civic community excluded from participatory citizenship not only women but also millions of Black slaves. But by the end of the first quarter of the nineteenth century, property requirements for voting by free white men had been largely abandoned. Citizens participated by voting for representatives and service on juries, although few Black Americans held civic rights before the Civil War finally ended slavery. While women had won the franchise by the 1920s, the notorious Jim Crow laws established in the southern states soon after the war prevented most southern Black Americans from exercising participation rights until the 1960s. The institutional framework, designed as a balance of powers among a bicameral representative system, president, and Supreme Court, has lasted for some 230 years. But American constitutional democracy had deep antecedents in the prerevolutionary experience of local and regional self-government. Some of America's civic practices and legal system were carried over from its British colonial period; once again, democracy developed over a long period.

Scale Challenges, Internal and External

In each of the four cases, citizens struggled with challenges of scale, and struck bargains to face those challenges. Each suffered periodic civil strife, rising to full-blown civil war. Internal disputes centered variously on political prerogatives, individual freedoms, civic rights and duties, property rights, foreign policy choices, and religious and national identities. Externally, they all struggled to mobilize enough human and resource capacity to defend themselves against hostile rivals. They all expanded state capacity by mobilizing citizens (or would-be citizens). They used that capacity to grow their wealth and power by establishing extensive overseas empires. The subjects of these empires were in some cases granted formal protection of laws, but not significant civic rights. The overseas territories controlled by the United States as colonies were more limited, but the post–World War II Pax Americana—secured by international troop postings and dominance in international organizations—could be seen as a de facto equivalent. Like the others, with minor exceptions, America has not extended rights of citizenship beyond its national borders.

In each case, the historical trajectory ending in democracy featured political bargains made long in advance of the civic bargain, establishing (or denying) the rights and responsibilities of different categories of state residents. In each case, democratic government was based in part on formal legislative, executive, and judicial institutions that were developed before the civic bargain was secured. The general trend before the civic bargain was struck was that those with decision power extended certain legal rights to certain others through political bargains, thereby enhancing the security and welfare of the shared community. Pressured by circumstances and popular demands, rulers first granted certain basic protections ("negative rights"—for example, freedom from threat of enslavement, unlawful seizure, and judgment without trial). Then at a later stage, participation ("positive") rights were extended across an extensive body of citizens. Those citizens either engaged directly in public decision-making or indirectly by voting for representatives.

In no case did reallocations of power, rights, and duties follow an easy path. The political bargains that led to the civic bargain were often painful, far from perfect, and frequently failed along the way. The civic bargain itself was always imperfect from the perspective of complete justice. In some instances, it was substantially revised. The first lesson arising from our case studies is that democracy is hard to get, not easy to keep, and never finished: democratic emergence and survival is never a sure thing.

How Comparable Are the Cases?

Before proceeding, we anticipate an objection: How much can we actually learn from comparing cases drawn from such different historical eras, each with its unique historical trajectory? Don't the significant differences among these diverse cases limit the value of any insights we might gain about democracy writ large? In chapter 1, we tackled two related concerns. We insisted on the distinction between democracy as self-government by a self-defined body of citizens and a just regime predicated on an egalitarian principle of distribution or full array of universal human rights. And we rejected the stark opposition of representative republic to direct democracy. We answer the "diverse cases" objection by reference to the seven essential conditions: at the relevant (albeit quite high) level of generality, each of the conditions is consistent enough across the cases to allow for meaningful comparisons.

Of course, there are huge differences between ancient Athens and Rome and early modern nation-states. The trope of contrasting ancient and modern states (to the detriment of one or the other) dates to the seventeenth century. We readily acknowledge obvious differences in economic development, technologies of production, religious beliefs and practices, and cultural assumptions. The demographic and economic scale of modernity is a major differentiator. Religious conflicts arising from competition among different forms of monotheism have created problems unknown to ancient pagans before the rise of Christianity.

Yet the conditions that enable a community to act collectively without a boss are, we believe, transhistorical. The core problem of achieving social order at scale may be solved by domination, through force and ideology, or a negotiated agreement that enables many diverse persons to share in power and participate in rule. In the first case, a boss rules over subjects. In the second, citizens rule themselves through managing benefits and costs, dividing both the moral and material payoffs of their political cooperation and the duties, including military service and the payment of taxes. They do so in a way that is regarded, for the time being, as fair enough. In each of our cases, that end was gained by creating and sustaining the conditions of no boss, security and welfare, defined citizenship, and citizen-led institutions; compromising with one another in good faith, on terms of civic friendship; and developing and sustaining effective forms of civic education. The rest of this chapter notes salient differences across time and space, while also seeking to vindicate our claim that attending to similarities among fundamental conditions allows for new insights into the general question of how democracy arises and persists over time.

Technologies of Travel and Communication

From the perspective of the civic bargain, it matters little if the weapons wielded by citizen-soldiers are spears or guns, or if they pay taxes in coined silver or fiduciary currency. Changes in technologies of travel and communication are, however, highly salient for our analysis of the survival of democracy. Travel in the ancient world was slow, relative to modernity, and transport was expensive. Ancient information technology was limited to the spoken and handwritten word. The relative difficulty of ancient travel limited direct civic participation in democratic institutions. That, combined with the limited communications technology available to organize and process large numbers of people wanting to speak or vote, helps to explain why the Athenians (who insisted on direct engagement—albeit augmented with representational institutions and practices) created a democracy that remained relatively small. Citizens were numbered in the tens of thousands; the home territory was about a thousand square miles.

Romans developed institutions that enabled them to grow their citizen body, but in light of travel and communication limitations, they were thrown back on virtual representation in ways that eventually exacerbated social and political tensions. All Roman citizens were in principle entitled to participate directly in assemblies, but in practice, most civic engagement and voting was done by those who lived in or near the city. As the republican rule expanded during the third and second centuries BCE, and different versions of Roman citizenship were packaged and extended further afield, citizenship became ever more virtual, less embodied. Romans had less and less lived experience in the work of doing self-government. With the end of the republic, citizenship was reduced to a legal status, divorced from political decision-making.

In Britain and early America, citizens entitled to vote cast ballots for representatives; improvements in transportation enabled them to do so from distant locations. British and American systems also offset limited national participation (primarily voting for representatives) by honoring local civic engagement. In Britain, freemen participated in local judicial and governmental duties as well as exercising rights to petition Parliament. American federalism, a substantial organizational advance on the methods of ancient federal states, combined political activity at the local and state levels with voting for representatives at the national level—an innovation that allowed its citizens to conceive of their country as at once big and small.

Modern advances in the speed and breadth of information dissemination and interpersonal communication are even more significant. The ancient states lacked the means of scaling up "one-to-many communications" other than speaker-to-audience or by the hand copying of written texts. The fifteenth-century invention of the printing press vastly increased one-to-many communication through the publication of books, pamphlets, and newspapers. By the seventeenth century, printed media

had become an integral aspect of British and colonial American societies, spreading new ideas while popularizing politically charged ideals
of freedom, resistance to tyranny, and popular governance to ever-
widening audiences. The broader, more rapid spread of new ideas
sparked political debate about the national economy, state finances, and
commercial opportunities among diverse stakeholders. That in turn created new pressures on policy making while increasing demands for political voice and vote. The added pressure for new and better bargains
shaped modern democratic development.

Ancient states lacked this transformative technology, putting a ceiling
on the size of any truly participative democracy. As they built empires,
there was no technology that could facilitate active civic engagement
across expanded populations and increased distances. The Athenian
polis expanded by building an empire of subjects answerable to citizen
bosses, not a larger state bound by shared civic values and deliberations.
When Athenian military power waned due to high casualties in disease
and war, imperial subjects rose in revolt. The Romans pursued scale in
ways that were more culturally integrative, granting different levels of
citizenship and building a network of alliances—but demands for full
inclusion by the Italian allies were settled only by war, and citizenship
was not extended to most residents of the far-flung empire. In a world
of better and faster mass communications, perhaps the outcome (or
longevity) of the Roman democratic republic might have been different.
That said, the nineteenth-century British Empire was better connected
with more modern communication, yet failed to bring its colonial subjects into participative citizenship. The idea was periodically considered
in Parliament—but always rejected.

Patterns in Historical Bargaining: First Steps

In each of our four cases, the state was at one point led by a boss—a
king, tyrant, or narrow oligarchy. Athens was ruled by aristocrats and
then a tyrant; the Rome kings were initially replaced by an oligarchy of
elite Patricians. England was ruled as a hybrid partnership of king,

nobles, and ecclesiastical elites; America was long ruled as a group of colonies, ostensibly controlled by Britain's parliamentary monarchy.

In every instance, the first steps toward democracy began with political bargains—when the interests of those ruled clashed with rulers' demands, and a decision was made to negotiate as an alternative to fighting. Artful bargaining created a political solution in which both sides gained some new advantage that better aligned the conflicting needs and created some sharing of power. In the early sixth century BCE, poorer Athenians were suffering from economic distress, land-related debt and bondage, and a threatened civil war. Noble landowners feared loss of labor and exploitation of their weakened state by acquisitive rivals. Shared recognition of the high cost of strife led to the appointment of Solon as mediator; the political bargain he brokered offered nonelite Athenians certain protections and a limited say in decision-making.

In early Rome, Plebeians went on strike when they tired of serving as soldiers, with little reward and no say in their future. Faced with the choice of bargaining with the Plebeians and conquest by hostile neighbors, the Patricians chose the latter, offering the Plebeians a share in government. In Britain, early Anglo-Saxon kings had to protect their new kingdoms from ravaging neighbors and overseas invaders. To increase their military and resource capacity, they used land grants to negotiate feudal relationships with nobles and local farmers. America's founders, having fought to gain independence from the English king, realized the new country would remain vulnerable unless it could organize the recruitment of an army, and ensure that taxes were paid into a central treasury and debts were paid in trustworthy currency. When the Articles of Confederation proved incapable of accomplishing those things, the representatives from twelve of the thirteen states met in Philadelphia in 1787 to address the problems. They struck a bargain for a new federalist system that created a stronger central government while addressing the concerns not only of slave owners determined to protect their rights to human property but also of the residents of small states fearful of being dominated by their larger neighbors.

Need and Opportunity

Each of these bargains was born from the requirement of a state to meet an external scale challenge by providing for collective security and welfare. The threat of external attack and conquest forced those with more power to make a deal with subjects or less powerful peers so as to gain their support in exchange for the guarantee of certain rights and benefits. The deal ensured a commitment of resources in anticipation of future threats. The process was repeated over time. The more democratic the state became, the more decision-making authority for such needs was shared—until it was taken into the hands of the citizens themselves.

Other early political bargains were struck to gain an opportunity: to realize the ambition of growth—often building more scale of power and wealth through conquest and expansion. As Rome grew, Patrician leaders realized the increasingly demanding military service required of Plebeians could be secured by acquiescing to their demands for more civic rights and protections. English kings, including John and Henry II, struck bargains to quell dissension at home to obtain the resources to lead campaigns of conquest abroad. The same theme is seen throughout much of the later rise and institutionalization of Parliament: kings making democratizing deals so they could raise taxes and borrow money for overseas expansion and continental wars.

As states became more citizen led, bargaining for the support necessary to pursue new opportunities remained important. As the Athenians built their empire in the fifth century BCE, the expanded duties and responsibilities for the ordinary citizens defending it were paid for by expanding civic privileges and material benefits for sharing in inherently risky common ventures. In Rome, the Gracchus brothers attempted new bargains in the late second century BCE with windfall resources gained from overseas expansion that could facilitate the distribution of land to needy citizens. Britain's parliamentary monarchy answered the desires of the voting population to capture commercial opportunities opened by overseas trade in the sixteenth and seventeenth centuries.

America's failed attempts at new bargains over slavery prior to the Civil War emerged from the opportunities of westward expansion and newly formed states. In this case, instead of finding some new bargain, political opponents in the North and South plunged into civil war.

That policy needs and opportunities were repeatedly the drivers of bargain making offers one other critical insight. The forging or modification of political bargains is never about changing the terms of governance under ideal deliberative conditions in which perfect justice is the goal and time for discussion is unlimited. Political bargaining about the rules and roles of decision-making has always been an instrument, or sometimes by-product, of pragmatic leaders pursuing new strategies to get something urgent and practical done. We return to this point below.

Contexts and Process

Bargaining, then, concerns practice, but as we survey the many political bargains struck across our four cases, we see patterns that confirm theories proposed by academic students of bargaining. First is the importance of context: the right people must come together with the right questions at the right time. Both "who's at the table" and "what issues are on the table" will be determinative of success or failure. Timeliness also matters: a pressing need or substantial desire must induce the relevant parties to come to the table in the first place. Threats and opportunities motivate bargainers to find ways to strike a deal that will increase human and resource capacity for achieving the goal. But the right people (to quote from the musical *Hamilton*) have to be in "the room where it happens" too—people with the necessary bargaining power and a clear enough understanding of the relevant issues to grasp what can and cannot be traded or offered in the dealmaking.[1] Additionally, these "right people" must be willing to negotiate in good faith, opening the chance for both sides to conclude that they will be better off inside the bargain than outside it.

We know only a few details of Cleisthenes's revolutionary bargain in 508 BCE. But given that it was so participatively successful and quickly accepted, we can guess that multiple leaders and citizens-to-be worked together to hammer it out. The founders in Philadelphia, though officially delegates of the several states, understood the new Constitution would never be realized unless it was subsequently ratified by popular vote. Despite their differences and the document's imperfect compromises, a majority of the delegates stood together behind the final draft, thereby helping to ensure final confirmation. Moreover, through the editorials collected as *The Federalist* (authored by Hamilton, Madison, and Jay) and pamphlets written by the Anti-Federalists, leaders encouraged ordinary citizens to engage with their reasoning; justifying or challenging a proposed new bargain is itself an important form of civic education.

The initially failed bargain of the English Magna Carta was likely doomed for reasons to do with those at—and not at—the table. Judging by his subsequent behavior, King John clearly didn't intend to surrender as much authority as he promised at Runnymede; he was bargaining in bad faith. And when the nobles and clergy tried to hold him accountable with a clause invoking the wider community to enforce the deal, that mechanism failed because it was an unrealistic allocation of responsibility that few people in the kingdom even knew about. The broader population was not even virtually at the table for that issue. On the other hand, because the negotiation with John had identified wide support for complaints about royal overreach—the right issues—it was easier for more sympathetic kings to revive Magna Carta in later years. So Magna Carta's terms were progressively incorporated into English law. The sacrifices and loyalty to duty shown by British citizens in the trenches of World War I signaled the right moment to MPs, who saw that in 1918, it was high time to widely extend the voting franchise.

Incremental and Accelerated Change

Two other process commonalities are observable across the cases. First, the achievement of democracy was not the result of any one bargain but rather several: self-governance was achieved through an ongoing and cumulative effort to solve problems through positive-sum agreements. Second, the move toward democracy, though often incremental, periodically accelerated with episodic breakthroughs—punctuated equilibrium. In Athens, we observe major breakthroughs in its archaic age that clearly created forward momentum: Solon's great compromise of 594 BCE, followed by Cleisthenes's revolutionary innovations in 508 BCE. But there was also some backsliding during the rule of tyrants in the years between those two reformers. After Cleisthenes's revolution, the citizen body was not expanded, but the gives and gets of citizenship were revised repeatedly over the fifth and fourth centuries. The political standing of Rome's Plebeians advanced relatively slowly across the fifth to third centuries BCE. Yet what pushed it ahead were the repeated secessions of the masses in the face of existential external threats.

In England, the rise of Parliament (which eventually grounded British representative democracy) is traceable to the late Middle Ages. The major expansions of its powers against the monarch, though, occurred in response to periodic eruptions of civil war or major domestic conflict in the twelfth through seventeenth centuries. After a dramatic push to expand the franchise in 1832, further extension of the franchise proceeded slowly for close to another century. America's successful constitutional civic bargain, born of patriotic revolution and then the civic friendship on display at the Philadelphia convention as well as the educative process of ratification, then evolved mostly incrementally until the Civil War forced a radical restructuring of citizenship. Issues of race and identity have periodically dominated bargaining among American citizens into contemporary times.

Attending to the combination of incremental and accelerated change also explains why some of the agreements struck were tangible and literal (notably, the American Constitution), while others, like Cleisthenes's new civic order, are implicit, visible as a civic bargain only retrospectively. We know about certain specific laws that defined the contours of Athenian democracy, but many of its critical norms and even statutory requirements can be understood only secondhand—for example, inferred through claims or beliefs attested over time, visible in courtroom speeches, political narratives, or public dramas.

Similarly, the Roman Republic's architecture of assemblies, magistrates, and Senate powers are partly documented through attested laws with a certain assigned date, or through references to negotiated agreements made at key moments in history. But the all-important norms of *mos maiorum* ("customs of our ancestors") and civic virtues that embodied shared respect for res publica are known only by contemporary stories or literary references. Those norms comprised the important gives and gets of being a Roman citizen, but they formed only slowly and informally in the culture. In early Britain, the critical development of the common law was a cumulative evolutionary process. It was kick-started but by no means completed by Henry II; over centuries, many other individuals helped shape its content and culture. The bargain it ultimately created went far beyond what was first enacted by the Norman king.

Imperfection

One theme we have stressed from the outset is democracy's inherent imperfection when viewed from the standpoint of ideal justice or morality. Imperfection is a result of the hard bargaining that enables civic self-governance. Negotiation means no one gets all that they want, and compromise is how citizens (or would-be citizens) can keep adjusting and realigning agreement on the various conditions that, as we have argued, are required to live without a boss. So it is unsurprising that looking across the many political bargains of the cases, we see that each was—from the perspectives of those at the table, those not at the table, or an impartial judge—in various ways imperfect.

Many of the political bargains profiled in the cases were exceedingly clever and pioneering. What made them imperfect was the compromises entailed in gaining agreement. No agreement arising from bargaining ever satisfies each party's complete wish list. Negotiation experts often talk of the baseline at which bargaining begins as the "best alternative to a negotiated agreement" (BATNA) for each party. BATNA is what that party will have if they walk away from the table without a deal. And that is what all parties must always consider: Keeping in mind what I know of the other parties' BATNA, what's the best possible deal I can expect to get? What compromises in various gives and gets am I, and other parties to the agreement, willing to make? And how does the best each of us can get compare with walking away (which may mean starting or resuming a war)?

As we see in our cases, the pressures of time and circumstances push bargainers to accept imperfection—that is, "to get practical and do a deal." In 1787, as the Articles of Confederation became more and more contentious after the war, the American founders knew they could not work indefinitely on designing and redesigning a new constitution. And as the weeks rolled by, it was clear that consensus on several thorny issues was impossible. So as Franklin noted in his final speech in Philadelphia, something far from perfect was agreed on. In 1689, the negotiators behind the English parliamentary monarchy had to finalize its terms quickly—and imperfectly, in the minds of many in the room—when King William, who had upended the old monarchy, threatened to sail home. The parliamentarians couldn't risk losing the opportunity to have the Dutch conqueror on-site, publicly endorsing (and implicitly enforcing) the new, less autocratic governance model.

Furthermore, the lack of perfection in any political bargain results from the unforeseen consequences that follow any agreement, and the changing world in which the governing and governed will continue to live. What may have seemed to be a good enough, if imperfect, bargain in 1787 Philadelphia was regarded as a whole lot worse on the eve of the Civil War in 1860. Cleisthenes's admirable democratic inventions in 508 BCE spawned increasingly volatile lawmaking by the citizen assembly in the following century—ultimately requiring a revised bargain, which thereby established the stabilizing constitutional addition of the separation of policy making from fundamental law. The fifth-century BCE Roman republican bargain pushed by recalcitrant Plebeians and grudgingly accepted by Patricians created the office of tribunes and eventually led to a long period of republican stability. But divisions among tribunes later played a central role in sparking the citizen-on-citizen violence of the civil wars that ended the republic.

In sum, in political bargains, perfection is never achieved, and "good enough" may have a limited shelf life. That is why civic bargains are never final and must always be open to revision. Finding the right balance between the stability secured by a binding agreement and remaining open to revising the terms of the bargain as circumstances change is among the fundamental challenges that every democracy must answer if it is to survive.

Key Factors for Bargaining Success and Failure

Our discussion has focused on the various conditions for the successful conclusion of a civic bargain—and also bargaining failure, when essential conditions are not in place. We have emphasized the imperfection of every political bargain, but that does not mean abandoning the aspiration of progress toward a better, fairer, more secure, and more prosperous future. To highlight the major insights gained from the historical cases, we summarize the key factors that make for a less imperfect bargain and allow citizens (to borrow from the terms of the American constitutional preamble) to aim at a more perfect union.

First, leaders, those who can initiate (or block) a negotiation, must recognize the need or opportunity to pursue a bargain. Next is bringing the right people to the table at the right time, with the right issues to be negotiated and decided. Relatedly, another factor is recognizing who, among those who are not at the table, believe their interests are being directly or virtually represented—or who regard themselves as without representation of any kind. Success depends on understanding the risks and costs of not making a bargain as well; these can include falling into, or back into, bloody civil war or living with an oppressive and unstable status quo. Successful bargainers also take advantage of prior bargains to learn from and build on—and reform as needed—as circumstances change.

Success derives from bargainers having the skills and creativity to craft agreements with the potential to be "integrative" too—that is, provide more value for all parties—and to come as close as possible to maximizing social value in the sense of the Pareto optimal ideal of every party getting as much as possible without lessening the payoff for anyone. In most cases, this precludes bargains that are zero-sum or simply keep the peace for the moment, with nothing else substantially accomplished. The most productive bargains expand opportunity for the future—create agreements that encourage more collaboration, innovation, or the win-win creation of value, making for achievable aspirations beyond what can be seen or imagined in the initial deal.

What also enables such collaboration, innovation, and the win-win creation of future opportunities is an often-overlooked condition we have emphasized in each of the four cases. That is civic friendship, the concept we have adapted from Aristotle: attitudes and behaviors of citizens or would-be citizens working together in good faith; not treating those of opposing beliefs as mortal enemies; following public norms that are reliable and predictable in a way that builds trust; and accepting that mutual respect for the common good may limit personal gains in various circumstances. Civic friendship makes coming to the bargaining table more palatable and develops further when those at the table maintain its spirit and then manifest the appropriate social attitudes. But the deeper value of civic friendship is realized when it runs through the whole society—because that constantly nourishes the potential to find new bargains and improves the likelihood that future bargains will be better in the sense of getting more for more people. When civic friendship is deep enough, the distinction between gives and gets is blurred: doing the right thing as a citizen, because others will benefit, becomes a valued end in itself.

Civic friendship can be seen in varying forms in each our cases. For the Athenians, it appeared in the intense reverence for the polis, manifest in public rhetoric and the artistic expressions of Athenian democratic culture. In republican Rome, it was reflected in the unifying respect that early and middle republic Romans held for res publica along with the traditional virtues and *mos maiorum* passed down through stories of military heroes of earlier generations. The development of the English common law, Magna Carta, and parliamentary governance was pushed forward by civic-friendly leaders who constantly invoked respect for "our ancient liberties." The goodwill that finally opened up the voting franchise to all in the early twentieth century was an outgrowth of the shared sense of progress and moral purpose that arose in British society during the Victorian imperial era. It was American civic friendship that enabled the Philadelphia delegates to forge the great compromise of the US Constitution and encouraged so many citizens in the thirteen states to vote for its ratification.

On the other side of the equation, the many bargains that failed vividly demonstrate the cost and existential threat for democracy when civic friendship erodes or disappears. Our examples included when democracy in late fifth century BCE Athens temporarily collapsed into terrorism and civil war; the Gracchus brother reformers were set on by senators and their clients in late republican Rome; party politics replaced the governing agreement between monarch and Parliament with civil war in seventeenth-century England; and America's constitutional agreement was convulsed by southern secession from the union in 1861.

All four cases endured bargaining failures. All four also demonstrated the resilience to learn, adapt, and bounce back from failure. But the inherent dilemmas of any democracy and persistent difficulty of maintaining a vital civic bargain are important warnings—because sustaining democracy is never guaranteed. Even the strongest civic bargains will fail if they are not renewed and revised as circumstances change.

The demise of the ancient self-governing regimes is a stark reminder of how bargaining failure leads to the death of democracy. Despite hundreds of years of vital self-governance, and major comebacks from wars, oligarchic revolution, and civil conflict, the ancient Athenian democracy ended after being defeated in battle by Macedonian warlords, overwhelmed by a large, well-led, and well-equipped fighting force. It was a devastating challenge of scale that the Athenians might have met with an expanded citizen body—but they failed even to begin negotiating the kind of new bargain that would have been required. The Romans, after hundreds of years of prosperous and stable expansion, built on a bargain among the masses and elites, finally suffered collapse of their res publica. This too was ultimately a failure of a civic bargain— abandoned by greedy elites and self-aggrandizing generals willing to sacrifice the collective good in search of their own private advantage. They were also eagerly followed by thousands of impoverished soldiers who found better reward in the bribes of captured farmland than dutiful service to republican tradition.

History can tell us what is required for democratic survival, but not whether the requirements will be met in the future. Both of our modern democracies are still standing. But nobody can predict if the troubles now swirling around Britain's parliamentary governance or America's constitutional order will be overcome, as other challenges have in the past, or will spell the end of genuine self-governance. Optimists can look backward at the civil wars and social conflict that both nations have endured and survived. Pessimists point to the increasing political polarization in these societies, rising impulses to rally around boss-like populists, ongoing tensions over immigration and expanded citizenship, the loss of agreement on basic matters of factual truth, and the growth of technologically capable adversaries. What history certainly does teach us is that there is every reason to ask—and with some urgency— whether today's civic bargains are resilient and adaptable enough to meet such challenges.

Leadership

In political history, although great leaders are not the sole drivers of meaningful change, leadership matters. Leadership is manifest in the successful bargains seen in each of our cases. Not every leader at each historical moment has had the opportunity, sense of timing, understanding of opponents, and creativity of mind to craft a true civic bargain. The bargain of Cleisthenic democracy was a pioneering and ingeniously engineered system that enabled the subsequent success of democratic Athens. In Rome, the (temporary) dictator Quintus Hortensius, who crafted the compromise law in 287 BCE, resolved what became the last secession of the Plebeians, and established a phase of the Roman Republic that created 150 years of social harmony and growth. In England, William of Orange, with his judicious combination of practicality and restrained threat of force, deftly nudged quarreling Whigs and Tories toward a settlement that ended civil war. His leadership and the agreement he encouraged certainly contributed to the subsequent stability of British governance along with its unprecedented imperial accomplishment. America's founders, collaborative leaders committed to the common good, forged a constitution that although imperfect from the start, and under great pressure today, has survived immense changes in scale and bloody civic conflict. Effective leadership is demanding even in an autocracy. Truly effective leadership is that much harder in a democracy, in which leaders advise but seldom command, and in which citizens must employ the talents and skills of leaders, while also collaborating in resisting any leader who seeks to take over as boss.

Future Lessons?

The practical lessons about the art of political bargaining visible in the historical cases reinforce what skilled negotiators already know. The deeper lesson, made vivid in different ways in the historical cases, concerns the requirement of periodically rethinking what democracy requires of individuals and groups, and what it offers to them. We have argued that the necessary rethinking begins by recognizing, at the most basic level, that the practice of democracy is citizens negotiating with one another (directly or through representatives)—about the why and how, the gives and gets, of self-governance. And that those negotiations, to be productive, must be grounded in some demanding conditions. History allows us to see that it is bargaining, and the conditions that facilitate good faith compromise, that develops democracy, moves it ahead, and allows it to weather seemingly profound setbacks.

This perspective is a warning about today's too frequent pursuit of unproductive absolutism concerning the ends sought by participants in democratic politics and the dangers of hyperpolarized partisanship aimed at winning, when winning is defined as destroying our enemies on the other side. When politics is reduced to whose rights override whose, or when it devolves into zero-sum competition between parties out to secure their own interests and careless of the common good, democracy is in serious trouble. In the final chapter, we propose practical measures that we believe could sustain the essential conditions of democracy in the face of the current crises of confidence.

7

KEEPING THE DEAL REAL

We began this book challenging the pessimistic view that today's democracies are fated to die. Drawing from our conceptual and historical analysis, we conclude that past experience offers no guarantees for any democracy's survival—but also that more optimistically, paths to renewal *are* available, if citizens have the acumen and courage to pursue them. Prominent cases of long-surviving democracies (ancient Athenian democracy, republican Rome, Great Britain's parliamentary system, and the United States' federalist constitutionalism) suggest that to keep today's democratic systems alive, citizens must now rebuild their current civic bargains. Whether that means further amending a constitution, revising rules, regulations, and civic practices, or restoring norms of public behavior (or perhaps all of the above), we'll need to renew the processes and values that built self-governance: accepting the commitments citizens make and expect of one another to live with one another as civic equals in the freedom of no boss. These must include guaranteeing security and basic welfare, defining citizenship, and ensuring and protecting citizen-led institutions. And they must include being able to forge and honor those commitments through bargaining with compromise, adopting a disposition of civic friendship with one another, and ensuring for all the knowledge and skills of a civic education that will bind us together.

We'll sketch our envisioned path to renewal as it would apply to the current American democracy. Securing the democratic future of the

United States is of special concern to us and likely many of you reading this book. But the same general recommendations would be relevant to other modern democracies too. Our argument for why and how to re-build the civic bargain is framed around the seven essential conditions of democracy—strengthening and adapting them to today's new chal-lenges and circumstances. We'll argue that the most urgent priority—and way to get started—is to invigorate and deepen civic education. A new civic education is not a short-term fix. It will take a long time to achieve real impact. Yet it is the surest means by which tomorrow's citi-zens will recover understanding of the fundamental bargain on which democracy is based, and what they must be willing to take on, to make democracy work as well as possible for as many as possible.

Obstacles to Democratic Renewal

American democracy's survival is threatened today by both impersonal forces and the dysfunctional behaviors of citizens and civic leaders. If democracy is self-governance by citizens and survives only through bar-gaining and good faith compromise, the most damaging forces and be-haviors are those that block us from finding common ground—both in what we do and how we govern ourselves. There are many such obsta-cles and destructive behaviors; these are ultimately interrelated. Four are particularly threatening.

First is the changing structure and incentives of our political process. Increasing citizen dissatisfaction with government has undone the es-tablished paths to agreement within and between our two main political parties. Abetted by media-scaled negative messaging and more expan-sive fundraising, new political factions have arisen, fragmenting party solidarities. These factions are characterized by their staunch rejection of bargaining with the other side. To keep up with the new independent disrupters, the traditional parties have resorted to building "tribal soli-darity," mobilized by constant attack on political opponents—no longer fellow citizens but now enemies. Maintaining solidarity demands ever more extremism, with primary elections favoring those candidates who are most fierce and antagonistic against the rival gang. Compromise becomes the kiss of death.

Meanwhile, with little recourse to good faith bargains, the ability of Congress to pass bills—or do much of anything—has steadily declined. Instead of working on needed legislation, members stage public relations stunts to finger point and proclaim righteous anger against their enemies. This in turn stokes even greater citizen dissatisfaction, and the negative cycle of tribalism only grows stronger. Disrupters and faction leaders keep attacking the status quo, promising that they alone can "fix the problem," thereby allowing them to raise even more money to cement loyalties and demonize enemies. They claim to be saving democracy's house; what they are doing is burning it down.

The second obstacle is the new media environment, which provides tools and fuel to fan the bonfires of acrimonious political discourse. The greater the viewership of news and social media by citizens, the greater the revenue stream for profit-seeking platform and content providers. Because media research shows viewership rises with programming that promotes fear, anger, and resentment, including across differences in race and economic status, these enterprises aggressively promote such content. Conspiracy theories and disregard for truth follow accordingly. Comity and trust in public conversation have become endangered species.

The third obstacle is that many citizens, overwhelmed by the changing environment, rising tribalism, and proliferating discord, are now simply disengaging from political life. They turn away from any participation, self-consciously ignore the news, and don't bother to vote. In so doing, they are undermining their own democratic bargain of self-governance. And the more they disengage, the harder it will be to restore the bargain.

The fourth obstacle is in many ways the most pressing now: citizens' lack of understanding about how to tackle the problems at hand. This manifests itself in two ways. First is widespread confusion about the difference between making short-term policy versus repairing the essential conditions of democracy itself. Hashing out decisions about changes in taxes, climate remediation, or aid for foreign allies—examples of the kind of actions that our democracy may choose to pursue—is not the same as defining and finding agreement about what democracy is and how it works: the purpose, membership, civic rights and responsibilities, institutions, and values that are needed to live freely and responsibly without a boss. Below we'll see examples of how this confusion is diverting energy away from real democratic reform.

The second troubling manifestation is that as citizens, we are losing our ability to even agree about getting agreement. We no longer recognize that democracy depends on coming to terms with one another, whether it's about specific policies or the "what, why, and how" of democracy itself. Today one often hears comments such as "Most of us really want the same things. Why can't we just agree and get on with those?" The question is well-intentioned but reveals a historical ignorance of how hard it is for self-governing citizens to reach and live by agreement. Though bound to one another in a democracy, we never really do "want all the same things"—nor is democracy defined by consensus. It is instead based on finding workable compromises so that as citizens, we can move ahead together. Centuries of conflict and hard bargaining went into making democracy what it is today, and will determine what it will be too, if it survives tomorrow. We must rebuild understanding of all that and the civic disposition that moves understanding into action. If we don't, we'll fail to repair America's tattered civic bargain, with predictably dire consequences. America's democratic future now depends on reeducating its citizens—especially those of rising generations.

Battling the Civic Knowledge Gap

What is it that citizens today and tomorrow must now learn to address these many problems? A full-blown "learning diagnostic" for America's next generation of citizens is beyond our current scope. But we can sketch the terrain by returning to democracy's essential conditions, and using those to highlight how a better educated citizenry might renew its current civic bargain. We'll conclude with a few forward-looking lessons from the recently launched Stanford Civics Initiative developed by Josiah Ober and other colleagues in his university.

No Boss, and Security and Welfare

Most Americans today still endorse the democratic principles of political liberty and civic equality—and by implication, governing themselves together without a boss. They worry (as they have through history) about overly intrusive government officials and unaccountable bureaucrats. But now, with rising political stalemates and inability of Congress to legislate, many citizens are beginning to believe that only a boss can fix what's broken. Thus partisans of the Left and Right periodically push for more executive action by the president or a more forceful Supreme Court to bypass stalled constitutional processes. Recent polls also report a growing desire for "stronger, more authoritarian leadership" to shortcut or even replace the hard work of democratic decision-making. At least some of those who stormed the Capitol on January 6, 2021, were acting on similar preferences, while millions of Americans are now also telling researchers that "armed revolt" against our government is sometimes justified.[1]

The willingness to embrace the rule of a boss may be driven by the conviction that an autocratic leader will better ensure security and welfare. For example, with limited historical perspective, many take for granted domestic safety and freedom from foreign interference. After all, following the collapse of the Soviet Union and before the rise of China, the United States was, for a short while, the only global superpower left standing. In the same period, brisk economic growth raised prospects that most people's standard of living would improve in the foreseeable future; a high baseline of welfare seemed to be guaranteed by an ever-growing average gross domestic product and wide availability of cheap consumer goods. In the second decade of the new century, those assumptions became contestable or even blatantly false. The cost-benefit calculation of the new global economic order convinced many to blame democracy and its "governing elites," and thus consider more authoritarian alternatives—and this despite the growing threat of emboldened autocratic states.

Citizenship Defined and Citizen-Led Institutions

The essential question of who is a citizen, and therefore who has a place at the bargaining table of democracy, is now often framed in zero-sum terms. In recent years, many current citizens have come to regard immigrants as rivals for scarce goods, including jobs and political power. That obscures the nation's strategic need for talent and innovation that greater mass of population and diversity in fact can provide; both, given declining birth rates, will be critical for America's future flourishing. The fears and suspicions about immigration are now played out in narrow partisan fights about border control as well as the rights and responsibilities of both visa holders and undocumented people.

We have emphasized that a democracy requires clarity about borders and civic membership in the state. Expanding the citizen body is frequently the answer to scale challenges; our historical cases show how achieving security and welfare often demanded and benefited from citizenship expansion. But expanding the citizen body in turn raises its own challenges, triggering new demands and needs for adjustments to the gives and gets of citizenship. In America, when a polarized Congress is unable to reach a compromise on citizenship questions, when advocates of a fixed national cultural identity square off against advocates of a universal human right to movement and entry, frustration mounts and gridlock follows. Both sides embrace bossy solutions. We can't keep our democracy if we can't learn how to bargain about who should be the "we" in "We the People."

Major democratic institutions, including the three branches of government, federalism, and election procedures, have also become intense arenas of factional wrangling. Instead of focusing on reforms promoting greater fairness while sustaining the conditions of no boss as well as security and welfare, partisans seek institutional changes that will deliver short-term tribal victories at the other side's expense. Seeking only to control institutions, as prizes in a competitive, zero-sum game, blocks exploration of new and more effective approaches to decision-making and civic participation. And that only makes it harder to address our ever-growing challenges of scale.

Good Faith Compromise and Civic Friendship

These two complementary conditions are critical to making self-governance work and yet are also too often ignored by contemporaries seeking to save democracy through institutional reform. These conditions are less about formal rules than the citizen mindset and behaviors needed to make the civic bargains of democracy feasible and functional. Lacking an understanding of democracy's long history, citizens fail to appreciate that self-governance has always required compromise, or that tribal warfare and partisanship aimed at "absolute victory" undermines the good faith negotiations on which democracy depends.

Civic friendship is about creating and maintaining a disposition among citizens that preserves the future *potential* for seeking and finding compromise. It's a longer-term insurance policy against the failure of bargains—providing a reservoir of goodwill so that citizens and their representatives can always renew their attempts to find agreement, if earlier negotiations fail. The gap of understanding about the essential role of compromise and civic friendship exacerbates counterproductive tribal warfare and political stalemates.

Civic Education

Civic education supports compromise and fosters friendship by teaching citizens what democracy really is and what it takes to keep it. Civic education also provides the skills and behaviors required to keep democracy functioning and offers the historical perspective to reinforce what makes democracy different from other forms of governance. It reminds us of the harsh and frequently brutal alternatives when democracy is lost. Civic education foregrounds what we share as citizens so that we can better appreciate and protect what living in a democracy provides for each of us.

Civic education is not an administrative task but rather a strategic process. Self-government requires people of differing backgrounds and beliefs to find ways to live and work together, even when they frequently disagree. If they devolve into perpetual conflict, democracy fails. Civic education forges vital bonds of knowledge, values, and behaviors on which shared membership in the ongoing project of self-government stands or falls.

So what would a robust civic education look like today, and how should Americans go about expanding and strengthening it?

Civic Education through Informal Communal Practices

Looking back in history once more, as we have done throughout this book, can illuminate such questions. One critical lesson from the past is that much civic education has nothing to do with a classroom. Democracy has long been strengthened by a broad array of informal educational practices.

Our four historical cases demonstrate how citizens learned democratic values and behaviors from one another. They learned what self-government offers to citizens and what it requires of them in a variety of practical venues. They learned the benefits and costs of democracy through military service in which citizens shared in the often-dangerous and sometimes-fatal work of guarding or expanding their country. They learned through shared civic activities, including public parades, sacred rituals, and collective oath taking; participation in local government such as town meetings and public hearings; and membership in local voluntary associations and clubs in which individuals practiced the skills of public deliberation and speaking, giving and taking reasons for policies advancing some common interest. They also learned through active participation in making decisions for their country, whether by directly voting on policy proposals or electing representatives; public service as officials and jurors; and political activism, whether in support of the current institutional rules or in peaceful protest against them.

Much of this was not devised specifically as what we would today call citizen education. Its cumulative effect, however, was just that: clarifying and deepening citizens' understanding of important aspects of self-government. Working together with fellow citizens, members of a democracy historically learned for themselves how the processes of self-government operated in practice. Through engaging in symbolic and emotionally charged cooperative activities, they learned to embrace the identity of the citizen. Each participant gained knowledge of the participation of others, as others in turn did of their participation, thus building essential common knowledge: "I know that you know that I know (and so on), and that we are in this together." Common knowledge of this kind builds the capacity to do things together. It creates rational trust of others because their commitment to the shared enterprise is manifest in their choice to engage with others in its living practice.

Through history, the sense of shared civic identity was further strengthened via repetition—practices and rituals that were performed over and again, across generations and a diverse population. For ancient Athenians, civic rituals included the oath taken by young men on entering training for military service, the annual All-Athens parade, local- and polis-level sacrifices to the gods of the community, and the distribution of sacrificial meat that followed the sacrifice. It included the oath taken by all jurors to listen to both sides impartially and judge by the law. And it included the expectation of occasionally entering a lottery that decided who would serve on boards of state officials. Republican Roman citizens learned similar lessons through their military service, in assemblies and courts, and in the public rituals of res publica. British subjects en route to democratic citizenship learned about shared duty and responsibility as well as communal benefits by serving on local juries, fighting Napoléon as part of armies and navies, attending political clubs and coffeehouses, and celebrating patriotism and the progress of their empire by participating in parades and royal jubilees. For modern Americans, the relevant rituals may be as solemn as the process of taking an oath as a juror or soldier, festive as marching in an Independence Day parade, simple as setting up a lawn sign for a preferred candidate, salient as going to the polls to vote on election day, and intimate as joining together with friends to watch the election returns on television.

Formal Civic Education

Our democratic case histories also suggest that more structured education—from government programs and schools to private instruction—complemented, in differing ways, the rituals and community experiences of social civic learning.

Athenian democracy supplies a vivid example. In Aristotle's day, cadets aged eighteen and nineteen received two years of state-sponsored education. Their military training included learning to use the traditional weapons of the hoplite infantry, but also state-of-the-art catapult artillery. Supervisors for the cadets took the title of masters of moderation. Cadets were expected to learn from and exemplify this prime civic virtue. On taking up duties, the cadets swore an oath never to disgrace their arms nor abandon a comrade, and always to protect sacred and civic spaces. They swore also to obey legitimate democratic leaders as well as to respect the existing laws and any new, democratically established ones. And they swore to oppose, together, any attempt to overthrow the constitution.

Military training in our other cases also provided structured civic education, but otherwise, formal education varied. In republican Rome, most childhood learning was supplied through the family, and included domestic skills but also an emphasis on *pietas*, respect for virtues such as the duty to honor gods, family, and nation. Older boys from well-to-do families were tutored in rhetoric and the reasoning skills necessary for advocacy in the law courts and other roles in public life. Such training was essential for the ambitious men who pursued the cursus honorum, the well-structured progression of elective offices designed to build ever-deeper civil and military knowledge along with the skills for ever more responsible positions of public leadership.

In Britain, formal civic education has been an outgrowth of the nation's relatively recent development of full democracy. But that built on earlier traditions relevant to freedom and duty in the predemocratic age.

During the Victorian era, the moral aspirations for the British Empire were reinforced by teaching the history of its development. Curricula in schools and universities stressed how the virtues and public duties of exemplary British heroes carried over to the art of parliamentary governance. This, plus the preparation for the civil service examinations that chose young men seeking government posts, helped create the culture of meritocracy, public service, and sacrifice that in turn paved the way for expanding the voting franchise during the nineteenth and twentieth centuries.

American Civic Education

There is a long tradition of civic education in America, encompassing both informal and formal learning. Literacy rates in colonial America were high in comparison to contemporary boss-ruled countries. Literacy promoted knowledge of current events and ancient history. It fostered the culture of critical thought, reasoned argument, and frank debate that was a precondition for the revolution. Ratification of the Constitution was driven in part by the editorials of *The Federalist*, published to inform Americans about the issues and decisions that went into the creation of the nation's new charter. Many of the founders understood the importance of educating citizens to make the new democracy work, though they differed on the exact purpose and type of knowledge to emphasize. When Jefferson established the University of Virginia (1819), his intent was to "advance human knowledge, educate leaders, and cultivate an informed citizenry."[2]

Civic education content appears in some late eighteenth-century school materials but became more prominent in school curricula during the first part of the nineteenth century when a movement arose for more coherent and widespread public education. Horace Mann, a key leader, emphasized that free, standardized, and universal schooling was essential to American self-governance, observing, "It may be an easy thing to make a Republic, but it is a very laborious thing to make Republicans; and woe to the republic that rests upon no better foundation than ignorance, selfishness and passion."[3] During this same general era,

Tocqueville's observations in his *Democracy in America* underscored the significance of Americans learning about and reinforcing the all-important values of "equality of condition" in their many voluntary associations. He also noted how high rates of American literacy and widespread newspaper circulation contributed to democratic culture.

Before long, however, competing trends called into question the need for Americans' pursuit of civic education. The focus of educators shifted toward "more practical" subjects. President Lincoln signed the Morrill Act of 1862 (amid the Civil War) that launched land grant universities. The expanded opportunities for higher education increased demand for more vocational learning. For example, Montana Agricultural College—today Montana State University—was founded in 1893 and soon adopted as its motto "Education for Efficiency."[4]

But the vocational movement in turn created its own backlash. Early twentieth-century educators worried that if the commitment to civic education was lost, if shallow careerism replaced the foundational knowledge necessary for democracy, the country would suffer in the longer run. Drawing on a tradition of classical learning, American schools, colleges, and civic organizations symbolically adopted the ancient oath of Athenian cadets. Students swore a version of the oath on graduation, and politicians repeated it in radio broadcasts. Civic education regained momentum, with many American schools and universities building structured curricula centered on government processes, the history of democratic development, and a celebration of patriotic values. These were complemented in contemporary parades, holidays, and the growth of civically patriotic groups like the Boy Scouts.

During the mid- and later twentieth century, there was yet another swing of the pendulum that again de-emphasized civic education. The Sputnik and Cold War eras put urgent strategic priority on science, math, and engineering skills for Americans. Civic education was soon further pressured during the Vietnam War. Protesters argued against education that celebrated the history and decision-making of a government that was fighting an immoral war and lying to its citizens about it. Many other critics raised concerns about persistent racism in our society, notwithstanding progress driven by a rising civil rights movement.

Since then, the study of American history and its institutions has become a battlefield of moral debates and political antagonisms. To minimize controversy, schools reacted by watering down or eliminating civic educational offerings. Once celebratory—but also educational—public holidays (Memorial Day, Veterans Day, and Independence Day)—were reduced for many Americans to opportunities for family picnics or to buy a new mattress on sale.

Today's faded emphasis on educating citizens in the history, institutions, and values of democracy and self-governance is visible in doleful statistics. To take some selected and alarming samples, only 30 percent of Americans born since 1980 now say it is essential to live in a democracy; 44 percent of Americans cannot name all three branches of our government; one in three say they would consider abolishing the Supreme Court; and 30 percent of twelfth graders say they have never participated in any kind of debate. A civics assessment done by the National Assessment of Educational Progress has reported that less than one-third of eighth graders are able to identify the historical purpose of the Declaration of Independence, and fewer than one-fifth of all high school seniors can explain how citizen participation benefits democracy. Student achievement in civic knowledge for Black and Latino students typically lags behind their white counterparts, and those minority populations also generally have less access to civic education.[5] That said, even the best public schools typically fall short in their civic offerings. As one student of a nationally ranked high school told us, "My education offers nothing beyond a standard curriculum of American history, nor anything about civic engagement and involvement."[6]

Toward a Renewal of America's Civic Education

Throughout this book we have argued that for democracy to survive and continue to flourish, citizens must understand and support its essential conditions—binding one another in a civic bargain to govern themselves. We have also highlighted how, in an era of increasing polarization and distrust in government—and amid a historical expansion of immigration into the United States—it is more important than ever to educate citizens in the essential conditions that define democracy and make it work.[7] Thus our recommendation that America must now dramatically invest in renewing its civic education.

Fortunately, our call comes at a time when interest in civics appears to be growing. The question of the education of citizens is once again moving to the forefront for educators at all levels—from K–12 to universities. There is also increasing attention addressing that need among civic and nonprofit organizations as well as by some members of Congress. That said, this shift is still in the early days, and it remains to determine the best content, experiences, and approaches to pursue.

So what should twenty-first-century civic education look like? We cannot offer a detailed answer here, and there is no one-size-fits-all solution. Our research for this book, however, and insights from practical experience in the Stanford Civics Initiative suggest some general design principles. We hope these will contribute to the continuing development of renewed programs aimed at enabling tomorrow's citizens to rebuild their civic bargain with one another.

Build on Earlier Traditions

Civic education in surviving democracies looks ahead but also looks back because self-governance is fostered by understanding the origins of living without a boss and why it has been so highly valued. America's own rich tradition of civic education provides a platform on which to build—even if future programs must evolve or discard certain themes and certainties of the past. The history of civic education at Stanford University, where one of us teaches, offers one way of pursuing this balance.

In 1920, the year that the Nineteenth Amendment granted women the right to vote, Stanford (coeducational from its founding in 1885) inaugurated Problems of Citizenship, a yearlong course for all first-year students. Incoming students were told that the founders of their university "had in mind a preparation for citizenship as a problem in education, rather than the development of a technique in Political Science, Economics, or Law." In addition to laying the "foundations for work in your special field of interest," the university would also call on them "to build carefully and to prepare thoughtfully for your work as a citizen." They would learn that "citizenship is not a thing apart, something to be thought of only occasionally or left to the energies of a minority of our people, but that its proper understanding is at the very root of our daily life."[8]

Stanford's Problems of Citizenship, in common with similar courses in other universities, was prompted in part by a challenge of scale: not only had the enfranchised citizen population doubled now that women enjoyed voting rights, but in recent years there had been a sharp increase in immigration. Between 1890 and 1910, immigrants constituted between 14 and 15 percent of the total US population, up from about 10 percent in 1870. The citizenship course not only pushed back against merely vocational education but also sought to address concerns about the civic loyalties of immigrants (notably German speakers) in the aftermath of World War I. It was seen as imperative that millions of new citizens understand the principles and practices of democracy.

After 1930, due to restrictive legislation, immigration levels dropped sharply. The decline continued through the 1960s; by 1970, immigrants constituted less than 5 percent of the US population.[9] Accordingly, the educational focus shifted from citizenship as such to America's shared cultural inheritance. Stanford's educational evolution illustrates the trend. In 1935, Problems of Citizenship was replaced with a mandatory sequence in Western Civilization. A generation later, during 1960s' campus protests, Western Civ classes were under attack; the sequence was abandoned in 1969. After a decade without a common civics-related course, Stanford tried out a more inclusive multitrack Western Culture sequence. It morphed into Cultures, Ideas, Values, followed in the 1990s by Introduction to the Humanities. That was in turn replaced in 2012 by a smorgasbord of Thinking Matters courses, from which first-year students were asked to pick one. Civic education at Stanford had vanished into a Silicon Valley version of education for efficiency.

Meanwhile, however, faculty members were voicing concerns that without a civics-centered curriculum, Stanford's undergraduate education was impoverished—and dangerously so given the growing political malaise. Some, with knowledge of Stanford's earlier traditions, reflected on what had been lost. Others, cognizant of America's changing role in the world and increasing demographic diversity, saw opportunities for a new approach to educating citizens. In 2021, the university senate unanimously approved a new sequence of three courses aimed at remaking the educational experience of first-year students.

The central course in the new sequence became Citizenship in the 21st Century. More advanced courses, building on Citizenship in the 21st Century, are now being offered through the Civics Initiative. Stanford's recommitment to civic education builds on and has inspired similar initiatives at other universities. It is too early to predict a full-blown national movement for intensifying American civic education. But there are growing indications of an educational shift away from a single-minded focus on efficiency, and toward promoting the knowledge and leadership of participative democratic citizens. Tomorrow's reformers should take advantage of the lessons of the past while also pioneering new and innovative approaches that prepare citizens to rebuild the civic bargains by which democracy survives.

Knowledge and Approaches, Deep and Broad

As we are learning at Stanford, students differ widely in their readiness to engage with civic-related material. The content and approach of courses addressing democratic citizenship must be carefully designed to build a comprehensive body of knowledge and skills without devolving into propagandistic cheerleading or deflationary defeatism. The knowledge and skills for an informed and participatory democracy must include, but also go beyond, constitutional mechanics. In addition, young citizens and would-be citizens should receive a grounding in American political history to appreciate the origins of our democratic civic bargains, and in comparative political history to understand the different approaches to self-governance in other times and places as well as the reality of living under nondemocratic bosses. They must be trained in the critical and analytic tools necessary to make informed judgments about the pressing political issues of their day and participate in addressing them. Civic education must arm citizens to withstand the distractions and misinformation often offered by contemporary news and social media too.

Even the most robust K–12 and college-level curriculum is only one part of the learning that should extend over a citizen's lifetime. In each of our case studies of long-surviving democracies, civic education was built into the cultural practices and expectations of the society. It began in childhood with stories and games, and continued through various forms of military and public service. The twenty-first-century analogues of those cultural practices are still lacking. Just as the formal courses in civic education now being devised in American universities differ profoundly in form and content from their predecessors, a dynamic and engaging twenty-first-century civic culture cannot simply restore past practices. But by the same token, a renewed civic culture must aim at the traditional goal of sustaining the conditions of democracy.

Diversity and the Ordering of Loyalties

We believe that the central thesis of this book—that citizens of any democracy must understand and commit to the essential conditions of the bargain they make to have boss-free self-governance—should inform civic learning. The necessities of security, basic welfare, defined citizenship, citizen-led institutions, and the behaviors of compromise and civic friendship must be learned and embraced by future generations.

Understanding and honoring the essential conditions of democracy are not the same, though, as demanding conformity to any political ideology. Research shows that enforcing ideological conformity frequently backfires—on both sides of a political divide. Still, we also believe that the director of the original Stanford Problems of Citizenship course was correct in telling his students that "we are engaged in a right 'ordering of our several loyalties.'" The ideal of citizenship—as participative membership in a common project of people governing themselves—need not be at the top of that ordering of loyalties. Yet we believe that to save democracy, it must be higher up than it is at present. It is the job of tomorrow's civic education to make that case in a way that is not jingoistic, propagandistic, or tilted toward either end of the ideological spectrum.

A new approach to twenty-first-century civic education, both in formal schooling and the wider culture, must provide the basis for renewed civic friendship and the willingness to bargain with one another in good faith, without ideological absolutism. That will take time and good faith engagement—and ultimately compromise—by citizens from across the political spectrum. It will also require that our nation rethink the relationship between diversity, inclusion, a shared commitment to civic ideals, and a willingness to participate in identifying and promoting common goods.

Throughout this book we have argued that access to a diversity of experience, information, and knowledge is a prime source of democracy's competitive advantage. Because of that, a successful democratic citizen body must be relatively large and socially diverse. We have noted that the ratchet of civic membership tends toward more inclusion, and that democracy is put at risk when the ratchet is reversed. The historical trend is therefore toward a larger citizen body—one that is more diverse in origin, experience, and viewpoint. The question, then, is how diversity can accommodate the recognition that certain fundamental interests are those of the democratic community as a whole and a shared commitment to seeking common goods. As we have contended, without that shared commitment, democracy as self-government fails.

Unfortunately, in many organizations today and some aspects of government policy, diversity is being reified in a way that makes seeking the common good more difficult. When they narrowly seek diversity predicated on race, ethnicity, gender, and sexual orientation, diversity and inclusion programs may implicitly reject the notion that individuals can and should share, or even aspire to share, important interests with others unlike them.[10] Policies that focus intensely on racial, ethnic, and gender *differences* undermine democracy's goal of citizens working *together* on shared civic projects, and making the bargains needed to enjoy boss-free self-governance. Moreover, such policies may erode the productive diversity of experience and viewpoint that is essential for innovation. They can make it harder to see why good faith bargaining among those with different interests and goals is a condition of democracy.

The reification of diversity-promoting social identities also encourages the proliferation of demands for new group rights and protection against anything that might challenge those often-fragile, reified identities. This decreases a willingness to compromise for the common good and increases tendencies to degrade civic friendship—both of which, we have argued, are essential conditions for maintaining democratic self-government.

A Process of Experimentation and Innovation

The current state of democratic malaise need not be fatal, but it ought to be recognized as an existential threat, comparable to external threats and internal conflicts that destroyed ancient democracies. That recognition can and should provoke a willingness to join together in response to the threat as well as embark on meaningful change in the form of a thoughtful process of experimentation, dialogue, and compromise. And that is, we believe, just how the renewal of civic education for our democracy might now best proceed. New programs and attempts to educate young citizens are sprouting up across the country. As a citizenry, we must seize the opportunity to accelerate and expand those while also being patient not to declare too quickly or dogmatically the final best practice. In the coming years, civic educators should keep experimenting with new approaches, learning from one another and watching out for breakthroughs, while also consolidating the most successful content and methodologies that are having a positive impact. Over time, new standards and measures of success will evolve. Progress must come through learning by doing and citizens learning from one another.

No simple and standardized curriculum will suit the rich American ecology of K–12 or postsecondary education, nor the variety of local practices and priorities across our expansive nation, nor the diversity of civic-related programs already offered by hundreds of community-oriented organizations. Citizens, leaders, and educators in different constituencies will have their own ideas about what an adequate (or optimal) education for citizenship should be. Those differences must be taken into account as new curricula and participative practices evolve. We believe that a range of coherent approaches—variously reflecting conservative, libertarian, liberal, or progressive viewpoints—could potentially support the seven essential conditions for democracy highlighted in this book. Citizenship-centered American history courses, for example, might be located at different points on a spectrum from a focus on structural injustices to the ideals and aspirations of the founders. The choice of which political thinkers and texts to study, and degree of emphasis on social science methods, could also vary considerably.

Respect Core Principles of Democratic Engagement

Developing a new civic education, and following a process of experimentation and adaptation from differing viewpoints and approaches, will only be successful if it is pursued with a firm commitment by all to the deliberative principles inherent to civic friendship and good faith bargaining: open inquiry, critical reasoning, and lively but respectful debate in search of the best answers that can be embraced by the greatest number. Civic education that becomes ideological or lopsidedly partisan shuts down freedom of thought and speech, thereby betraying democracy itself; those who cancel the viewpoints of others set themselves up as a boss. Tomorrow's renewed civic education should frankly acknowledge the imperfection of past civic bargains—including America's constitutional founding—but must back the values of freedom, equality, and civic dignity. Whatever its trajectory, civic education must provide positive reasons for people to embrace the identity of the participatory citizen in today's democracy. Ultimately good civic education answers the questions of why democratic citizenship is worth striving for and why its costs are worth paying.

Saving Democracy

The central arguments of this book are aspirational and forward-looking; they offer a historically informed construct to help citizens reimagine what democracy is, and the obligations, values, and mindsets needed to keep it alive and flourishing. If we have been successful, you will start to think differently about democracy today—not as an impersonal form of government or some series of battleground institutions to be won by your party, but fundamentally as a bargain with fellow citizens, about the agreements, compromises, and behaviors that allow you and other members of the nation to govern yourselves without a boss. Like all changes in mindsets, effecting this one will take time, and many hands and voices working together. It will require a sustained educational commitment to inspire the next generation of citizens to keep up the momentum of change.

But what, now, can be done to get started on this reconstructive journey? We close with three urgent imperatives for you and your fellow citizens who worry about our democracy's survival.

1. *Learn about democracy's nature, fundamental conditions, and historical development—and engage others in discussing them.*
   Any attempt at reform must start not just by "understanding the problem" but even before that, understanding the subject. As a nation, we can't move ahead without firmly grasping what democracy is, how it arose, and how it has been kept. We have done our best to explain that by specifying characteristics and conditions drawn from the histories of long-surviving democracies. We urge you to continue to study history and explore the meaning of democracy with family and friends. More challenging but vitally important, be willing to talk about what you have learned with people who don't share your political views. What will it take to find common ground with them? One approach is discussing how enduring democracies have met the critical problems of self-governance—the repeated conflicts over how to deal with challenges of scale as well as conflict over the roles and responsibilities of sharing power; how past democracies granted freedoms and guaranteed individual rights, while still maintaining order and defense of the community; and how they inspired a willingness to compromise private interests for the public good.

Appreciating that today's seemingly intractable problems have been recognized and periodically overcome through history can help convince you and others that democratic renewal today is possible. Violent conflict can be replaced by good faith bargaining, thereby settling on compromises that, while imperfect, lay the foundation for people with diverse preferences and backgrounds to make progress together. Building civic friendship and other forms of self-moderating civic behavior can keep democracy alive while sustaining the ideal of working together for a more perfect union.

2. *Support and promote the development of expanded civic education.* The renewal path for democracy must begin by intensifying our commitment to a lifelong civic education that instills an appreciation of democratic history, builds skills and mindsets for compromise, and nourishes practices of civic friendship. Updating our civic bargain, with reforms led by civically educated citizens, is how America will keep its democracy. A renewed civic bargain will require changes—perhaps dramatic ones—to institutions and practices; these potentially include restructuring congressional representation or Supreme Court service, designing more participative practices using technology, reimagining citizenship freed from geographic definition, or innovating new forms of civic media and social learning. A new civic bargain might call for further amending the US Constitution—which the founders foresaw as necessary. As the history of democracy shows, however, future reform must be anchored in the foundational underpinning of what democracy is and what it requires of citizens. That knowledge and those behaviors must be strengthened among our next generation—those who will have the responsibility for making the changes required to continue governing themselves without a boss.

3. *Summon the courage to act now.* Nothing is gained by wallowing in despair over the current dysfunctions. Yes, today's democracies are being buffeted by unprecedented global economic forces and technology-magnified conflicts among citizens. But

democracies have always faced major disruptive discontinuities—
so why not summon the will to fix what's dragging us down by
grasping for the courage shown by earlier heroes of civic reform?
However modest, your own first steps can make a difference—
engaging with others, joining public dialogue, advocating for
better civic education, and teaching others through your own
commitment to civic behavior. Don't allow yourself to fall into
the cynical conviction that your voice and actions can't matter.
History teaches us that collective civic action is grounded in
individuals' courageous, willed choices. And it is those choices
that can tip the balance in favor of a saving our imperfect union
and making it better than it was.

Building democracy takes a long time and is the work of all. The job of
keeping it is never done, and the process is always contentious. Recognizing what's breaking and fixing what's broken is always part of the
deal. The future is in our hands. There's no time to waste.

NOTES

Introduction: Democracy's Real Deal

1. Powel had hosted delegates to the convention at her Philadelphia home, and later became a friend and confidante of Washington. The interchange between Franklin and Powel is briefly recorded in the diary of James McHenry, September 18, 1787, https://en.wikipedia.org/wiki/Elizabeth_Willing_Powel (section 3). The incident had a convoluted later history, in which McHenry's original report was edited and elaborated to make Franklin contrast an orderly republic to unruly democratic self-government (rather than to monarchy). On the false dichotomy between a republic and democracy, see chapter 1.

2. On Franklin's speech and its setting, see Rasmussen 2021, 1–2; "Constitutional Convention," Benjamin Franklin Historical Society, http://www.benjamin-franklin-history.org/constitutional-convention/; "Speech of Benjamin Franklin," U.S. Constitution, https://www.usconstitution.net/franklin.html.

Chapter 1. Fundamentals: Essential Conditions for Democracy

1. While we offer no specific parameters for *large* or *socially diverse*, what we mean by these terms is clarified in discussions of historical cases in chapters 2–5.

2. Aristotle discusses civic friendship in both the *Nicomachean Ethics* and *Eudemian Ethics*. See Ober 2022, 365–71.

3. Kant 1991.

4. The 1948 United Nations' Universal Declaration of Human Rights includes the right to life, liberty, and security of person; not to be enslaved, tortured, or subjected to cruel, inhuman, or degrading treatment or punishment; recognition everywhere as a person before the law and equal protection under the law; privacy, marriage, and family; freedom of thought, conscience, and religion; free choice of employment, just and favorable conditions of work, and protection against unemployment; education; and so on. "Universal Declaration of Human Rights," United Nations, https://www.un.org/en/universal-declaration-human-rights/.

5. Schumpeter [1950] 2008, 279, 277, 293.

6. Hamilton, Madison, and Jay 2003, no. 10, 14, 55. For more on *The Federalist*, see chapter 5.

7. Hamilton, Madison, and Jay 2003, no. 55.

Chapter 2. Athens: The Bargain That Invented the Power of the Citizenry

1. Plutarch, *Life of Solon*, 5.2–3.
2. Plutarch, *Life of Solon*, 15.2.

Chapter 3. Rome: The Compromises That Created the First Great Republic

1. Polybius, *Histories*, 1.1.
2. Hitchner, in progress.
3. Quoted in Plutarch, *Life of Pyrrhus*, 21.9.
4. Morstein-Marx 2019.

Chapter 4. Britain: The Royal Bargains That Made Parliament Sovereign

1. Quoted excerpts of Magna Carta throughout this section are adapted from the translation of the 1215 edition by the British Library, "English Translation of Magna Carta," https://www.bl.uk/magna-carta/articles/magna-carta-english-translation.

2. *Quod omnes tangit ab omnibus approbatur*. For further discussion on this initiative, and sources and usage, see Stasavage 2020, 115ff.

3. Martin Bucer," On Lawful Ordination," cited in Guy 1988, 225; Tombs 2014, 174.

4. Tombs 2014, 182, quoting Russell 1996, 280.

5. Quoted in Tombs 2014, 206.

6. Resolution of the House of Commons, January 4, 1649, quoted in Sharp 1998, 140.

7. Excerpt from a speech recorded by Thomas Salmon in his *Chronological Historian* (London, 1723), quoted in Tombs 2014, 247.

8. Excerpt from William's statement after the reading of the Declaration of Rights at his coronation, April 11, 1689, cited in Kishlansky 1996, 286.

9. "Edmund Burke, Speech to the Electors of Bristol," November 3, 1774, https://press-pubs.uchicago.edu/founders/documents/v1ch13s7.html.

10. Klein 2020, 875–76.

11. See Morris 2022, chap. 8.

12. The phrase was coined in Anderson 1983.

13. Ferguson 2002, 211.

14. Quoted in Tombs 2014, 561.

15. Quoted in Hyam 2010, 83.

16. Speech of Prime Minister Gascoyne-Cecil at the Queen's Diamond Jubilee (1897), quoted in Bennett 1962, 322.

17. Tombs 2014, 628.

18. Tombs 2014, 630.

19. Ogg 1918.

20. Tombs 2014, 634–35.

Chapter 5. United States: Painful Compromises
in Search of a More Perfect Union

1. Quoted in Farrand and Matteson 1937, 3:97; 1:125, cited in Hutson 1980, 73n7.

2. Quoted in Hutson 1980, 68. The proposal evidently never made it to the actual bargaining table; it is not mentioned in Madison's detailed notes.

3. Cited in Kloppenberg 2016, 401; Lander 1956, 145.

4. Fiske 1916, 265, cited in Hutson 1980, 73n8.

5. Cited in Kloppenberg 2016, 82.

6. Cited in Kloppenberg 2016, 61, 87.

7. The statistics are from Kloppenberg 2016, 71, 75, 177, 186. Property valued at forty shillings was the usual minimum.

8. The statistics are from Lockridge 1974, cited in Daniel Lattier, "Did Public Schools Really Improve American Literacy?," FEE Stories, https://fee.org/articles/did-public-schools-really -improve-american-literacy/.

9. Locke, *Second Treatise of Government*, sec. 208.

10. "Lee Resolution (1776)," National Archives, https://www.archives.gov/milestone -documents/lee-resolution.

11. "Estimated Population of American Colonies: 1610 to 1780," https://web.viu.ca/davies /H320/population.colonies.htm.

12. Allen 2015.

13. "The Declaration of Independence," National Archives, https://www.archives.gov /founding-docs/declaration.

14. "The Declaration of Independence," National Archives, https://www.archives.gov /founding-docs/declaration.

15. "Articles of Confederation," National Archives, https://www.archives.gov/historical-docs /articles-of-confederation.

16. "Articles of Confederation," National Archives, https://www.archives.gov/historical-docs /articles-of-confederation.

17. Letter to William Stephens Smith, the son-in-law of John Adams, 1787, Monticello, https://www.monticello.org/site/research-and-collections/tree-liberty-quotation.

18. Lander 1956, 53.

19. US Constitution, Article 4, sec. 3.

20. US Constitution, Article 3, sec. 1.

21. The Federalist papers are collected in Hamilton, Madison, and Jay 2003.

22. Introduction by Terence Ball in Hamilton, Madison, and Jay 2003, xv.

23. Brutus letter 1. The works of prominent Anti-Federalists are collected in Hamilton, Madison, and Jay 2003.

24. Quoted in Wilentz 2005, 34.

25. "U.S. Population, Land Area and Density, 1790–2020," https://www.u-s-history.com /pages/h986.html; "Black and Slave Population in the United States 1790–1880," Statista, https://www.statista.com/statistics/1010169/black-and-slave-population-us-1790-1880/; James P. Collins, "Native Americans in the Census, 1860–1890," National Archives, https://www

.archives.gov/publications/prologue/2006/summer/indian-census.html; "Historical Racial and Ethnic Demographics of the United States," Wikipedia, https://en.wikipedia.org/wiki /Historical_racial_and_ethnic_demographics_of_the_United_States.

26. Jefferson's first inaugural address, 1800, https://avalon.law.yale.edu/19th_century /jefinau1.asp.

27. Quotes from Wilentz 2005, 95, 96, 97.

28. Tocqueville et al., 1990, vol. 1, chap. 9.

29. According to the US Census, the number of enslaved people increased from under 1 million in 1800, to about 1.2 million in 1810, to 2.5 million in 1840, and then 3.2 million in 1850.

30. David Reader, "Appeal of Forty Thousand Citizens," Encyclopedia of Greater Philadelphia, https://philadelphiaencyclopedia.org/archive/appeal-of-forty-thousand-citizens/.

31. Declaration of Independence, https://www.nps.gov/wori/learn/historyculture /declaration-of-sentiments.htm.

32. Quoted in Wilentz 2005, 650.

33. In fact, in 1790 free Black men could vote on equal terms with whites in ten of the thirteen states, but the Supreme Court dispensed with historical niceties. Wilentz 2005, 712.

34. Hacker 2011.

Chapter 6. Patterns in Democratic Bargaining and Survival

1. "The Room Where It Happens," from *Hamilton*, music and lyrics by Lin-Manuel Miranda, featuring Leslie Odom Jr., Lin-Manuel Miranda, Daveed Diggs, Okieriete Onaodowan, and Original Broadway Cast of *Hamilton*, 2015, https://genius.com/Leslie-odom-jr-lin-manuel -miranda-daveed-diggs-okieriete-onaodowan-and-original-broadway-cast-of-hamilton-the -room-where-it-happens-lyrics.

Chapter 7. Keeping the Deal Real

1. MacWilliams 2020.

2. "About the University," University of Virginia, https://www.virginia.edu/aboutuva.

3. Cited in Winthrop 2020.

4. "The Early Years," Montana State University, https://www.montana.edu/marketing /about-msu/history/early_years.html.

5. "The Constitution Explained," Center for Civic Education, https://www.civiced.org /index.php?page=introduction; Gould, Jamieson, Levine, McConnell, and Smith 2011; Winthrop 2020; https://www.brookings.edu/wp-content/uploads/2020/04/BrookingsPolicy2020 _BigIdeas_Winthrop_CivicEducation.pdf; S. Healy 2022.

6. Interview with Julian Hong, July 21, 2022, Palo Alto, CA.

7. By 2000, the share of immigrants as a percentage of the American population was over 10 percent for the first time in sixty years; by 2022, it was above 14 percent and nearing the all-time highs of the late nineteenth and early twentieth centuries. Steven A. Camarota and Karen Zeigler, "Foreign-Born Population Hits Record 46.6 Million in January 2022," Center for

Immigration Studies, February 23, 2022, https://cis.org/Camarota/ForeignBorn-Population -Hits-Record-466-Million-January-2022.

8. Edgar E. Robinson, "Citizenship in a Democratic World," October 1931.

9. "U.S. Immigrant Population and Share over Time, 1850–Present," Migration Policy Institute, https://www.migrationpolicy.org/programs/data-hub/charts/immigrant-population -over-time.

10. See, for example, "Diversity Statement Resource Guide," American University, https:// www.wcl.american.edu/career/documents/diversity-statement-resource-guide/. The first four in the list of "diverse factors to consider" in answering the question "What makes me diverse?" are race, ethnicity, gender, and sexual orientation. These are followed by religious affiliation, socioeconomic status, and educational background.

WORKS CONSULTED *and* FURTHER READING

Introduction. Democracy's Real Deal

Widespread pessimism among citizens about democracy's future, especially in the United States, is reflected in ongoing public polling and analysis by research and news organizations. Some recent illustrative findings include:

"CNN Poll: Most Americans Feel Democracy Is under Attack in the US," CNN, September 15, 2021. https://www.cnn.com/2021/09/15/politics/cnn-poll-most-americans-democracy-under-attack/index.html.

"A House Divided," *Economist*, September 3, 2022. https://www.economist.com/interactive/briefing/2022/09/03/american-policy-is-splitting-state-by-state-into-two-blocs.

"Poll: Despite Record Turnout, 80 Million Americans Didn't Vote. Here's Why," NPR, December 15, 2020. https://www.npr.org/2020/12/15/945031391/poll-despite-record-turnout-80-million-americans-didnt-vote-heres-why.

"Public Trust in Government: 1958–2022," Pew Research Center, June 6, 2022. https://www.pewresearch.org/politics/2021/05/17/public-trust-in-government-1958-2021/.

"Satisfaction with Democracy," Pew Research Center, February 27, 2020. https://www.pewresearch.org/global/2020/02/27/satisfaction-with-democracy/.

Meanwhile, a torrent of work continues to pour forth, assessing democracy's current problems and proposing various solutions that might ward off its demise. We've found the following particularly informative:

Diamond 2015 (coining and exploring the concept of a new "democratic recession"); Fukuyama 2015 (democracy's capacity failure to meet the impatient demand for good government); Fuller 2015 (a neo-Athenian participative approach to reviving democracy); Deneen 2018 (rebuilding civic life with a Tocquevillian emphasis on community and private organizations as bulwarks against the modern state); Galston 2018 (on the dangers of antiliberal populism); Levitsky and Ziblatt 2018 (on the crisis of eroding democratic and political norms in today's society); Mounk 2018 (reconnecting liberalism to modern democracy); Mounk 2022 (addressing the political polarization of identity-driven diversity); Runciman 2018 (future scenarios for democracy's collapse); Lessig 2021 (on improving representation in current US democracy); Taylor 2020 (stressing rising inequality and its negative effects); Applebaum 2020 (on the spreading authoritarianism); Landemore 2020 (a normative vision combining a new liberalism with more participative democracy, building on James Fishkin's [2009] continuing work to foster more civic deliberations through regional citizen panel discussions).

Chapter 1. Fundamentals: Essential Conditions for Democracy

The recursive case-study-to-theory approach, as applied to problems of democratic survival, is exemplified and justified in Moss, Fung, and Westad (forthcoming). The external scale challenge was elaborated, with special reference to European history since the medieval period, in Tilly 1990. The general problem of rival organizations having to grow to stay equal to the competition is sometimes described as the "Red Queen problem" (Barnett 2008).

Some of the ideas that went into our definition and theory of democracy were developed in a preliminary, more academic form in Ober 2017. That democracy does not imply organized authority relations or even a state is argued in Graeber and Wingrow 2021. For a survey of anthropological studies that support the hypothesis that small foraging communities are strongly democratic in the basic sense of resisting the rule of a boss, see Boehm 2012; Christopher Boehm calls this "reverse dominance hierarchy." For a broad definition of democracy to include monarchs who employ a deliberative council not entirely of their own choosing, see Stasavage 2020. Influential minimalist definitions include Schumpeter [1950] 2008; Dahl 1989; Przeworski, Stokes, and Manin 1999.

"More demanding" definitions require a commitment to rights-based liberalism and/or the presence of competitive political parties. That democracy, in its most basic sense, *does not* require liberalism was the theme in Ober 2017. The most important foundational texts of classical liberalism include John Locke's *Second Treatise of Government* and John Stuart Mill's *On Liberty*. For an authoritative discussion of the development of modern liberalism, see Ryan 2014. For a persuasive argument that modern liberalism and modern republicanism developed in tandem rather than in opposition to one another, see Kalyvas and Katznelson 2008. For some of the best and most influential statements of contemporary liberalism, see Kateb 1992; Rawls 2001, 2005. See also the works on human rights cited below. On the role of political parties and the relationship of republic to democracy, see the works cited below.

The question of who has the authority to decide "who is a citizen," described by political theorists as "the boundary problem," is elucidated in Abizadeh 2012.

There is a vast literature on issues related to the extension of citizenship. Powerful recent discussions of contemporary cases include Hainmueller and Hangartner 2013; Fouka 2019, 2020.

The value of representative institutions for democracy, understood as collective self-government, is defended in Manin 1997; Urbinati 2006. The idea that any working democracy must be predicated on institutions that are self-enforcing is the subject of a growing literature in political science. See especially Weingast 1997; Fearon 2011. The potential contribution of diversity of information, experience, and knowledge to problem solving is discussed in Ober 2008; Landemore 2012.

On the basics of the theory and practice of bargaining, see Serrano 2008. Ken Binmore (2007) supplies a helpful and user-friendly introduction to game theory and its application to bargaining problems. Our discussion of the "armed robber" is inspired by Hart 1994. The organization of pirates and gangsters is discussed by Thucydides in his *History of the Peloponnesian War*, book 1, and more recently in Skarbek 2014. The importance of political bargains to social development was pioneered in the "New Institutional Economics" in North 1981, 1990, and further elaborated in North, Wallace, and Weingast 2009.

The idea of civic friendship was first elaborated by Aristotle in the *Nicomachean Ethics* and *Eudemian Ethics*. See discussions in Cooper 1999, chapter 16; Ludwig 2020. For a deep and thoughtful examination of the question of civic friendship in modern America, see Allen 2004. On the relationship of a culture of trust in institutions and democracy, see Putnam 1993. Works on civic education are listed below in the section on chapter 7.

Human rights may be imagined as either natural or a requirement of morality. The doctrine of "natural rights" is well presented in Locke's *Second Treatise* and the American Declaration of Independence; see further in the section on chapter 5 below. Leo Strauss (1953) remains influential on the topic. Immanuel Kant's *Groundwork for the Metaphysics of Morals* laid the foundation of human rights as a requirement of morality; much of contemporary liberalism remains Kantian in inspiration. For the Universal Declaration of Human Rights, see https://www.un.org/en/about-us/universal-declaration-of-human-rights. For an eloquent discussion by a legal scholar of some of the problems that arise with the proliferation of inherent, universal rights, see Greene 2021.

Fundamental works on the relationship of democracy and political parties include Schattschneider 1960; Schumpeter [1950] 2008; Michels 1962. For a powerful and thoughtful defense of the role of parties in modern democracy, see Rosenblum 2010.

The contrast between a democracy and republic was made by James Madison in several of the essays collected in *The Federalist*; see Hamilton, Madison, and Jay 2003. Among recent works arguing that the contrast is a false one, and that *democracy* and *republic* are close synonyms, see Amar 2005; Kloppenberg 2016. On the original meaning of *democracy*, see Ober 2017, chapter 2. The original meaning of *republic* is discussed below in the section on chapter 3. Jean-Jacques Rousseau's theory of the general will along with his objections to public deliberation and representation were developed in *The Social Contract* (2002, originally 1762). For a thoughtful and critical discussion of Rousseau's ideas, see Shklar 1985. Contemporary Rousseauian democrats include Benjamin Barber (1984) and Richard Tuck (2016).

Chapter 2. Athens: The Bargain That Invented the Power of the Citizenry

Each of us has been thinking and writing about Greek history for most of our careers, so our own work is overrepresented in what follows. For what remains a definitive study of the emergence and development of democratic citizenship at Athens, see Manville 1990. Among Ober's (1989, 1996, 1998, 2005, 2008, 2015) extensive body of work on Athens is a trilogy exploring how democracy was established, sustained, and critically evaluated, two collections of related essays, and a general account of the "rise and fall of classical Greece" that sets the framework for Athenian history. For the best general handbook of Athens's constitutional order, see Hansen 1999. The Athenian democratic revolution of 508 BCE, along with its antecedents and consequences, is discussed in Raaflaub, Ober, and Wallace 2007. Cleisthenes's organizational plan is analyzed in Manville 1990; Ober 2008, chapter 4.

The social collapse that ended the Bronze Age is detailed in Cline 2014. The subsequent Early Iron Age and the revival of the Greek economy and rise of the city-state as a new form of complex social order are well discussed in Morris 1987, 2006; Murray 2017. On Spartan history as well as the distinctive Spartan political and social regime, see Cartledge 2001.

The political bargain that made Solon's legislative reforms possible and the impact of his invention of Athenian citizenship are recounted in Manville 1990; Ober 2022, chapter 4. The tyranny of Peisistratus and his sons is discussed in detail in Lavelle 2005. The history of the Persian Wars, the primary topic of the great *Histories* of Herodotus, is recounted in lively fashion in Green 1996. For a compelling assessment of the key battle of Salamis and how it was won, see Strauss 2004.

The Athenian Empire and the complex historical sources for Athenian imperialism are discussed from different angles in Meiggs 1972; Morris 2009; Ma, Papazarkadas, and Parker 2009. Athenian culture in the imperial era and its relationship to empire are explored in the essays collected in Boedeker and Raaflaub 1998. The Peloponnesian War, the subject of Thucydides's magisterial history, is succinctly related in Kagan 2003—a work that sums up a distinguished four-volume history of the war, from its outbreak to its conclusion. For assessments of the leadership of Pericles and his role in the development of Athenian democracy, see Manville 1997; Azoulay 2014. The new civic bargain that enabled Athens to recover from defeat as well as rebuild both its democracy and economy is skillfully analyzed in Carugati 2019. The role of commerce in the growing Greek economy and the special place of Athens in the commercial networks of the Mediterranean are brilliantly elucidated in Bresson 2015. For the relationship of citizen self-government and economic development, see Ober 2015.

For a discussion of the failure of Athens to respond effectively to the scale challenge offered by the rise of imperial Macedon, see Ober 2015, chapter 10. The career of Philip II is detailed in Worthington 2010. For a thoughtful assessment of the ongoing influence of Athenian democratic institutions and norms in the wider Greek world during the period of Macedonian and Roman domination, see Ma 2018.

Chapter 3. Rome: The Compromises That Created the First Great Republic

For an overview of Roman history, see Boardman, Griffin, and Murray 1991; Beard 2015. For a good introduction to the republican period, see Crawford 1993. On the views of leading scholars on a range of specific aspects of the era, see Flower 2004. For a detailed and magisterial account of Roman political institutions and their historical development, see Lintott 1999. For a thoughtful and provocative analysis of discontinuities in Roman republicanism arguing that the several periods within republican history were distinct in their institutions and norms, see Flower 2010. On the historian Polybius and how his theory of politics influenced his historical account of Roman development, see Champion 2004.

The era of the Roman kings and early republic, and the complex literary and archaeological sources of evidence for early Roman history, are skillfully surveyed in Cornell 1995. On the tradition of the conflict between Plebeians and Patricians, see Brunt 1971b; Raaflaub and Cornell 1986. For what remains an authoritative work on the historical development of Roman citizenship, and the growth of the citizen body, see Sherwin-White 1973. For a detailed look at the role of Italian military forces (citizens, semicitizens, and allies) in Rome's rise to power, see Brunt 1971a.

The Roman conquest of Italy and the slow Romanization of the peninsula are well covered in Salmon 1982. For a lively account of Rome's series of wars with Carthage, see Miles 2011. For a bold and controversial theory that a background culture of aggressive competition drove Roman imperialism, see Harris 1992. A more nuanced view of the Roman expansion into the eastern Mediterranean and western Asian Hellenistic Greek world is presented in Gruen 1984. For an analysis on the impact of imperialism, and especially the import of vast numbers of slaves, on Roman economy and society, see Hopkins 1978. On economic growth during republic, see Kay 2014. For a discussion of the central role played by Roman religion, see Peralta 2020.

The history of the later Roman Republic, and the crisis era that began with the reforms of the Gracchus brothers and reaction by the senatorial oligarchy, is narrated in Scullard 2010. For elucidations on social conflicts, see Brunt 1971b; Nippel 1995. For a discussion of changes in the organization of the Roman army introduced by Marius, see Smith 1958. For the career of Sulla and his ambition to reconstitute the republic, see Keaveney 2005. The careers of Mithridates of Pontus and the leader of a slave uprising, Spartacus, and their wars with Rome are skillfully recounted in Mayor 2009; Strauss 2009.

The dramatic and well-documented era that began with the collapse of Sulla's new order, and the forces that sustained Rome through an era of crisis, are well discussed in Gruen 1974, although the reader may remain puzzled about why the republic ended. For a classic and still-influential account of the kinship relationships among Rome's elite, and how those relations were exploited by a group of leading families, see Syme 1939. For insights on the relations between patrons and clients, see Saller 1982. For a demonstration that the power of the Senate was far from absolute, see Morstein-Marx 2019. On the orator and statesman Cicero, and the political thought of this period, see Connolly 2007; Straumann 2016; Atkins 2018. The career of Caesar along with his complicated role as both a traditional Roman aristocrat and revolutionary are subtly analyzed in Morstein-Marx 2021, which also offers a thorough and evenhanded discussion of earlier biographies. For a detailed look at the death of Caesar and the last days of the republic, see Strauss 2015. For a work that relates the doomed alliance between Antony and Cleopatra, and Octavian's final victory, see Strauss 2022.

The question of whether Rome is rightly described as a democracy in the republican era is debated in Millar 1998, 2002; Morstein-Marx 2004, 2013. Quintus Cicero's election manual is available in a lively translation: Cicero and Freeman 2012.

Chapter 4. Britain: The Royal Bargains That Made Parliament Sovereign

Our British case study takes a traditional, English-centric perspective on the nation's development of democracy, acknowledging but not including other contemporary governance systems of Scotland, Wales, Northern Ireland, or other parts of the "North Atlantic archipelago"—as some historians now want to call Britain. We follow familiar (if not always precise) national nomenclature, differentiating pre–United Kingdom "English" from later (post-1707) "British" history. See "The UK and Great Britain—What's the Difference?," Historic UK, https://www.historic-uk.com/HistoryUK/HistoryofBritain/The-UK-Great-Britain-Whats-the-Difference.

Our chronological narrative draws from three recent and complementary English histories: Jenkins 2011 (a lively but traditional retelling); the savvy analysis in Morris 2022 (emphasizing the significance of England's geographic position for foreign policy and governance); and the magisterial Tombs 2014 (blending a wide array of primary and secondary sources, with valuable discussions of English-French comparisons and the differing traditions of English historiography). Several other more specialized studies that informed this case are noted further below.

For the essential reference on Magna Carta, see Holt 2015. For its broader contribution to later English law, see Baker 2017.

Our discussion of the "hybrid platform of governance" was informed by modern business concepts about shared central and decentralized authority and decision-making: Galbraith 1995; Kotter 2011. But it also draws from previous debates about the nature and contingencies of power between English monarchs and their Parliaments, often described as "government by consent" (see, for example, multiple essays in Jones 2009).

One of the more interesting questions of this debate is whether and how the English monarchy-Parliament relationship was unique versus similar to monarchy-aristocrat governing models in other European nations, and whether the English case was wholly "exceptional" for its role in promoting later democratic governance. On the latter, for arguments that it was, see Maddicott 2010, 376ff.; Stasavage 2020, especially 113–36. We've adopted much of John Maddicott's argument that Anglo-Saxon kings' approach to public councils and meetings was critical to the institutionalization of Parliament as well as English democratic evolution more generally. But we remain agnostic about true English exceptionalism or specific sources of parliamentary differences with later continental self-governance. For Britain's lack of a written constitution, see Colley 2021, 203–43.

For an excellent survey of the socioeconomic, religious, and political background of the Middle Ages, critical to the first millennium of post-Roman English history, see Cantor 1993. Anglo-Saxon society, security, and social organization are thoughtfully woven together in Lambert 2017, emphasizing intersecting customs and laws. For valuable insights and examples documenting Anglo-Saxon military organization and culture, see Hill 2012.

For the development and social impact of the English common law, see Potter 2015; Hudson 2018, both of which also reflect on Magna

Carta's place in its tradition. A more specific discussion of the thorny but critical issues of the development of trial by jury is available in Levy 1999.

For the authoritative work on the history and institutional development of Parliament, see Maddicott 2010. Details of the body's historical membership, size, procedures, and legislative powers are sketched, era by era and chamber by chamber, in concise essays collected in Jones 2009. The numbers, population percentages, and social profiles of enfranchised adult male voters are often debated, but the overall trends are generally agreed on. For this period, we followed research in Dickinson 1994; Payling 1999; Maddicott 2016. For an invaluable and easy-to-access resource for information and historical background related to today's Parliament, see "The Evolution of Parliament," UK Parliament, https://www .parliament.uk/about/living-heritage/evolutionofparliament/.

Examples and discussion of traditions and service in medieval local and shire courts, assemblies, and juries appear throughout Lambert 2017; Hudson 2018; Potter 2015. For profiles and details of contemporary parish life, see French 2001 and 2011.

For a masterful narrative of the sixteenth- and seventeenth-century rise of parliamentary monarchy and the broader context of the period— and also a royal-empathetic corrective to most Whig-slanted histories, see Kishlansky 1996. On the sixteenth-century background of Henry VIII's break with Rome and Tudor rule, see Elton 2019, which remains required reading; see also Guy 1988. Colorful detail and background on the English Civil Wars are offered in Braddick 2009. For a forceful argument for the major significance of socioeconomic partisan struggles in determining the course of the Revolution of 1688, see Pincus 2009.

Debates and references about the growth of readership and literacy in this period are collected by Hailwood 2014. For a wide-ranging discussion of the political ideas and debates of the era (Milton, Hobbes, Locke, etc.), and a helpful way to position them against the legacy of Greco-Roman and Renaissance traditions, see Rahe 1992.

The evolution of parliamentary political parties has been variously explained. For useful starting discussions, see Bulmer-Thomas 1965; also, "The Politics of the House," History of Parliament, https://www

.historyofparliamentonline.org/volume/1690-1715/survey/politics
-house.

We owe the phrase and ideas of "institutionalized disunity" to Tombs 2014, 263ff.

An excellent analysis, combining political, social, and intellectual history into a story of the formation of the British nation during the eighteenth and early nineteenth centuries, is offered in Colley 2005. Linda Colley's research shaped much of our point of view about the period and specifically the emergence of British national identity; the cultural, social, and political reform; and extension of the franchise prior to and after the Great Reform Act of 1832. We have also used her data in our discussion of that major act. For additional insights into the society and ideology of the same period, in a work that is contrarian but comprehensive, see Clark 2000. For a crisp monograph that specifically focuses on the post-1688 stabilization of the government and the rise of Robert Walpole, see Plumb 1967. For an analysis of the partisan dynamics of elections during Walpole's political dominance, see Morris 2022, 281–85.

The story of the 1791 rioting in Birmingham over the celebration of Bastille Day is discussed in Rose 1960 (cited in Tombs 2014, 386). On the persisting dominance of landed gentry in the House of Commons into the nineteenth century, see Whiteley 1970, 172.

The British Empire along with the attendant intellectual and social values of the nineteenth century are once again topics of great controversy, particularly about the nature of the empire's impact on the world and the morality of imperialism relative to contemporary standards. For works that are both excellent and balanced, but with differing ethical assessments, see Jackson 2013; Ferguson 2002; Lester, Boehm, and Mitchell 2021. For another helpful overview, supplemented by more commercial, military, religious, and governing detail during the mature imperial period, see multiple essays in Porter 1999.

Our data related to and discussions of the later nineteenth-century voting reforms follow Tombs 2014, 507–12, with additional discussion in Smith 2004; O'Gorman 1989, 182ff.

On the comparative figures and analysis of World War I soldiers, including volunteers, recruiting, battlefield deaths, and research about troop motivation, see Tombs 2014, 614ff. with references. On the Representation of the People Act, see Ogg 1918.

Chapter 5. United States: Painful Compromises in Search of a More Perfect Union

Two magisterial works on the history of democracy in the United States provided the framework for our account of American history. James Kloppenberg (2016) surveys, in the words of his book's subtitle, "the struggle for self-rule in European and American thought." He presents a sweeping intellectual history of democracy in America from colonial times into the nineteenth century (and beyond) in relationship to developments in western Europe (especially Britain and France). Kloppenberg situates writers and thinkers in their social and especially political contexts. Without claiming that ideas were the unique driver of events, Kloppenberg shows his reader how important ideas were in shaping new conceptions of what was possible and desirable in American political life. Sean Wilentz (2005) traces "the rise of American democracy" from Jefferson to Lincoln. His book introduces readers to the many individuals and organizations whose ambitions and actions led to the development of American political parties and the expansion of the franchise.

Both Kloppenberg and Wilentz argue that the ideal and practice of democracy, as collective self-government by citizens, runs deep in American history. They each emphasize, we believe rightly, that the ideals of freedom, equality, and dignity were central to American political thought and practice from early on—and that the profound and increasingly intolerable contradiction between those ideals and the practice of slavery (along with the exclusion of women from participatory citizenship) was among the central drivers of American political development. Participation in local politics in early Massachusetts, even by those who did not meet the property qualification, is documented in Zuckerman 1968.

On Madison as a leading figure in the writing of the Constitution, careful recorder of the proceedings of the Constitutional Convention of 1787, and ardent defender of the result, see Rakove 1997, 2006. The documents related to the writing of the Constitution are collected in Farrand and Matteson 1937; see also "Farrand's Records," Library of Congress, https://memory.loc.gov/ammem/amlaw/lwfr.html. Butler's notes on the convention are collected and discussed in Hutson 1980. On Butler and the South Carolina delegation in Philadelphia, see Lander 1956. For the social context of Philadelphia in the later eighteenth century, see Smith 1990. On the later doubts of several founders about their project, see Rasmussen 2021.

For a demonstration that the advantage of Britain over France in public borrowing in the eighteenth century was due to their different political systems, and had powerful effects on warfare outcomes, see North and Weingast 1989. On Locke and his theory of popular sovereignty, see Franklin 1978; Dunn 1982. On Montesquieu, see Shklar 1987. For a survey of the founders' knowledge of Greek and Roman texts, and the influence of ancient political thought on them, see Ricks 2020. The essays collected in Onuf and Cole 2013 focus on the influence of the classical world on Jefferson.

Whether the American Revolution was fundamentally radical and democratic, or conservative and concerned with protecting the rights of property, is much debated. Our sympathies are with the former; see Wood 1982; Rakove 2011. Danielle Allen's (2015) reading of the Declaration of Independence, and the circumstances of its composition, is inspiring and deeply thoughtful. The text of the Declaration of Independence with commentary is available at "The Declaration of Independence," National Archives, https://www.archives.gov/founding-docs/declaration.

For the text of the Articles of Confederation, see "Articles of Confederation," National Archives, https://www.archives.gov/historical-docs/articles-of-confederation. For Madison on the failure of the articles, see "Vices of the Political System of the United States, April 1787," National Archives, https://founders.archives.gov/documents/Madison/01-09-02-0187. On the democratic character of the US Constitution, our views have been influenced by Amar 2005. For the text of the Constitution, see "The Constitution of the United States," National Archives, https://www.archives.gov/founding-docs/constitution.

For the Federalist papers, along with the letters of Brutus, see Hamilton, Madison, and Jay 2003. For a history of the Constitution's ratification, see "The Documentary History of the Ratification of the Constitution," University of Virginia Press, https://rotunda.upress .virginia.edu/founders/RNCN.html; Kaminski and Leffler 1998. For a state-by-state analysis, see Maier 2010.

Anti-Federalists and their arguments are discussed in Storing and Dry 1981; Cornell 1999, with the latter focusing on decentralization, localism, constitutional textualism, and public debate. For an investigation of how the concept of constitutionalism evolved in the United States, from the period prior to the drafting and ratification of the Constitution through to its early implementation during the first Congress, see Gienapp 2018. For a look at the complex notion of "we the people" as the source of constitutional authority as it played out in the postrevolutionary American context, see Frank 2010.

For a new edition of the *Narrative of the Life of Frederick Douglass,* with added materials, see Douglass 2016. Tocqueville's (1990) immensely influential account of American democracy is assessed in the context of his other work in Wolin 2001; the essays in Schleifer 2012 offer a range of appreciations. For estimates of the casualties of the American Civil War, employing statistical methods, see Hacker 2011. For a classic account of the Civil War era, see McPherson 1988. For the postwar amendments to the Constitution, see "The Constitution: Amendments 11–27," National Archives, https://www.archives.gov/founding-docs /amendments-11-27. The movement for women's suffrage is chronicled in Crawford 2003. For a highly influential history of the suppression of the rights of American Blacks after the Civil War, see Woodward 2002; see also Litwack 1998, 2009.

Chapter 6. Patterns in Democratic Bargaining and Survival

On the seventeenth-century "quarrel of the ancients and moderns" and its resonance in the culture war debates of the late twentieth century, see DeJean 1997. The speed of travel in antiquity is analyzed and visualized on the immensely useful Stanford ORBIS website, https://orbis.stanford.edu/. For an analysis of how travel time affects modern voting in a modern democracy, using a case study in New Zealand, see Gibson et al. 2013. On the political ramifications, especially in seventeenth-century England, of the invention of the printing press and the wide dissemination of printed materials, see Zaret 2000. On the importance of BATNA in practical bargaining, see Pinkley, Neale, and Bennett 1994; Dixit and Skeath 1999, chapter 16.

Chapter 7. Keeping the Deal Real

Many works influenced this chapter's argument. In addition to those already cited in the introduction, we'd note others particularly relevant to the American context. On changing party and political structures, see Issacharoff, Karlan, and Pildes 2006; Pildes 2022.) On the damaging effects of social media, see Rauch 2021; Persily and Tucker 2022; Susskind 2022. On disagreements, distrust, and tribal enmity among citizens, see Haidt 2012; Mason 2018; Fukuyama 2019; Klein 2020; Zuckerman 2021.

For background on civic education (both formal and informal), see the helpful overview in Crittenden and Levine 2018. For civic education in Athens, see Ober 1989, 157–91; Ober 2005, 128–56; Ober 2015, 232–36; Strauss 2000. In Rome, see Bonner 1977. In Great Britain, see Heater 2006, 56–57, 115–16, 213–16; Colley 2005, 226ff., passim; Beck 2011. In America, see Marquette and Mineshima 2002; Winthrop 2020. For a demonstration of the failure of forced language assimilation to Americanize descendants of German immigrants in the early and mid-twentieth century, see Fouka 2019, 2020.

Edgar Robinson's 1931 opening lecture is available in Stanford's archives; a slightly later version was published in Robinson 1934, 50–62. For a brief history of the programs that followed Problems of Citizenship at Stanford, see Manuel 1997. On The new Citizenship in the 21st Century course, see "Citizenship in the 21st Century," Stanford University, https://college.stanford.edu/courses/citizenship; "Stanford Pilots a New Citizenship Course for First-Year Students," Stanford

University, https://news.stanford.edu/report/2021/03/17/citizenship -course-piloted/. On the new Stanford Civics Initiative, see "Welcome to the Stanford Civics Initiative," Stanford University, https://civics .stanford.edu/.

Recent initiatives and organizations promoting improved civic education (variously defined) across America comprise a growing list, including: Educating for American Democracy 2021 (https://www .educatingforamericandemocracy.org/); Lenore Annenberg Institute for Civics (https://www.annenbergpublicpolicycenter.org/political -communication/leonore-annenberg-institute-for-civics/); iCivics (https://www.icivics.org/about); the Center for Civics Education (https://www.civiced.org/); the Democratic Knowledge Project at the Harvard Safra Center for Ethics (https://www.democraticknowledgeproject .org/); CivicLex (https://www.civiclex.org/); "Civics at Work" at the Center for Strategic and International Studies (https://www.csis.org /programs/international-security-program/civics-work-initiative); Sphere Summit for Educators at the Cato Institute (https://www.cato .org/sphere/about-sphere); Community Colleges for Democracy (https://compact.org/current-programs/affinity-networks /community-colleges-for-democracy?f%255B0%255D%3Dresource _tag=667); Tufts University CIRCLE (Center for Information and Research on Civic Learning and Engagement (https://circle.tufts.edu/); and the Georgia Center for Civic Engagement (https://georgiacivics .org/).

Also on the rise are other related initiatives and research discussions: a comprehensive approach to reforming our democratic system and citizenship by the Commission on the Practice of American Citizenship (2020); legislative proposal of the US Congress, the Educating for Democracy Act (authorizing grants to expand state programs and assess civics and history programs in public education, H.R. 8295, https://www .congress.gov/bill/116th-congress/house-bill/8295). Johns Hopkins University's president's recent book calls for adding civic education to college curricula (Daniels 2021). For reflections on the history of unifying stories of America's purpose and identity, and suggestions for new narratives for the next generation of civic education, see Goldman 2021.

The vision advanced in our book is not intended to discourage other, more institutional and cultural solutions being voiced for improving our democracy. In some cases, the concepts forwarded by the civic bargain could complement those. In other instances, they might reframe approaches to improve the chances of success. Readers might consider such opportunities when reviewing other reform proposals—those in the works cited earlier as well as others coming forth in the future.

Ideas from related disciplines about improving current democracy might also be complemented by civic bargain approaches. One emerging discussion from technology and economics proposes using the real-time behavioral data of citizens to dynamically legislate national policies, increasing their relevance and impact for society. See "Enter Third-Wave Economics" 2021.

From sociology, certain practical ideas for fostering civic friendship are now being floated (such as requiring congressional members to live together when the legislature is in session): Cooper 2018. Others are more wide-ranging and ambitious, like the suggestion to translate the cultural practices of the early twentieth-century progressive era to today's civic-starved society. See Putnam 2020.

Business leaders are also seeing the need and opportunity to strengthen American democracy, such as by adopting certain civic practices within their companies (first explored in Manville and Ober 2003), pursuing socially responsible practices to complement those (Henderson 2020), or employing business-style strategies to accelerate political reform itself (Gehl and Porter 2020).

REFERENCES

Abizadeh, Arash. 2012. "On the Demos and Its Kin: Nationalism, Democracy, and the Boundary Problem." *American Political Science Review* 106:867–82.

Allen, Danielle. 2004. *Talking to Strangers: Anxieties of Citizenship since Brown v. Board of Education.* Chicago: University of Chicago Press.

———. 2015. *Our Declaration: A Reading of the Declaration of Independence in Defense of Equality.* New York: W. W. Norton and Company.

Amar, Akhil Reed. 2005. *America's Constitution: A Biography.* New York: Random House.

Anderson, Benedict. 1983. *Imagined Communities: Reflections on the Origins and Spread of Nationalism.* London: Verso.

Applebaum, Anne. 2020. *Twilight of Authoritarianism: The Seductive Lure of Authoritarianism.* New York: Penguin.

Atkins, Jed W. 2018. *Roman Political Thought.* Cambridge: Cambridge University Press.

Azoulay, Vincent. 2014. *Pericles of Athens.* Princeton, NJ: Princeton University Press.

Baker, John. 2017. *The Reinvention of Magna Carta 1216–1616.* Cambridge: Cambridge University Press.

Barber, Benjamin R. 1984. *Strong Democracy: Participatory Politics for a New Age.* Berkeley: University of California Press.

Barnett, William P. 2008. *The Red Queen among Organizations: How Competitiveness Evolves.* Princeton, NJ: Princeton University Press.

Beard, Mary. 2015. *SPQR: A History of Ancient Rome.* New York: W. W. Norton and Company.

Beck, John. 2011. "A Brief History of Citizenship Education in England and Wales." In *Debates in Citizenship Education,* edited by James Arthur and Hilary Cremin, 3–16. London: Routledge.

Bennett, George. 1962. *The Concept of Empire: Burke to Attlee, 1774–1947.* London: Black.

Binmore, Ken G. 2007. *Game Theory: A Very Short Introduction.* Oxford: Oxford University Press.

Boardman, John, Jasper Griffin, and Oswyn Murray, eds. 1991. *The Oxford History of the Roman World.* Oxford: Oxford University Press.

Boedeker, Deborah D., and Kurt A. Raaflaub, eds. 1998. *Democracy, Empire, and the Arts in Fifth-Century Athens.* Cambridge, MA: Harvard University Press.

Boehm, Christopher. 2021. *Moral Origins: The Evolution of Virtue, Altruism, and Shame.* New York: Basic Books.

Bonner, Stanley F. 1977. *Education in Ancient Rome: From the Elder Cato to the Younger Pliny.* Berkeley: University of California Press.

Braddick, Michael. 2009. *God's Fury, England's Fire: A New History of the English Civil Wars.* London: Penguin Books.

Bresson, Alain. 2015. *The Making of the Ancient Greek Economy: Institutions, Markets, and Growth in the City-States.* Princeton, NJ: Princeton University Press.

Brunt, P. A. 1971a. *Italian Manpower, 225 B.C.–A.D. 14.* Oxford: Oxford University Press.

———. 1971b. *Social Conflicts in the Roman Republic.* New York: W. W. Norton and Company.

Bulmer-Thomas, Ivor. 1965. *The Growth of the British Party System: Volume I: 1640–1923.* London: John Baker.

Camarota, Steven A., and Karen Zeigler. 2022. "Foreign-Born Population Hits Record 46.6 Million in January 2022." Center for Immigration Studies, February 23. https://cis.org /Camarota/ForeignBorn-Population-Hits-Record-466-Million-January-2022.

Cantor, Norman. 1993. *The Civilization of the Middle Ages.* Revised ed. New York: Harper-Collins.

Cartledge, Paul. 2001. *Spartan Reflections.* London: Duckworth.

Carugati, Federica. 2019. *Creating a Constitution: Law, Democracy, and Growth in Classical Athens.* Princeton, NJ: Princeton University Press.

Champion, Craige Brian. 2004. *Cultural Politics in Polybius's Histories.* Berkeley: University of California Press.

Cicero, Quintus Tullius, and Philip Freeman. 2012. *How to Win an Election: An Ancient Guide for Modern Politicians.* Princeton, NJ: Princeton University Press.

Clark, J.C.D. 2000. *English Society 1660–1832: Religion, Ideology and Politics during the Ancien Régime.* Cambridge: Cambridge University Press.

Cline, Eric H. 2014. *1177 B.C.: The Year Civilization Collapsed.* Princeton, NJ: Princeton University Press.

Colley, Linda. 2005. *Britons: Forging the Nation 1707–1837.* Revised ed. New Haven, CT: Yale University Press.

———. 2021. *The Gun, the Ship, and the Pen: Warfare, Constitutions, and the Making of the Modern World.* New York: Liveright.

Commission on the Practice of American Citizenship. 2020. *Our Common Purpose: Reinventing American Democracy for the 21st Century.* Cambridge, MA: American Academy of Arts and Sciences.

Connolly, Joy. 2007. *The State of Speech: Rhetoric and Political Thought in Ancient Rome.* Princeton, NJ: Princeton University Press.

Cooper, John M. 1999. *Reason and Emotion: Essays on Ancient Moral Psychology and Ethical Theory.* Princeton, NJ: Princeton University Press.

Cooper, Rory. 2018. "Want to Drain the Swamp? Build Congress a Dorm." *Politico,* November 20. https://www.politico.com/magazine/story/2018/11/20/want-to-drain-the-swamp -build-congress-a-dorm-222641/.

Cornell, Saul. 1999. *The Other Founders: Anti-Federalism and the Dissenting Tradition in America, 1788–1828.* Chapel Hill: University of North Carolina Press.

Cornell, Tim. 1995. *The Beginnings of Rome: Italy and Rome from the Bronze Age to the Punic Wars (c. 1000–264 B.C.).* London: Routledge.

Crawford, Elizabeth. 2003. *The Women's Suffrage Movement*. New York: Routledge.

Crawford, Michael. 1993. *The Roman Republic*. Cambridge, MA: Harvard University Press.

Crittenden, Jack, and Peter Levine. 2018. "Civic Education." In *Stanford Encyclopedia of Philosophy*. https://plato.stanford.edu/archives/fall2018/entries/civic-education.

Dahl, Robert Alan. 1989. *Democracy and Its Critics*. New Haven, CT: Yale University Press.

Daniels, Ronald J. 2021. *What Universities Owe Democracy*. Baltimore: Johns Hopkins University Press.

DeJean, Joan. 1997. *Ancients against Moderns*. Chicago: University of Chicago Press.

Deneen, Patrick. 2018. *Why Liberalism Failed*. New Haven, CT: Yale University Press.

Diamond, Larry. 2015. "Facing up to the Democratic Recession." *Journal of Democracy* 26 (1): 141–55.

Dickinson, H. T. 1994. *The Politics of the People in Eighteenth-Century Britain*. Houndmills, UK: Macmillan Press.

Dixit, Avinash K., and Susan Skeath. 1999. *Games of Strategy*. New York: W. W. Norton and Company.

Douglass, Frederick. 2016. *Narrative of the Life of Frederick Douglass, an American Slave: Written by Himself*. Edited by John R. McKivigan and Peter P. Hinks. New Haven, CT: Yale University Press.

Dunn, John. 1982. *The Political Thought of John Locke: An Historical Account of the Argument of the "Two Treatises of Government."* Cambridge: Cambridge University Press.

Educating for American Democracy. 2021. "Educating for American Democracy: Excellence in History and Civics for All Learners." https://www.educatingforamericandemocracy.org/.

Elton, Geoffrey R. 2019. *England under the Tudors*. 3rd ed. New York: Routledge.

"Enter Third-Wave Economics." 2021. *Economist*, October 23. https://www.economist.com/briefing/2021/10/23/enter-third-wave-economics.

Farrand, Max, and David Maydole Matteson, eds. 1937. *The Records of the Federal Convention of 1787*. New Haven, CT: Yale University Press.

Fearon, James. 2011. "Self-Enforcing Democracy." *Quarterly Journal of Economics* 126:1661–708.

Ferguson, Niall. 2002. *Empire: The Rise and Demise of the British World Order and the Lessons for Global Power*. London: Allan Lane.

Fishkin, James S. 2009. *When the People Speak: Deliberative Democracy and Public Consultation*. Oxford: Oxford University Press.

Fiske, John. 1916. *The Critical Period of American History, 1783–1789*. Boston: Houghton Mifflin Company.

Flower, Harriet I., ed. 2004. *The Cambridge Companion to the Roman Republic*. Cambridge: Cambridge University Press.

———. 2010. *Roman Republics*. Princeton, NJ: Princeton University Press.

Fouka, Vasiliki. 2019. "How Do Immigrants Respond to Discrimination? The Case of Germans in the US during World War I." *American Political Science Review* 113 (2): 405–22.

———. 2020. "Backlash: The Unintended Effects of Language Prohibition in U.S. Schools after World War I." *Review of Economic Studies* 87 (1): 204–39.

Frank, Jason. 2010. *Constituent Moments: Enacting the People in Postrevolutionary America*. Durham, NC: Duke University Press.

Franklin, Julian H. 1978. *John Locke and the Theory of Sovereignty: Mixed Monarchy and the Right of Resistance in the Political Thought of the English Revolution*. Cambridge: Cambridge University Press.

French, Katherine L. 2001. *The People of the Parish: Community Life in a Late Medieval Diocese*. Philadelphia: University of Pennsylvania Press.

———. 2011. "Rebuilding St. Margarete's: Parish Involvement and Community Action in Late Medieval Westminster." *Journal of Social History* 45 (1): 148–71.

Fukuyama, Francis. 2015. "Why Is Democracy Performing So Poorly?" *Journal of Democracy* 2 (1): 11–20.

———. 2019. *Identity: The Demand for Dignity and the Politics of Resentment*. London: Profile Books.

Fuller, Roslyn. 2015. *Beasts and Gods: How Democracy Changed Its Meaning and Lost Its Purpose*. London: Zed Books.

Galbraith, Jay R. 1995. *Designing Organizations: An Executive Briefing on Strategy, Structure and Process*. San Francisco: Jossey-Bass.

Galston, William. 2018. *Anti-Pluralism: The Populist Threat to Liberal Democracy*. New Haven, CT: Yale University Press.

Gehl, Katherine M., and Michael E. Porter. 2020. "Fixing U.S. Politics." *Harvard Business Review*, July–August. https://hbr.org/2020/07/fixing-u-s-politics.

Gibson, John, Bonggeun Kim, Steven Stillman, and Geua Boe-Gibson. 2013. "Time to Vote." *Public Choice* 156 (3–4): 517–36.

Gienapp, Jonathan. 2018. *The Second Creation: Fixing the American Constitution in the Founding Era*. Cambridge, MA: Harvard University Press.

Goldman, Samuel. 2021. *After Nationalism: Being American in an Age of Division*. Philadelphia: University of Pennsylvania Press.

Gould, Jonathan, Kathleen Hall Jamieson, Peter Levine, Ted McConnell, and David B. Smith, eds. 2011. *Guardian of Democracy. The Civic Mission of Schools*. Philadelphia: Leonore Annenberg Institute for Civics of the Annenberg Public Policy Center at the University of Pennsylvania, 2011. https://www.carnegie.org/publications/guardian-of-democracy-the -civic-mission-of-schools/.

Graeber, David, and David Wengrow. 2021. *The Dawn of Everything: A New History of Humanity*. New York: Farrar, Straus and Giroux.

Green, Peter. 1996. *The Greco-Persian Wars*. Berkeley: University of California Press.

Greene, Jamal. 2021. *How Rights Went Wrong*. New York: Houghton Mifflin.

Gruen, Erich S. 1974. *The Last Generation of the Roman Republic*. Berkeley: University of California Press.

———. 1984. *The Hellenistic World and the Coming of Rome*. Berkeley: University of California Press.

Guy, John. 1988. *Tudor England*. Oxford: Oxford University Press.

Hacker, J. David. 2011. "A Census-Based Count of the Civil War Dead." *Civil War History* 57 (4): 307–48.

Haidt, Jonathan. 2012. *The Righteous Mind: Why Good People Are Divided by Politics and Religion*. New York: Pantheon Books.

Hailwood, Mark. 2014. "'The Rabble That Cannot Read'? Ordinary People's Literacy in Seventeenth-Century England." *The Many-Headed Monster* (blog). October 13. https:// manyheadedmonster.com/2014/10/13/the-rabble-that-cannot-read-ordinary-peoples -literacy-in-seventeenth-century-england/.

Hainmueller, Jens, and Dominik Hangartner. 2013. "Who Gets a Swiss Passport? A Natural Experiment in Immigrant Discrimination." *American Political Science Review* 107 (1): 159–87.

Hamilton, Alexander, James Madison, and John Jay. 2003. *The Federalist.* Edited by Terence Bell. Cambridge: Cambridge University Press. First published 1788.

Hansen, Mogens Herman. 1999. *The Athenian Democracy in the Age of Demosthenes: Structure, Principles and Ideology.* Norman: University of Oklahoma Press.

Harris, William V. 1992. *War and Imperialism in Republican Rome, 327–70 B.C.* Oxford: Oxford University Press.

Hart, H.L.A. 1994. *The Concept of Law.* Oxford: Oxford University Press.

Healy, Shawn. 2022. "Momentum Grows for Stronger Civic Education across States." American Bar Association, January 4. https://www.americanbar.org/groups/crsj/publications /human_rights_magazine_home/the-state-of-civic-education-in-america/momentum -grows-for-stronger-civic-education-across-states/.

Heater, Derek. 2006. *Citizenship in Britain: A History.* Edinburgh: Edinburgh University Press.

Henderson, Rebecca M. 2020. *Reimagining Capitalism in a World on Fire.* New York: Public Affairs.

Hill, Paul. 2012. *The Anglo-Saxons at War, 800–1066.* Barnsley, UK: Pen and Sword Books.

Hitchner, R. Bruce. In progress. *An Evolutionary History of Roman Imperialism under the Republic.*

Holt, J. C. 2015. *Magna Carta.* 3rd ed. Cambridge: Cambridge University Press.

Hopkins, Keith. 1978. *Conquerors and Slaves.* Cambridge: Cambridge University Press.

Hudson, John. 2018. *The Formation of the English Common Law.* 2nd ed. New York: Routledge.

Hutson, James H. 1980. "Pierce Butler's Records of the Federal Constitutional Convention." *Quarterly Journal of the Library of Congress* 37 (1): 64–73.

Hyam, Ronald. 2010. *Understanding the British Empire.* Cambridge: Cambridge University Press.

Issacharoff, S., Pam Karlan, and Richard H. Pildes. 2006. *The Law of Democracy: Legal Structure of the Political Process.* Saint Paul: Foundation Press.

Jackson, Ashley. 2013. *The British Empire: A Very Short Introduction.* Oxford: Oxford University Press.

Jenkins, Simon. 2011. *A Short History of England: The Glorious Story of a Rowdy Nation.* New York: Public Affairs.

Jones, Clyve, ed. 2009. *A Short History of Parliament: England, Great Britain, the United Kingdom, Ireland and Scotland.* Woodbridge. UK: Boydell Press.

Kagan, Donald. 2003. *The Peloponnesian War.* New York: Penguin Books.

Kalyvas, Andreas, and Ira Katznelson. 2008. *Liberal Beginnings: Making a Republic for the Moderns.* Cambridge: Cambridge University Press.

Kaminski, John P., and Richard Leffler. 1998. *Federalists and Antifederalists: The Debate over the Ratification of the Constitution.* Madison, WI: Madison House.

Kant, Immanuel. 1991. "Perpetual Peace: A Philosophical Sketch." In *Kant: Political Writings*, edited by H. S. Reiss, 93–130. Cambridge: Cambridge University Press. First published 1795.

Kateb, George. 1992. *The Inner Ocean: Individualism and Democratic Culture*. Ithaca, NY: Cornell University Press.

Kay, Philip. 2014. *Rome's Economic Revolution*. Oxford: Oxford University Press.

Keaveney, Arthur. 2005. *Sulla, the Last Republican*. London: Routledge.

Kishlansky, Mark. 1996. *A Monarchy Transformed: Britain 1603–1714*. London: Penguin Books.

Klein, Ezra. 2020. *Why We're Polarized*. New York: Simon and Schuster.

Kloppenberg, James T. 2016. *Toward Democracy: The Struggle for Self-rule in European and American Thought*. New York: Oxford University Press.

Kotter, John P. 2011. "Hierarchy and Network: Two Structures, One Organization." HBR.org, May 23. https://hbr.org/2011/05/two-structures-one-organization.

Lambert, Tom. 2017. *Law and Order in Anglo-Saxon England*. Oxford: Oxford University Press.

Landemore, Hélène. 2012. *Democratic Reason: Politics, Collective Intelligence, and the Rule of the Many*. Princeton, NJ: Princeton University Press.

———. 2020. *Open Democracy: Reinventing Popular Rule for the Twenty-First Century*. Princeton, NJ: Princeton University Press.

Lander, Ernst M. 1956. "The South Carolinians at the Philadelphia Convention, 1787." *South Carolina Historical Magazine* 57 (3): 134–55.

Lavelle, B. M. 2005. *Fame, Money, and Power: The Rise of Peisistratos and "Democratic" Tyranny at Athens*. Ann Arbor: University of Michigan Press.

Lessig, Lawrence. 2021. *They Don't Represent Us: Reclaiming Our Democracy*. New York: William Morrow.

Lester, Alan, Kate Boehm, and Peter Mitchell. 2021. *Ruling the World: Freedom, Civilization and Liberalism in the Nineteenth-Century British Empire*. Cambridge: Cambridge University Press.

Levitsky, Steven, and Daniel Ziblatt. 2018. *How Democracies Die*. New York: Broadway Books.

Levy, Leonard. 1999. *The Palladium of Justice: Origins of Trial by Jury*. Chicago: Ivan R. Dee.

Lintott, Andrew W. 1999. *The Constitution of the Roman Republic*. Oxford: Oxford University Press.

Litwack, Leon F. 1998. *Trouble in Mind: Black Southerners in the Age of Jim Crow*. New York: A. A. Knopf.

———. 2009. *How Free Is Free? The Long Death of Jim Crow*. Cambridge, MA: Harvard University Press.

Locke, John. 1988. *Two Treatises of Government*. Edited by Peter Laslett. Cambridge: Cambridge University Press.

Lockridge, Kenneth A. 1974. *Literacy in Colonial New England: An Enquiry into the Social Context of Literacy in the Early Modern West*. New York: W. W. Norton and Company.

Ludwig, Paul W. 2020. *Rediscovering Political Friendship in Aristotle's Theory and Modern Identity, Community, and Equality*. Cambridge: Cambridge University Press.

Ma, John. 2018. "Whatever Happened to Athens? Thoughts on the Great Convergence and Beyond." In *The Hellenistic and Early Imperial Greek Reception of Classical Athenian Democracy and Political Thought*, edited by Benjamin Gray and Mirko Canevaro, 277–97. Oxford: Oxford University Press.

Ma, John, Nikolaos Papazarkadas, and Robert Parker, eds. 2009. *Interpreting the Athenian Empire*. London: Bristol Classical Press.

MacWilliams, Matthew C. 2020. "Trump Is an Authoritarian. So Are Millions of Americans." *Politico*, September 23. https://www.politico.com/news/magazine/2020/09/23/trump-america-authoritarianism-420681.

Maddicott, John. 2010. *The Origins of the English Parliament, 924–1327*. Oxford: Oxford University Press.

———. 2016. "Parliament and the People in Medieval England." *Parliamentary History* 35 (3): 336–51.

Maier, Pauline. 2010. *Ratification: The People Debate the Constitution, 1787–1788*. New York: Simon and Schuster.

Manin, Bernard. 1997. *The Principles of Representative Government*. Cambridge: Cambridge University Press.

Manuel, Diane. 1997. "Reshaping the Humanities." *Stanford Today*, May–June. https://web.stanford.edu/dept/news/stanfordtoday/ed/9705/9705ncf1.html.

Manville, Philip Brook. 1990. *The Origins of Citizenship in Ancient Athens*. Princeton, NJ: Princeton University Press.

———. 1997. "Pericles and the 'both/and' Vision for Democratic Athens." In *Polis and Polemos: Essays on Politics, War, and History in Ancient Greece, in Honor of Donald Kagan*, edited by Charles D. Hamilton and Peter Krentz, 73–84. Claremont, CA: Regina Books.

Manville, Philip Brook, and Josiah Ober. 2003. *A Company of Citizens: What the World's First Democracy Teaches Leaders about Creating Great Organizations*. Boston: Harvard Business School Press.

Marquette, Heather, and Dale Mineshima. 2002. "Civic Education in the United States: Lessons for the UK." *Parliamentary Affairs* 55 (3): 539–55.

Mason, Lilliana. 2018. *Uncivil Agreement: How Politics Became Our Identity*. Chicago: University of Chicago Press.

Mayor, Adrienne. 2009. *The Poison King: The Life and Legend of Mithridates, Rome's Deadliest Enemy*. Princeton, NJ: Princeton University Press.

McPherson, James M. 1988. *Battle Cry of Freedom: The Civil War Era*. New York: Oxford University Press.

Meiggs, Russell. 1972. *The Athenian Empire*. Oxford: Oxford University Press.

Michels, Robert. 1962. *Political Parties: A Sociological Study of the Oligarchical Tendencies of Modern Democracy*. New York: Collier Books.

Miles, Richard. 2011. *Carthage Must Be Destroyed*. New York: Viking.

Millar, Fergus. 1998. *The Crowd in Rome in the Late Republic*. Ann Arbor: University of Michigan Press.

———. 2002. *The Roman Republic in Political Thought*. Hanover, NH: University Press of New England.

Montesquieu, Charles de Secondat. 1968. *Considerations on the Causes of the Greatness of the Romans and Their Decline*. Edited by David Lowenthal. Ithaca, NY: Cornell University Press.

———. 1989. *The Spirit of the Laws*. Edited by Anne M. Cohler, Basia Carolyn Miller, and Harold Stone. Cambridge: Cambridge University Press.

Morris, Ian. 1987. *Burial and Ancient Society: The Rise of the Greek City-State*. Cambridge: Cambridge University Press.

———. 2006. "The Collapse and Regeneration of Complex Society in Greece, 1500–500 BC." In *After Collapse: The Regeneration of Complex Societies*, edited by Glenn M. Schwartz and John J. Nichols, 72–84. Tucson: University of Arizona Press.

———. 2009. "The Greater Athenian State." In *The Dynamics of Ancient Empires*, edited by Ian Morris and Walter Scheidel, 99–177. Oxford: Oxford University Press.

———. 2022. *Geography Is Destiny: Britain's Place in the World: A 10,000-Year History*. New York: Farrar, Straus and Giroux.

Morstein-Marx, Robert. 2004. *Mass Oratory and Political Power in the Late Roman Republic*. Cambridge: Cambridge University Press.

———. 2013. "'Cultural Hegemony' and the Communicative Power of the Roman Elite." In *Community and Communication*, edited by Catherine Steel and Henriette van der Blom, 29–47. Oxford: Oxford University Press.

———. 2019. "Fear of the People." *Rivista Storica Italiana* 131:515–33.

———. 2021. *Julius Caesar and the Roman People*. Cambridge: Cambridge University Press.

Moss, David, Archon Fung, and Odd Arne Westad. Forthcoming. *When Democracy Breaks: Studies in Democratic Erosion and Collapse, from Ancient Athens to the Present Day*. Oxford: Oxford University Press.

Mounk, Yashcha. 2018. *The People vs. Democracy. Why Our Freedom Is in Danger and How to Save It*. Cambridge, MA: Harvard University Press.

———. 2022. *The Great Experiment: Why Diverse Democracies Fall Apart and How They Can Endure*. New York: Penguin Press.

Murray, Sarah. 2017. *The Collapse of the Mycenaean Economy: Imports, Trade, and Institutions, 1300–700 BCE*. New York: Cambridge University Press.

Nippel, Wilfried. 1995. *Public Order in Ancient Rome*. Cambridge: Cambridge University Press.

North, Douglass Cecil. 1981. *Structure and Change in Economic History*. New York: W. W. Norton and Company.

———. 1990. *Institutions, Institutional Change, and Economic Performance*. Cambridge: Cambridge University Press.

North, Douglass Cecil, John Joseph Wallis, and Barry R. Weingast. 2009. *Violence and Social Orders: A Conceptual Framework for Interpreting Recorded Human History*. Cambridge: Cambridge University Press.

North, Douglass Cecil, and Barry R. Weingast. 1989. "Constitutions and Commitment: The Evolution of Institutions Governing Public Choice in Seventeenth-Century England." *Journal of Economic History* 49:803–32.

Ober, Josiah. 1989. *Mass and Elite in Democratic Athens: Rhetoric, Ideology, and the Power of the People*. Princeton, NJ: Princeton University Press.

———. 1996. *The Athenian Revolution: Essays on Ancient Greek Democracy and Political Theory*. Princeton, NJ: Princeton University Press.

———. 1998. *Political Dissent in Democratic Athens: Intellectual Critics of Popular Rule*. Princeton, NJ: Princeton University Press.

———. 2005. *Athenian Legacies: Essays in the Politics of Going on Together*. Princeton, NJ: Princeton University Press.

———. 2008. *Democracy and Knowledge: Innovation and Learning in Classical Athens*. Princeton, NJ: Princeton University Press.

———. 2015. *The Rise and Fall of Classical Greece*. Princeton, NJ: Princeton University Press.

———. 2017. *Demopolis: Democracy before Liberalism in Theory and Practice*. Cambridge: Cambridge University Press.

———. 2022. *The Greeks and the Rational: The Discovery of Practical Reason*. Berkeley: University of California Press.

Ogg, Frederic A. 1918. "The British Representation of the People Act." *American Political Science Review* 12 (3): 498–503. https://www.jstor.org/stable/1946102.

O'Gorman, Frank. 1989. *Voters, Patrons, and Parties: The Unreformed Electoral System of Hanoverian England, 1734–1832*. Oxford: Oxford University Press.

Onuf, Peter S., and Nicholas P. Cole, eds. 2013. *Thomas Jefferson, the Classical World, and Early America*. Charlottesville: University of Virginia Press.

Payling, Simon J. 1999. "County Parliamentary Elections in Fifteenth-Century England." *Parliamentary History* 18 (3): 237–59.

Peralta, Dan-el Padilla. 2020. *Divine Institutions*. Princeton, NJ: Princeton University Press.

Persily, Nathaniel, and Joshua A. Tucker, eds. 2020. *Social Media and Democracy. The State of the Field, Prospects for Reform*. Cambridge: Cambridge University Press.

Pildes, Richard H. 2022. "It's Not Just Us. Western Democracies Are Fragmenting." *Washington Post*, July 17. https://wapo.st/3BajxqN.

Pincus, Steven. 2009. *1688: The First Modern Revolution*. New Haven, CT: Yale University Press.

Pinkley, Robin L., Margaret A. Neale, and Rebecca J. Bennett. 1994. "The Impact of Alternatives to Settlement in Dyadic Negotiation." *Organizational Behavior and Human Decision Processes* 57 (1): 97–116.

Plumb, J. H. 1967. *The Growth of Political Stability in England, 1675–1725*. Atlantic Highlands, NJ: Humanities Press.

Porter, Andrew, ed. 1999. *The Oxford History of the British Empire: The Nineteenth Century*. Oxford: Oxford University Press.

Potter, Harry. 2015. *Law, Liberty and the Constitution: A Brief History of the Common Law*. Woodbridge, UK: Boydell Press.

Putnam, Robert D. 1993. *Making Democracy Work: Civic Traditions in Modern Italy*. Princeton, NJ: Princeton University Press.

———. 2020. *The Upswing: How America Came Together a Century Ago and How We Can Do It Again*. New York: Simon and Schuster.

Przeworski, Adam, Susan Carol Stokes, and Bernard Manin. 1999. *Democracy, Accountability, and Representation*. Cambridge: Cambridge University Press.

Raaflaub, Kurt, Josiah Ober, and Robert W. Wallace. 2007. *The Origins of Democracy in Ancient Greece*. Berkeley: University of California Press.

Raaflaub, Kurt A., and Tim Cornell. 1986. *Social Struggles in Archaic Rome: New Perspectives on the Conflict of the Orders*. Berkeley: University of California Press.

Rahe, Paul A. 1992. *Republics Ancient and Modern*. Chapel Hill: University of North Carolina Press.

Rakove, Jack N. 1997. *Original Meanings: Politics and Ideas in the Making of the Constitution*. New York: Vintage.

———. 2006. *James Madison and the Creation of the American Republic*. New York: Pearson.

———. 2011. *Revolutionaries: A New History of the Invention of America*. Boston: Mariner Books.

Rasmussen, Dennis C. 2021. *Fears of a Setting Sun: The Disillusionment of America's Founders*. Princeton, NJ: Princeton University Press.

Rauch, Jonathan. 2021. *The Constitution of Knowledge: A Defense of Truth*. Washington, DC: Brookings Institution.

Rawls, John. 2001. *Justice as Fairness: A Restatement*. Cambridge, MA: Harvard University Press.

———. 2005. *Political Liberalism*. Expanded ed. New York: Columbia University Press.

Ricks, Thomas E. 2020. *First Principles: What America's Founders Learned from the Greeks and Romans and How That Shaped Our Country*. New York: Harper.

Robinson, Edgar E. 1934. *American Democracy in Time of Crisis*. Stanford, CA: Stanford University Press.

Rose, R. B. 1960. "The Priestly Riots of 1791." *Past and Present* 18:68–88.

Rosenblum, Nancy L. 2010. *On the Side of the Angels*. Princeton, NJ: Princeton University Press.

Rousseau, Jean-Jacques. 2002. *The Social Contract and the First and Second Discourses*. New Haven, CT: Yale University Press.

Runciman, David. 2018. *How Democracy Ends*. New York: Basic Books.

Russell, Conrad. 1996. "The Reformation and the Church of England, 1550–1640." In *The Oxford Illustrated History of Tudor and Stuart Britain*, edited by John Merrill, 258–92. Oxford: Oxford University Press.

Ryan, Alan. 2014. *The Making of Modern Liberalism*. Princeton, NJ: Princeton University Press.

Saller, Richard P. 1982. *Personal Patronage under the Early Empire*. Cambridge: Cambridge University Press.

Salmon, Edward Togo. 1982. *The Making of Roman Italy*. Ithaca, NY: Cornell University Press.

Schattschneider, Elmer Eric. 1960. *The Semisovereign People: A Realist's View of Democracy in America*. New York: Holt, Rinehart and Winston.

Schattschneider, Elmer Eric, and Sidney A. Pearson Jr. 1942. *Party Government*. Piscataway, NJ: Transaction Publishers.

Schleifer, James T., ed. 2012. *The Chicago Companion to Tocqueville's Democracy in America*. Chicago: University of Chicago Press.

Schumpeter, Joseph Alois. (1950) 2008. *Capitalism, Socialism, and Democracy*. New York: Harper.

Scullard, H. H. 2010. *From the Gracchi to Nero: A History of Rome from 133 BC to AD 68*. New York: Taylor and Francis.

Serrano, Roberto. 2008. "Bargaining." In *The New Palgrave Dictionary of Economics*, edited by Matías Vernengo, Esteban Pérez Caldentey, and J. Barkley Rosser. New York: Palgrave Macmillan. https://link.springer.com/referencework/10.1057/978-1-349-95121-5.

Sharp, Andrew, ed. 1998. *The English Levellers*. Cambridge: Cambridge University Press.

Sherwin-White, A. N. 1973. *The Roman Citizenship*. Oxford: Oxford University Press.

Shklar, Judith N. 1985. *Men and Citizens: A Study of Rousseau's Social Theory*. Cambridge: Cambridge University Press.

———. 1987. *Montesquieu*. Oxford: Oxford University Press.

Skarbek, David. 2014. *The Social Order of the Underworld: How Prison Gangs Govern the American Penal System*. Oxford: Oxford University Press.

Smith, Billy G. 1990. *The "Lower Sort": Philadelphia's Laboring People, 1750–1800*. Ithaca, NY: Cornell University Press.

Smith, Michael S. 2004. "Parliamentary Reform and the Electorate." In *A Companion to Nineteenth-Century Britain*, edited by Chris Williams, 156–73. Oxford: Blackwell.

Smith, Richard Edwin. 1958. *Service in the Post-Marian Roman Army*. Manchester: Manchester University Press.

Stasavage, David. 2020. *The Decline and Rise of Democracy: A Global History from Antiquity to Today*. Princeton, NJ: Princeton University Press.

Storing, Herbert J., and Murray Dry. 1981. *What the Anti-Federalists Were For*. Chicago: University of Chicago Press.

Straumann, Benjamin. 2016. *Crisis and Constitutionalism: Roman Political Thought from the Fall of the Republic to the Age of Revolution*. Oxford: Oxford University Press.

Strauss, Barry S. 2000. "Democracy, Kimon, and the Evolution of Athenian Naval Tactics in the Fifth Century B.C." In *Polis and Politics: Studies in Ancient Greek History*, edited by Pernille Flensted-Jensen, Thomas Heine Nielsen, and Lene Rubinstein, 315–26. Copenhagen: Museum Tusculanum Press.

_____. 2004. *The Battle of Salamis: The Naval Encounter That Saved Greece—and Western Civilization*. New York: Simon and Schuster.

———. 2009. *The Spartacus War*. New York: Simon and Schuster.

———. 2015. *The Death of Caesar: The Story of History's Most Famous Assassination*. New York: Simon and Schuster.

———. 2022. *The War That Made the Roman Empire*. New York: Simon and Schuster.

Strauss, Leo. 1953. *Natural Right and History*. Chicago: University of Chicago Press.

Susskind, Jamie. 2022. *The Digital Republic: On Freedom and Democracy in the 21st Century*. London: Bloomsbury Publishing.

Syme, Ronald. 1939. *The Roman Revolution*. Oxford: Oxford University Press.

Taylor, Astra. 2020. *Democracy May Not Exist, but We'll Miss It When It's Gone*. New York: Metropolitan Books.

Tilly, Charles. 1990. *Coercion, Capital, and European States, AD 990–1990*. Cambridge, MA: B. Blackwell.

Tocqueville, Alexis de. 1990. Translated by Henry Reeve, revised by Francis Bowen. Edited by Phillips Bradley. Introduction by Daniel J. Boorstin. *Democracy in America*. 2 vols. New York: Vintage Books. First published 1835.

Tombs, Robert. 2014. *The English and Their History*. New York: Vintage.

Tuck, Richard. 2016. *The Sleeping Sovereign: The Invention of Modern Democracy*. Cambridge: Cambridge University Press.

Urbinati, Nadia. 2006. *Representative Democracy: Principles and Genealogy*. Chicago: University of Chicago Press.

Weingast, Barry R. 1997. "The Political Foundations of Democracy and the Rule of Law." *American Political Science Review* 91:245–63.

Whiteley, William H. 1970. "The Social Composition of the British House of Commons, 1868–1885." *Historical Papers* 5 (1): 171–85.

Wilentz, Sean. 2005. *The Rise of American Democracy: Jefferson to Lincoln*. New York: W. W. Norton and Company.

Winthrop, Rebecca. 2020. "The Need for Civic Education in 21st-Century Schools." Brookings. https://www.brookings.edu/wp-content/uploads/2020/04/BrookingsPolicy2020_BigIdeas_Winthrop_CivicEducation.pdf.

Wolin, Sheldon S. 2001. *Tocqueville between Two Worlds: The Making of a Political and Theoretical Life*. Princeton, NJ: Princeton University Press.

Wood, Gordon S. 1992. *The Radicalism of the American Revolution*. New York: A. A. Knopf.

Woodward, C. Vann. 2002. *The Strange Career of Jim Crow*. Oxford: Oxford University Press. First published 1955.

Worthington, Ian. 2010. *Philip II of Macedonia*. New Haven, CT: Yale University Press.

Zaret, David. 2000. *Origins of Democratic Culture: Printing, Petitions, and the Public Sphere in Early-Modern England*. Princeton, NJ: Princeton University Press.

Zuckerman, Ethan. 2021. *Mistrust: Why Losing Faith in Institutions Provides the Tools to Transform Them*. New York: W. W. Norton and Company.

Zuckerman, Michael. 1968. "The Social Context of Democracy in Massachusetts." *William and Mary Quarterly* 25:523–44.

INDEX

abolitionist movement, 196–98; British, 156, 196; Underground Railroad of the American, 197. *See also* slavery

Act of Settlement (1701), 145. *See also* Britain

Acts of Union (1801), 145. *See also* Britain

Adams, Abigail, 171

Adams, President John, 171, 193

Aegean Sea, 55, 66, 70

Aemilius Lepidus, Marcus, 106

Afghanistan, 154

agriculture: Athenian lands for, 57; British fragmentation of lands for, 153; commercialization of English, 126; development of, 3; Spartan institutions of enslavement and rents in, 56

Alexander III ("the Great"), King, 74, 76; death of, 74; military tradition of, 92

Alien and Sedition Acts (1796), 193

Allen, Danielle, 178

American Revolution, 148, 160, 164, 170, 178–82, 196. *See also* Intolerable Acts (1774); Stamp Act (1765); Townshend Acts (1767); Treaty of Paris (1783); United States

Anatolia: southwestern, 73; western, 99. *See also* Asia

Angevin Empire, 120. *See also* Henry II, King

Anne, Queen, 145

Anti-Federalists, 186–88, 190–91, 249n23

Antiochus III, King, 95

Antony, Marc, 105–6

aristocracy, 15; Athenian, 58–61, 75; English, 111–16, 119, 121–24, 127–28, 131; French loyalist, 119; property rights of local English, 121–23; rebellion of the English, 128; social habit of deference to the, 164; Spartan, 55–56. *See also* oligarchy

Aristophanes, *The Assemblywomen*, 77

Aristotle, 22, 36–37, 48, 61, 233; concept of civic friendship adapted from, 220; Lyceum of, 72

Articles of Confederation, 6–8, 160, 180–86, 212, 218. *See also* United States

Asia, 79, 95–96; revolt in the Roman province of, 102; taxation of the Roman province of, 100. *See also* Anatolia

Athenian Empire, 66–69, 211, 213; dismantling of the, 70; loss of the, 72; scaling up the, 69, 211. *See also* democratic Athens

Athens: Acropolis of, 60, 63, 65, 68; basic rights for citizens of, 56–57; civic festivals of, 75, 232; geography of, 56, 64; new civic institutions of, 61, 75; public offices on the basis of annual income in, 57; regime of the Thirty Tyrants in, 70; revolt against Rome led by Mithradates of Pontus of, 74–75, 102, 104; social crisis and political bargain in, 56–58; social diversity of the population of, 64. *See also* Athenian Empire; democratic Athens; *polis* (city-state); Thirty Tyrants

Australia, 157

authoritarianism, 2, 16, 228–29. *See also* autocracy; bosses

autocracy, 15–16, 25, 30, 169; command-and-control power of, 19–20; effective leadership in, 223; and political parties, 43; security and welfare as ensured by, 228. *See also* authoritarianism; bosses